CAPITAL SPICE

21 INDIAN RESTAURANT CHEFS I MORE THAN 100 STUNNING RECIPES

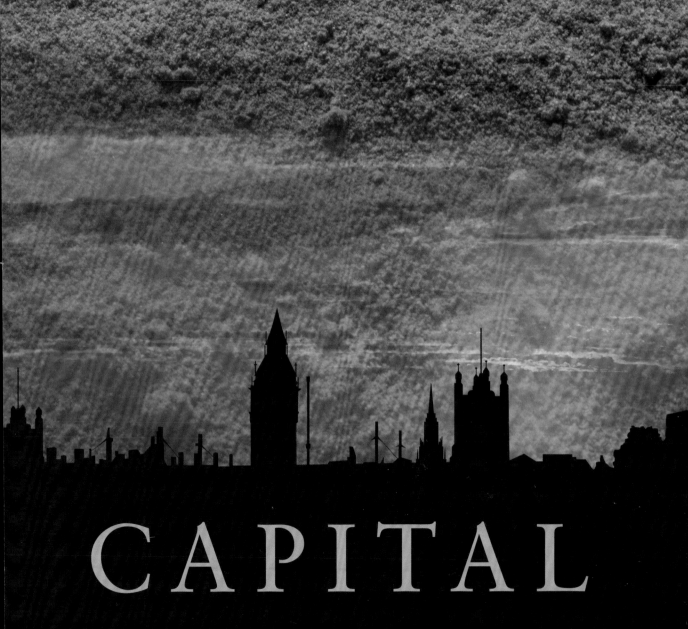

CAPITAL SPICE

21 INDIAN RESTAURANT CHEFS I MORE THAN 100 STUNNING RECIPES

First published in Great Britain
in 2012 by Absolute Press,
an imprint of Bloomsbury Publishing Plc

Absolute Press
Scarborough House
29 James Street West
Bath BA1 2BT
Phone 44 (0) 1225 316013
Fax 44 (0) 1225 445836
E-mail info@absolutepress.co.uk
Website www.absolutepress.co.uk

Publisher Jon Croft
Commissioning Editor Meg Avent
Art Direction and Design Matt Inwood
Photographer Lara Holmes
Editor Gillian Haslam
Indexer Ann Parry

Photo of Naved Nasir on page 88 by Sim Canetty-Clarke

ISBN 9781906650728

Printed in China by C&C Offset Printing Co. Ltd.

A note about the text
This book was set using Sabon and Hitchock. Sabon was
designed by Jan Tschichold in 1964. The roman design is
based on type by Claude Garamond, whereas the italic
design is based on types by Robert Granjon. Hitchcock is
a font designed by Matt Terich – and is a homage to the
iconic lettering that so often appeared in the title sequences
designed by the artist Saul Bass, which notably included the
films of Alfred Hitchcock.

Bloomsbury Publishing Plc
50 Bedford Square, London WC1B 3DP
www.bloomsbury.com

FOREWORD
BY SANJEEV KAPOOR

Sanjeev Kapoor is a chef, entrepreneur, restaurateur and author. His celebrated TV show, Khana Khazana *is the longest-running cooking show in Asia. It is watched by home cooks and food professionals in 120 countries and has more than 500 million viewers. He is the most recognised face of Indian cuisine in Asia. In January 2011, Sanjeev launched his FoodFood channel, available on Indian TV, mobile and web. He has a chain of restaurants across the globe and has published dozens of cookbooks.*

We in India are so pleased to see that regional Indian food is beginning to get genuine recognition and has been enthusiastically embraced.
Indian dishes in good restaurants throughout the world are becoming healthier and more authentic, and these will continue to evolve as Indian food itself has done throughout the centuries. It will become more inventive and bolder. It will change as we change.

I have been honoured to serve on the panel of the Ministry of Tourism for the Government of India. This post was made specifically to document Indian cuisine and to present a classic version of it for Indians to follow and rest of the World to understand. Through both my food TV channel 'Foodfood' and my books, I have tried to educate and inspire food lovers, but those who live outside India often have only restaurants as their introduction to our rich culinary heritage.

Indian cuisine is now loved worldwide, and the quality available outside the Subcontinent has improved beyond measure over the last decades, particularly in cosmopolitan London. Each country seems to have evolved its own hybrid menu – a melange of Indian classics with a style deemed appropriate for the host population – but sometimes unrecognisable to any native Indian.

There is in London a renaissance of Indian cuisine. Yes, the British "curry house" still exists and the dishes found there are craved by many who have had a lifetime of enjoying this Bangladeshi touch. But there are now alternatives offering authentically Indian dishes as well as Indian nouvelle cuisine. These days there are Michelin-star restaurants that are frequented by visiting Indians, transplanted Indians and non-Indians from across the globe.

I have known Chrissie Walker for a number of years. She is mostly British but has an Indian heart and a passion for Indian food. She first came to notice with her cookbook reviews and later her restaurant and hotel reviews. She has penned this book which offers a personal overview of some of the best, the most iconic and the most fascinating Indian restaurants in London. It's a book that will entice the reader and encourage visitors to London to explore its increasing wealth of worthy Indian restaurants.

It's my aim to make Indian cuisine the most popular in the world and to have it recognised for being as refined as, but different from, that of French or Japanese. Books such as *Capital Spice* offer diners outside India a list of restaurants and recipes that will persuade them that real Indian food has more to recommend it than ever before.

INTRODUCTION

There have been many books written by chefs. Some of them have been Indian, and a few of those gentlemen are included between these covers. But I believe that this book is the first to focus purely on a collection of some of the most worthy Indian restaurants.

Whilst it's true that I am a proud Londoner, I have chosen to explore the Indian restaurant scene here rather than nationally simply because there are so many exceptional establishments in the capital, and because they are accessible to those from every corner of these isles... and indeed the whole world.

I confess I am no Indian food expert although I have worked in the kitchen of an Indian restaurant. I have merely taken the words of these chefs and massaged them into pocket-sized biographies. The recipes are theirs, not mine. It's a book written in homage to their skills. My intention has been to portray Indian cuisine as one of the true classics, offering high-end smart fare as well as the most casual of snacks. Many a volume has been published in praise of French restaurants but we now have Michelin-starred Indian restaurants, and still more Indian restaurants that rank among the best in the world.

This isn't a book that pretends to be a definitive guide to all things delightful and delicious in the Sub-continental food forum. In fact it does not even include all those on my own list of preferred restaurants. This is a collection of noteworthy venues that have been happy to donate some time and recipes to my project. There are others that I would have liked to have included, and the reader will doubtless have his/her own suggestions. Remember, the ones you yourself would have included might well be amongst those that have not been able to participate, for various reasons beyond the control of this author. There are still more that I would have liked to have had here, but they were just outside our designated geographic area served by red buses and black cabs.

These chefs and restaurants cover a good cross-section of taste and style. There are Northern Indian gravy curries, Goan specialities, and dishes from the length of the Grand Trunk Road, as well as street food. There are recipes from the Parsi community and others with a hint of French je ne sais quoi. Every Indian food aficionado should be able to find something to tantalise the palate. Michelin-star restaurants share the stage with casual neighbourhood favourites. Each has something to offer, and they all do that with unique flair whilst maintaining a great deal of respect for their diverse cuisines.

Some of these amazing men and women (yes, we get everywhere) were friends before I started this endeavour; others have become friends during its progress. They have given their support and have often strived above and beyond the call of duty to assist and encourage. It has been heartwarming and humbling. Talented chums that actually feed me – I have been truly blessed.

Each establishment has its own character, but there has been a surprising common thread binding all the restaurants together: a regard for good British produce, and the enthusiasm to take advantage of it wherever possible. All of the chefs revel in our fresh fish, meat and vegetables. They have adapted dishes to showcase seafood that was never available in India. Some, like Cyrus and Pervin Todiwala, have become outspoken ambassadors for British meat.

The recipes are for dishes found in their respective restaurants, or for dishes that the chefs cook at home for their own families and friends. There are recipes to appeal to every taste and appropriate for every skill level, but don't be a cookbook slave. Make the dishes for the first time using the chef's original recipe but then tweak the ingredients to suit your own taste. Be faithful to the tradition, but a little more chilli here or a little less salt there will offend nobody: firstly because we won't tell the chef, and secondly if we did he would say "make it your way – that's how I cook."

Talking of chilli, there are dozens of varieties of fresh chillies available in high-street supermarkets and Asian stores; racks are full of different packs of dried chillies, either whole or in powder form. Use your favourite brand as you'll know its strength. If you find the finished dish a bit too strident then cut down the volume of chilli or mix with paprika – remember, you can put it in, but you can't take it out. If unsure, err on the side of discretion, and taste at every stage of the recipe. Recipes use chillies including seeds, unless otherwise stated, but feel free to remove seeds if you prefer a less spicy end result. A collection of 6 or 7 spices will provide you with all you need to make the majority of these recipes, and you will probably already have several of them lingering at the back of your larder. If they have been there since Indian independence then throw them out and buy some fresh.

There will be no need to invest in exotic appliances or gadgets to cook from this book (apart from a striking brass sev-maker for the Ganapati Idiappams). A tandoor in the corner of your studio flat might give the impression that you know a thing or two about naan, and it would take the place of central heating, but in truth you are better off with a domestic grill or garden barbecue. The recipes have been written with the home cook in mind. Get all your mise en place ready before you start these dishes, in other words, measure out all your ingredients in advance.

I trust that all lovers of Indian food will visit the restaurants showcased. I am sure enthusiastic home chefs will take pleasure in cooking the recipes. I have eaten every single dish offered for inclusion in this book and many of them are now putting in a regular appearance chez nous. I hope you will cook, eat and enjoy just as much as I have.

Chrissie Walker, London
May 2012

ATUL KOCHHAR

BENARES

In 2001 Atul Kochhar became one of the first Indian chefs to gain a Michelin star. Tamarind (see pages 241–251) was his professional stage in those days, and this was the restaurant that changed the perception of Indian cuisine in the UK. Atul moved on from Tamarind to open Benares and won another Michelin star in 2007.

Benares is a contemporary restaurant with Asian accents, understated opulence which successfully balances hints of exotic charm and practical comfort, unintimidating and well-cushioned luxury. The restaurant design concept is that of Ou Baholyodhin (an acclaimed Thai designer working in London), who was inspired by the old houses in Benares on the banks of the Ganges, in the Indian state of Uttar Pradesh, where the designer used to live. He introduced features like the infinity pool, the screens and the iconic boat-heads that he brought back from India.

Atul defines his restaurant with these words: 'I wanted to make a restaurant which was comfortable, and (not to sound too sexist) it had to be female-friendly – if women like it, men will come and eat here too. If a restaurant is shy of showing its loos and its kitchen, it's not worth eating there.' Atul is clearly a chef very much in tune with the needs of his guests.

Atul is not only a celebrated restaurant chef – he is also one of the familiar faces of Indian food on our TV screens where his ready smile and natural manner have endeared him to viewers. Atul grew up in a family where food was central. 'I often cooked when I was a child. Mum was a good cook and I had four older sisters, so it often felt like I had five mothers, especially when I was being told off! Only when my younger brother came along was I left alone!'

His father ran a catering business, and this helped him decide from an early age that his future would take a food-related path. His parents, however, like all other Indian parents it seems, wanted their son to be a doctor. They encouraged him to take the medical school exam and – unfortunately for Atul! – he passed. However, even as an adolescent Atul showed his customary enterprise – he had secretly studied for the hotel school exam, without telling his parents, and passed that, too.

'My father did help me when choosing the location for my studies. My family is from north India and I was born in east India, so I understood the cultures of two parts of the country really well, but my father said that it would be great if I went to south India and learnt about that, as none of the family had been there for many generations, and we knew very little about it.' Atul's association with various regions of India has stood him in good stead for his presentation of Benares' authentic pan-Indian menu.

'When I landed in Chennai (Madras at that time), it was like being in a foreign country – the people didn't look like me, the language was different, the eating style was different, the living style was different. For three years I immersed myself in it and loved it, and tried to visit every part of south India. I saw lots of Kerala – it was a paradise – and some of my college mates were from there. We would spend the afternoons and evenings fishing in backwaters, or sitting in the barn or on top of a tractor doing nothing, just eating good food and understanding the country. It was fun,

but I was learning without realising it, and when I started cooking it had a profound effect on what I produced.

'I come from a region which is landlocked, so fish was a very distant thing for my family. Spending time in south India really opened my mind. I took several tours of the country to learn more: Gujarat, Maharashtra, Goa, Kerala, Karnataka, Chennai, Andra Pradesh, Bangladesh. That gave me a clear idea of how well we eat on the coast, and we had never taken notice of that, which is sad. Now, as a chef I always take pride in cooking fish.

'I worked for Oberoi Hotels until 1994, when I was given the opportunity to become head chef at a new restaurant in London called Tamarind. I spent a year or so understanding what this country is all about: its demographics, its agriculture, what comes in from Europe and beyond. Until I acquired that knowledge, I had been writing a menu as if I was a curry-house chef, and that was a most frustrating part of my life. But slowly, as I gained confidence, I began creating menus that I was very happy to cook.

'There was also the responsibility of training the palates of the British. The problem was that we had to explain to customers demanding Prawn Rogan Josh that such a dish did not exist in the classic Indian food repertoire, and Tamarind was a classic restaurant. I would say "I can make one if you like, but let me give you Lamb Rogan Josh; try it, and if you don't like it, I will make whatever you want." So from those times we eventually landed two Michelin stars, and had kitchens into which any chef could walk and he would find it familiar. (In those days kitchens were shoved into a cupboard – a 150-seater restaurant might have a kitchen just 4 metres square, and some "chefs" were content to open boxes of frozen food.) To elevate your ambitions to the point where you are eagerly anticipating the ingredients arriving in the market, looking forward to your sea trout, your sugar-snap peas coming in, those things which excite one about the changing seasons – waiting for the chance to take your combination of four spices and try it on that sea trout is a marked change of attitude, and now young lads really are thinking in those terms.'

Atul modernised the cuisine at Tamarind and bagged a Michelin star for his efforts. However, the style of cooking still reflected the ethos of those who owned the restaurant, and Atul wanted to find his own more individual culinary path.

'There came a time when I needed to express myself more openly; I didn't want to become a British chef, but a chef who knew what British people would like to eat, and how to use fresh ingredients available to us, how to modernise, to push the envelope.'

Benares was opened with that philosophy – marrying the freshness of British ingredients and the vibrancy of Indian spices. It is a quintessentially British-Indian restaurant. Atul has a platform for dishes that unite the two culinary cultures to produce a contemporary menu that is respected and emulated far beyond these shores, and is even being exported to India.

'I think it's going in the right direction, it's taken time to get here, and it can only get better. Indians are now coming to Britain to find inspiration and are taking it back to India. Oberoi Hotels sent three young chefs to the UK to visit Benares and some other contemporary Indian restaurants, and then to go back and open a modern Indian restaurant in New Delhi. That was the proudest moment of my life!'

'My ambition for the future is to make sure that Vatika, my restaurant near Southampton, is recognised with a Michelin star. It's a spectacular restaurant, and nowhere in the world apart from England can you imagine a restaurant with an Indian influence in a vineyard. It's a beautiful, picturesque restaurant and I want to push the boundaries there.'

Benares has a contemporary and near-anonymous entrance, with a view across Berkeley Square. It offers no hint of the striking cuisine within, but it continues to attract a host of regular visitors as well as those wanting to see for themselves the reason why Atul Kochhar has been awarded his Michelin stars and a great deal of celebrity. It's evidently for more than just his boyish good looks.

Benares Restaurant & Bar
12a Berkeley Square House, Berkeley Square, London
W1J 6BS **Phone** 020 7629 8886
www.benaresrestaurant.com

SQUID SALAD

Dishes from the western coast of India are my inspiration for this salad. I tried it first in Goa, and the two things that are essential to Goan food are seafood and sour fruits like passionfruit or lime – they really appreciate those flavours on the coast, so I combined those two. Squid is so loved in the UK, and this makes a nice salad. I serve it with a sweet chilli vinaigrette, and you can add a passionfruit chutney to go with the crisp-fried squid if you wish.

SERVES 4

500g squid rings
20g ginger-garlic paste
juice of 1 lime
2 tablespoons rice flour
2 tablespoons cornflour
½ teaspoon red chilli powder, or to taste
1 teaspoon chaat masala
salt
vegetable oil, for deep frying

For the sweet chilli vinaigrette
100g sugar
100ml red wine vinegar
½ teaspoon chilli flakes
2 teaspoons honey

For the garnish
mixed salad leaves

First, make the vinaigrette: Put the sugar in a small pan and heat gently over a medium heat, stirring occasionally, until the sugar dissolves. Increase the heat slightly. After a few minutes the sugar will start to take on the characteristic amber colour – when all the sugar has changed colour add the red wine vinegar. Be careful at this stage, as the molten sugar will bubble up. Stir, add the chilli flakes and allow to simmer for a minute or so. Remove the pan from the heat, add the honey and stir to combine. Set aside to cool.

Put the squid rings in a small bowl, add the ginger-garlic paste and lime juice and stir to coat the squid. In a larger bowl mix together all the remaining ingredients apart from the vegetable oil. Add the squid rings one at a time to the dry mix and coat thoroughly; remove to a dry plate.

Heat the vegetable oil in a deep pan or fryer to a temperature of about 180°C (when dropped into the oil, a small cube of bread should become golden in 45–60 seconds). Carefully drop a few of the squid rings into the oil, and deep fry until golden and crispy – this will take about a minute. Remove from the pan onto crumpled kitchen paper to drain, and keep warm until serving. Continue until all the squid is cooked.

Dress the squid rings with a few tablespoons of the sweet chilli vinaigrette and serve the remainder of the vinaigrette separately. Toss together a colourful selection of salad leaves and serve as a garnish.

MANGSHO GHUGNI
LAMB RUMP WITH CHICKPEAS

This is a classic recipe from Kolkata (formerly Calcutta), West Bengal. Bengalis are very good at mixing beans with meat. This is one of those recipes, and there are three flavours which are quite distinct: bay leaf, black cardamom and clove. *Mangsho* means meat, and generally meat for Hindus from Bengal means goat.

SERVES 4

For the chickpeas
150g *chickpeas, soaked in water overnight*
1 *bay leaf*
1 *black cardamom pod*
1 *clove*
1 *teaspoon salt, or to taste*

For the lamb
100ml *vegetable or mustard oil*
6 *cloves*
2 *bay leaves*
3 *black cardamom pods*
200g *onions, thinly sliced*
1 *tablespoon ginger-garlic paste*
1 *teaspoon ground coriander*
1 *teaspoon red chilli powder*
1 *teaspoon ground cumin*
1 *teaspoon salt, or to taste*
200g *tomatoes, chopped*
4 *lamb leg steaks (100g each)*
2 *tablespoons chopped coriander leaves*
$\frac{1}{2}$ *teaspoon garam masala (ideally Bengali)*

To finish
2 *tablespoons mixed spices –*
 coriander seeds, cumin seeds, sesame seeds, black peppercorns, in equal proportions
1 *tablespoon Dijon mustard*
mixed cress, to garnish

Drain the water from the chickpeas, put them in a saucepan and cover with fresh water. Add the spices and salt, bring to the boil, cover with a lid and cook until the chickpeas are tender – about 1–1½ hours. Drain and set aside until required.

In a separate pan, heat the oil and sauté the cloves, bay leaves and cardamom pods until the cloves swell a little. Add the sliced onions and sauté until translucent, then add the ginger-garlic paste and cook over a medium heat for 1–2 minutes, until the paste is no longer raw.

Add the powdered spices and salt and cook for a couple of minutes; add the tomatoes and lamb steaks and enough water to cover the mixture; cover with a lid and cook for about 20–30 minutes or until the lamb is tender (the meat will no longer be pink inside).

Remove the bay leaves, add the chickpeas and simmer for a few more minutes.

Preheat the oven to 180°C/Gas Mark 4.

Roast the mixed spices for the crust in a dry frying pan over a medium heat for a minute or so, until they give off their aroma. Transfer to a separate bowl and allow to cool before grinding to a coarse mix.

Separate the steaks from the chickpeas; add the coriander leaves and garam masala to the chickpea mixture, and salt to taste.

Pat the steaks dry with kitchen paper, brush them with Dijon mustard, and roll them over the ground spices to coat. Place on a baking tray and roast in the oven for 5–6 minutes.

To serve, divide the chickpea mixture between four plates and place a lamb steak on top; garnish with mixed cress. Serve hot with some rice or Indian bread.

ROGAN JOSH
KASHMIRI LAMB CURRY

A classic Kashmiri dish, traditionally made with lamb, although elsewhere in India it's made with goat. The colour of the rogan josh comes from the bark of a tree called *ratan jote*. It's made by boiling the bark in oil, then using that oil to cook the lamb. *Rogan* means oil, and *josh* means to boil, so 'boiling oil' is the literal translation. We don't get *ratan jote* easily in this country, so we substitute it with tomato paste, putting more spicing in to compensate for the flavours we have lost from the omission of the bark.

SERVES 4

For the whole garam masala
1½ *teaspoons cumin seeds*
6 *green cardamom pods*
2 *black cardamom pods*
2.5-cm *stick of cinnamon*
8 *cloves*
1 *star anise*
2 *blades of mace*
1 *teaspoon black peppercorns*

For the rogan josh
1kg *leg of lamb*
150ml *yoghurt*
30g *finely-crushed almonds*
a large pinch of saffron
½ *teaspoon salt, or to taste*
50g *ginger-garlic paste*
100ml *vegetable oil*
1 *teaspoon garam masala*
  (see method below)
350g *onions, thinly sliced*
water or lamb stock, optional
1–2 *teaspoons red chilli powder,*
  or to taste
2 *teaspoons ground coriander*
2 *teaspoons ground turmeric*
60g *tomato paste*

For the garnish
3 *tablespoons roughly chopped*
  coriander leaves,
10g *ginger, cut into juliennes*
  (fine matchsticks)

To make the garam masala, pound the whole spices using a mortar and pestle. Store any remaining spice mix in an airtight jar, to use in your next recipes, while the flavours are still fresh.

Trim and remove the bone from the lamb and cut the meat into 2-cm cubes. Whisk the yoghurt in a bowl, then stir in the almonds, saffron, salt and half the ginger-garlic paste. Put the lamb in a glass dish, coat with the marinade mixture, cover with clingfilm and put in the fridge or somewhere cool to marinate for 2 hours.

Heat the oil in a large heavy-based pan, add 1 teaspoon of the garam masala and stir until the spices start to crackle. Add the sliced onions, stir and cook over a medium heat for a couple of minutes until golden brown; add the remaining ginger-garlic paste and cook for a minute or two until the paste is no longer raw.

Add the lamb with the marinade, stir and cook over a medium heat for a few minutes until the meat is browned and is starting to cook through. (When the lamb is added, it will exude its juices and cook in its own stock. If there isn't much liquid in the pan, add some water or lamb stock. Once the meat is browned, it may stick to the base of the pan, so you have to keep stirring and scraping the bottom of the pan. This is important for the development of the characteristic flavours.)

Add the dry spices and cook for a further 5 minutes. Add the tomato paste and stir for a few more minutes, until the lamb is thoroughly cooked.

Serve it in a bowl, garnished with coriander and ginger juliennes. Rogan josh can be served with saffron rice or an Indian bread.

CHICKEN TIKKA PIE WITH SPICED BERRY COMPOTE

This is a true fusion dish, created for the UK. Britain is very big on pies, yet it only occurred to me about two years ago to bring the 'pie' element into our menu. We were serving pigeon as a starter at the time, so we made a pie with this first and it worked really well. I thought, 'Chicken Tikka is the most-loved dish from an Indian kitchen, why can't we have a pie with that?' We came up with a jolly good pie, and obviously berries were the right partner for that, so we devised this berry compote to serve alongside. You could use 450g of good-quality readymade shortcrust pastry, or make your own, as below.

SERVES 4–6

For the shortcrust dough
300g plain flour
pinch of salt
75g unsalted butter, well chilled, cut into small cubes
75g lard or vegetable fat, cut into small cubes
cold water
1 egg, beaten, for sealing and glazing

For the pie filling
2 tablespoons vegetable oil
4–6 large garlic cloves, chopped
1 onion, chopped
2 tablespoons ginger-garlic paste
1 tablespoon ground coriander
1–3 teaspoons red chilli powder, or to taste
1 tablespoon ground turmeric
1 tablespoon garam masala
200g tomatoes, chopped
1/2 bunch (approximately 50g) coriander leaves, chopped

750g cooked chicken, diced (use either readymade Indian chicken tikka or diced roast chicken)
pinch of salt

For the spiced berry compote
500g blackberries (wild or shop-bought)
2 tablespoons ground cumin
2 teaspoons ground coriander
70g sugar

To make the pastry, mix the flour with the salt in a large bowl. Add the fats to the flour and gently, with your fingertips, rub the fat into the flour. This stage will be completed when you have a bowl of something that looks like breadcrumbs. Add the water a little at a time, and stir in with a knife. When the dough starts to stick together, use your hands to press into a ball. Wrap this in clingfilm and allow it to rest in the fridge for around 30 minutes.

Pre-heat the oven to 170°C/Gas Mark 3½.

For the filling, heat the oil in a pan over a medium heat, then add the chopped garlic and onion and sauté until translucent. Add the ginger-garlic paste and cook until the onions are golden brown. Add all the powdered spices and stir for a minute or two until they give off their delicious aroma.

Add the chopped tomatoes, stir to combine and cook until they become soft; add the chopped coriander. Season to taste. Toss the cooked chicken into the spicy mixture. Remove from the heat.

Roll out two-thirds of the pastry and line the base of a greased round pie tin about 26cm in diameter. Pour the chicken mixture into the lined pie tin.

Roll out the remaining pastry to make a lid. Brush the edges of the pastry base with beaten egg, lay the lid over the filling, and crimp the edges to seal. Brush the top of the pie with the remaining egg. Cut a small slit in the centre to allow steam to escape.

Place on a baking sheet and bake for 30 minutes or until the pastry is golden.

To make the compote, mix all ingredients in a saucepan and cook over a gentle heat for 20–25 minutes, until the berries are soft and the sugar has dissolved. Transfer to a small serving bowl and serve hot with the pie.

Chef's Tip
Instead of making a double-crust pie, simply fill a pie dish with the chicken filling, and cover with a readymade short-crust or puff pastry.

CRISP-FRIED SPICY JOHN DORY WITH GURKHA CHUTNEY

I met John Dory for the first time when I came to the UK, and became very friendly with it! Since then, I have had it constantly on the menu. I devised this recipe based on an Indian classic called *Amritsari Machhi*, where fish is cut into small strips and deep-fried in batter, with ajwain (carom seeds).

Gurkha chutney is a Nepalese chutney. When the Gurkha soldiers are at war, food rationing is very tight, but they will always have with them tomatoes, salt and chillies, so they would make a fire, grill the tomatoes, chop coriander and any other herbs they have, add salt and lime juice. It's as simple as that, and works very well with the fish.

SERVES 4

For the gurkha chutney
4 tomatoes, lightly grilled
2 garlic cloves, peeled and lightly grilled
3 tablespoons roughly chopped
    coriander leaves
1–2-cm piece of ginger, finely chopped
$1/2$ teaspoon cumin seeds, toasted in a
    dry pan and crushed
1 small green chilli, finely chopped
1 tablespoon olive oil
2 tablespoons lime juice
salt

For the fish
4 fillets of John Dory, each 100–120g
1 tablespoon lime juice
salt
1 teaspoon chaat masala, to garnish

For the batter
1 tablespoon ginger-garlic paste
$1/2$ teaspoon ground turmeric
$1/2$ teaspoon red chilli powder or
    crushed black pepper, or to taste
$1/4$ teaspoon garam masala

$1/2$ teaspoon mango powder (amchur)
$1/4$ teaspoon ajwain seeds (optional)
100g chickpea (gram) flour
1 tablespoon cornflour
1 drop of orange food colouring
    (optional)
120ml sparkling water
vegetable oil, for deep frying

To make the chutney, place all the ingredients on a large cutting board. Using a large knife, chop everything to a chunky consistency and combine. Store in the refrigerator until required.

Place the fish in a non-metallic bowl, coat with the lime juice and salt to taste. Place in the fridge or somewhere cool to marinate for 20 minutes.

Make a thin batter by whisking all the dry ingredients together in a large bowl, slowly pouring in the sparkling water until you have a smooth paste.

Remove the fish from the lime juice marinade and pat dry with kitchen paper to remove excess moisture. Place the fish in the bowl of batter and marinate for a further 10 minutes.

Heat the oil in a wok or deep frying pan until a haze appears. Fry the fillets over medium heat until crisp, turning after 2–3 minutes when the batter begins to become crisp and golden. Remove onto kitchen paper and sprinkle with chaat masala powder.

To serve, spoon some of the chutney onto a large warm plate, and place the fish next to it. Put the remaining chutney in a small serving bowl. Serve a portion of the Crushed Peas (right) and a spoon of Cucumber Salad (right) alongside. Serve immediately.

Crushed peas
2 teaspoons vegetable oil
1 tablespoon unsalted butter
pinch of asafoetida
$1/2$ teaspoon cumin seeds
$1/2$ teaspoon red chilli flakes, or to taste
100g garden peas, blanched
1 tablespoon vegetable stock or water
1 tablespoon single cream
salt

Heat the oil and butter together in a pan. Add the asafoetida; as it foams, add the cumin seeds. As the seeds crackle, add the chilli flakes and blanched peas. Cook for 3–4 minutes on a low heat. Add the stock and cream, stir and season. Remove the pan from the heat and, using a wooden spoon, gently crush the peas. Keep warm until required.

Cucumber salad
1 small cucumber, peeled and cut into
    juliennes
2 tomatoes, halved, pips removed, cut
    into juliennes
$1/2$ red onion, thinly sliced
leaves from 10 sprigs of coriander

For the dressing
1 tablespoon chilli jam
1 teaspoon lime juice
$1/2$ teaspoon olive oil
sea salt, to taste

Mix all the salad ingredients together and keep chilled in the fridge until required. Mix the dressing ingredients together and keep in the fridge until required. Toss the salad in the dressing when ready to serve.

PRAHLAD HEGDE

BOMBAY BRASSERIE

Bombay Brasserie and Bar seems to have been at the top of its game for decades. It has never been out of vogue and remains the haunt of not only the A-listers but also ordinary folk who hanker for some fine Indian food in the most opulent of surroundings.

The restaurant opened on 10th December 1982 (an auspicious date recommended by an Indian astrologer) and became one of London's first Indian fine-dining destinations. It was refurbished in 2009 and now is much lighter and more contemporary than its original incarnation, which had a distinct 'Raj' theme. It was unquestionably sumptuous and much admired by its habitués, but fashion changes and so must restaurants.

There is still the air of Raj-esque opulence before one even enters the restaurant, and the imposing front door gives a hint to the quality that awaits beyond. Diners are first welcomed into a bar area that now sports a working fireplace which is a magnet for guests to lounge by, while sipping their preprandial cocktails or after-dinner nightcaps on cold winter evenings. It is a charming space with calming ambiance and comfy chairs.

The extensive revamp was a bold step and much remarked-upon by those associated with the Indian food industry in London. Chhada Siembieda and Associates, one of the world's most reputable and respected interior design companies, gave Bombay Brasserie a new look, but they have managed to retain the much-loved Bombay Colonial ambiance. The soft furnishings are still rich, but in muted tones and old gold. The black-and-white pictures show Maharajas, but this is not a Taj Mahal theme park. It's a vision of tasteful and understated high-end comfort. There are well-spaced and intimate tables, as well as curved booths with banquette seating to accommodate larger groups. And, of course, the seamless and polished service remains unchanged.

Bombay Brasserie has grown in size. The airy and impressive conservatory has been transformed and there is a central open kitchen and counter seating. The walls are covered with murals wafting one far away from the grime, black taxis and red buses of grey London. The conservatory is a destination venue for those looking for a convenient location for memorably well-catered private events, and its Sunday Brunch is considered to be one of the best in town,

allowing families the opportunity to savour the restaurant's culinary delights in a less formal setting.

The restaurant is the dining room of choice for many a media face and the front-of-house team is acquainted with the famed, who include Hollywood stars, politicians from the international arena and notables from these shores and beyond. They have welcomed numerous celebrities, from Sydney Poitier and Marlon Brando to Elton John. Anthony Hopkins held his 60th birthday party here, and Tom Cruise was sufficiently impressed to appoint Bombay Brasserie as his preferred 'take-away', buying meals to take aboard his private jet. The staff have refined the art of unobtrusively running the well-oiled machinery of an iconic restaurant. Their high-profile guest list requires that they are discreet and unobtrusive, allowing those in the entertainment spotlight to enjoy some welcome anonymity, while savouring Bombay Brasserie's outstanding food.

Executive Chef Prahlad Hegde is the most modest and charming of men. Quietly spoken with an air of confident calm, he is the last person who will mention that the Brasserie's long list of awards and accolades which include the British Curry Awards, Best in Britain Awards and a Lifetime Achievement Award from the *Good Curry Guide*. He is the culinary face (mostly hidden in the kitchen) of Bombay Brasserie. 'I have always been interested in the production side, rather than being involved with the running of front of house.' He prefers that each and every member of Team BB takes credit for the success of the restaurant as a whole.

'We come from a Mangalorean community called Bunts associated with restaurants in India, small family-run businesses where there was no professional training – a young cook just started in the kitchen and worked his way up. My family inspired me – Mum and Dad were both great cooks, and we would all join in with food preparation. Similarly, my children want to come and help when I am working in the kitchen at home; my wife, too, is a very good cook.'

Prahlad did have a dream of becoming a chef: 'I studied chemistry and graduated from Wilson College, and later joined the reputed Institute Of Hotel Management, Mumbai to get into the professional side of the catering industry. There was a lot of competition for jobs, and everyone had either the Taj or Oberoi at the top of their wish list. Although I was accepted by several other hotels, I chose the Taj Hotel Group.' The culinary department was in the process of changing its outlook, and it was very open to innovation. This appealed to the young chef.

'My first year at Taj was scheduled and planned: you go to the various kitchens – Continental, Chinese, Indian, Banqueting, French – and you move through all of them learning from scratch, and that is where you build the foundations for your own skills. This is very important, and is the reason why the Taj Group is where it is today.

'There were only limited opportunities abroad, but I was asked to attend a food festival in Ireland, and then to come to London. We arrived in December – it was cold and dark! Bombay Brasserie was by then a well-known restaurant.

The chef at that time was the late Udit Sarkhel, and I already knew him as we had worked together in Mumbai.

'The style of food at Bombay Brasserie was very much what you would get back home, but the curry scene in the UK in general was so unrepresentative of what was being served in India. The Taj wanted to introduce authentic regional cuisine – what Indian food is really all about. So there was an elite team from the Taj Group here, and I am proud to have been a part of that since 1991.'

In the last two years, along with the redecoration, the menu has changed, and so has the presentation of the food, and even the crockery, but Bombay Brasserie still clings to the

essence of good Indian cooking. A quarter of a century was a long time to maintain the initial, successful format and food must evolve and menus must be revitalised.

Whilst Bombay Brasserie must assure the continuation of its enviable reputation as an outstanding Indian restaurant, in a city that boasts so many, it's the food that keeps the discerning diner returning. Dishes like the refined and melting Duck Shikampuri and Palak Patta Chat are stunning in texture and taste, but there is also a traditional Chicken Tikka Makhani that is comforting. Prahlad's presentation is always thoughtful and underlines the reasons why the restaurant is still held in such fond regard.

Prahlad remembers the past, and looks forward to the future: 'The emphasis is still on basics, and we want the guests to remember the great meals that they've had.' And I'm sure they'll be returning for years to come. The continued success of Bombay Brasserie is a testament to its quality and innovation, endeavouring to push the boundaries, while remaining true to the ethos of traditional and classic Indian cuisine.

Bombay Brasserie
Courtfield Road, London SW7 4QH
Phone 020 7370 4040
www.bombaybrasserielondon.com

SCALLOPS ON TOMATO KUT

Here freshly-grilled scallops have been marinated in spices, then flashed in the pan, served on tomato chutney, with curry leaves and jaggery to give a combination of sweet and sour. Scallops are particularly popular in the UK – they were once a special treat, but they are now much more accessible. Don't cook scallops for too long or they will go rubbery.

SERVES 4

2 tablespoons lemon juice
1/4 teaspoon ground turmeric
1 teaspoon curry leaves, pulverised
   to a powder in a blender
16 king scallops, without shell
salt, to taste
1 tablespoon vegetable oil

For the tomato chutney
2 tablespoons vegetable oil
2 teaspoons ginger-garlic paste
1/2-1 teaspoon red chilli powder, or
   to taste
1/2 teaspoon ground turmeric
8 tomatoes, quartered
2 tablespoons gram flour, roasted
   (dry-stir for a few minutes in a
   warm pan)
salt, to taste

To temper the chutney
2 tablespoons vegetable oil
1 teaspoon cumin seeds
1/4 teaspoon black mustard seeds
8 whole dried red chillies
8 curry leaves

To garnish
16 curry leaves, crisply fried
8 cherry tomatoes, halved (optional)

Preheat the oven to 180°C/Gas Mark 4.

Place the lemon juice, turmeric and powdered curry leaves in a bowl and mix; add the scallops and coat with the spices. Season with salt.

Heat the oil in a non-stick frying pan and sear the scallops on each side over a high heat for just a minute or so, until they become opaque. Remove the scallops from the pan and place in an ovenproof dish; continue to cook for 3–5 minutes in the oven. Remove from the oven, set aside and keep warm.

To make the tomato chutney, heat the oil in a frying-pan over a medium heat and sauté the ginger-garlic paste for a minute or so, until it is no longer raw. Add the chilli powder, turmeric and tomatoes and cook for 10 minutes, stirring frequently.

Mix the gram flour with 120ml water to make a thin paste, and add it to the cooking tomato mix. Simmer, uncovered, for 5 minutes.

Blend the tomato sauce and strain through a sieve. Season with salt, return the mix to the frying-pan, cover and simmer for a further 10 minutes.

To temper the chutney, in another frying pan heat the vegetable oil over a medium heat for a few minutes, then add the spices and cook until the seeds crackle, then mix in with the tomatoes.

Spoon the tomato chutney on to a serving plate. Gently lift the scallops and place them on top of the chutney. Garnish each scallop with a toothpick skewered through a crisply-fried curry leaf and half a cherry tomato, if using.

MASALA SEA BASS

We use Chilean sea bass, because we find the texture and flavour perfect for this dish. This is a basic masala of chilli and turmeric marinated into the fish, pan-grilled then cooked in the oven. The fish is served on a bed of mushrooms and spinach (*khumb-palak*) – be sure to slice the mushrooms thinly.

SERVES 4

4 skin-on fillets of Chilean sea bass, approximately 180g each
½–2 teaspoons chilli powder, or to taste
2 teaspoons ground turmeric
juice of 4 limes
salt
2 tablespoons vegetable oil

For the vegetable base
1 tablespoon vegetable oil
4 teaspoons cumin seeds
1 garlic clove, finely chopped
80g mushrooms, thinly sliced
200g baby spinach, shredded

For the garnish
4 chives
4 lemon wedges
a few drops of chilli oil

To make the garnish of chilli flowers, snip off the tip of a chilli, leaving the stalk intact, then make a few lengthwise cuts from the stalk to the snipped end. Place the chilli in a bowl of iced water. After a while the lengths of chilli will curl up like a flower.

In a non-metallic bowl, mix the chilli powder, turmeric and lime juice and season with salt. Spoon this over the sea bass. Cover with clingfilm and put in the fridge or somewhere cool for 20 minutes to marinate.

Preheat the oven to 180°C/Gas Mark 4.

Heat the vegetable oil in a non-stick pan and sear the marinated sea bass on both sides. Place on a tray and bake in the oven for 5 minutes.

To make the spinach and mushroom base, heat the oil in a pan, add the cumin and chopped garlic, and fry until the garlic turns golden brown. Add the mushrooms and shredded spinach and stir-fry for a few minutes on medium heat until cooked. Season with salt.

To serve, divide the spinach and mushroom mixture between four large plates. On each base, place a sea bass fillet (skin-side up), and garnish with a chive and a lemon wedge. Drizzle a few drops of chilli oil (or a sprinkle of paprika powder) around the plate.

MURGH KHATTA PYAZ

A version of chicken tikka – spiced chunks of chicken, combined with onions, tomatoes and pickled shallots. The tanginess of the pickled onions enhances the spices. It's a very comforting down-to-earth recipe. We make our own pickled onions here – place peeled shallots in a jar with white vinegar and some beetroot to give a reddish colour. They will be ready after a couple of weeks; store in a cool, dark place.

SERVES 4

400g boneless, skinless chicken, breast or thigh, cut into cubes

For the marinade
2 tablespoons ginger-garlic paste
½ teaspoon salt, or to taste
juice of 1 lemon
3 tablespoons red chilli paste, or to taste (made by soaking dried, deseeded Kashmiri chillies in water for several hours until they soften, then pulverising them into a fine paste in a blender), or ground paprika
1 tablespoon mustard oil or any vegetable oil
1 teaspoon garam masala
50ml Greek yogurt

For the gravy
3 tablespoons vegetable oil
1 teaspoon cumin seeds
1 onion, finely chopped
1 tablespoon ginger-garlic paste
1 tomato, finely chopped
2 teaspoons red chilli paste (as above) or paprika

To finish
1 tablespoon vegetable oil
1½ teaspoons finely chopped fresh ginger
1 garlic clove, finely chopped)
1 green chilli, chopped
8 pickled shallots

To garnish
1 teaspoon chaat masala
pinch of ground fenugreek
½ bunch (approximately 50g) coriander leaves, roughly chopped

In a non-metallic dish mix the ginger-garlic paste, salt and lemon juice together. Add the chicken pieces and coat well. Cover with clingfilm and put in the fridge or somewhere cool to marinate for 20 minutes.

Add a mix of the red chilli paste, mustard oil, garam masala and yogurt to the dish and coat the chicken; marinate in the fridge for a further 4 hours.

Preheat the oven to 230°C/Gas Mark 8.

Place the pieces of chicken on a wire rack over a deep baking tray and cook for 8–10 minutes until completely cooked, turning them occasionally. Remove from the oven and set aside.

To make the gravy, heat the oil in a pan, add the cumin seeds and cook for a minute or so until they crackle. Add the onion and sauté over a low heat until a light golden colour. Add the ginger-garlic paste, tomato and red chilli paste or paprika, and cook for 20 minutes, stirring occasionally, over a medium heat. Add a little water if your tomatoes are not very juicy. Put the gravy to one side.

Heat the oil in a frying pan and sauté the chopped ginger, garlic and green chilli for a minute or so. Add the gravy, cooked chicken and pickled shallots and mix together. Season with salt.

Finish with chaat masala, ground fenugreek and chopped coriander leaves.

KHURMANI KI TIKKI

These are very popular North Indian home-style patties. You have the mildness of the potatoes and the punch in the apricot stuffing, spiced with a little chilli and ginger, so you get the combination of the cold and the hot, the mild and the spicy. The potatoes need to be well-mashed, and the patties need to be quickly, but lightly fried, to get a crisp top with a soft inside.

SERVES 4

400g potatoes, unpeeled
30g butter, melted
20g cornflour
salt

For the filling
2 tablespoons vegetable oil
2 teaspoons cumin seeds
1 teaspoon fresh ginger, chopped
1–2 green chillies, or to taste, finely
    chopped
80g ready-to-eat, no-soak dried
    apricots, chopped
1 teaspoon ground cumin
1/2–1 teaspoon chaat masala
salt
handful of coriander leaves, finely
    chopped

For the sweet yoghurt
100ml yoghurt
20g sugar

For the garnish
1 teaspoon chaat masala
4 tablespoons Sweet Chutney
    (see recipe, opposite page)
4 tablespoons Mint Coriander
    Chutney (see recipe, opposite page)
8 whole ready-to-eat, no-soak dried
    apricots
Boil the unpeeled potatoes until tender.

Drain, allow to cool, then peel. Pass through a fine sieve or potato ricer to make a smooth mash. Tip the mashed potatoes into a bowl and mix well with the melted butter, cornflour and salt.

Whisk the yoghurt and sugar together; keep chilled in fridge until ready to serve.

To make the apricot garnish, put the whole apricots in a small pan and cover with sweet chutney. Simmer over a low heat for 10 minutes or so, until the apricots are soft and cooked through.

To make the filling, heat 1 tablespoon of oil in a small frying pan. Add the cumin seeds, chopped ginger and green chillies, and sauté for a couple of minutes. Add the chopped apricots and mix well. Sprinkle in the ground cumin, chaat masala, salt and chopped coriander and stir.

Divide the mashed potato into eight equal balls. Flatten each slightly and make an indention in the centre with a teaspoon. Fill with a little of the apricot mixture and reform the patty to completely enclose the apricot mixture, then slightly flatten again. Heat the remaining oil in a large non-stick frying pan over a medium heat. Add the patties and fry for a few minutes until they are golden brown on both sides. Drain well on crumpled kitchen paper.

To assemble, place 2 hot patties on each plate. Sprinkle with chaat masala. Spoon 4 tablespoons sweet yoghurt, 2 tablespoons sweet chutney, and 1 tablespoon mint and coriander chutney on top. Garnish with whole apricots cooked in sweet chutney.

MINT CORIANDER CHUTNEY

Ubiquitous on restaurant menus, mint and coriander chutney is easy to make at home. Our recipe is somewhat different from the more usual, as we add raw mango (a small green mango used only for cooking, and labelled as 'raw') and radish. If you prefer a milder chutney, remove the seeds from the green chillies before adding them to the other ingredients.

Makes more than a cup of chutney (can be stored in the fridge, covered, for a week).

2 bunches (approximately 200g) of coriander
1 bunch (approximately 100g) of mint
2 green chillies
30g raw mango (a small green mango used only for cooking, and labelled as 'raw'), peeled and stone removed
40g Asian white radish
salt, to taste

Remove and discard the bigger stalks from the coriander and mint. Finely chop all the ingredients, then blend to a fine paste. You may need to do this in several batches.

SWEET CHUTNEY

The sweet chutney is a tangy preparation using mango powder, which gives a distinct astringency.

25g mango powder (Amchur)
25g sugar
1 teaspoon jaggery or brown sugar
2 dates, stoned and finely chopped)
1/2 teaspoon red chilli powder, or to taste
1 teaspoon ground ginger
1/2 teaspoon black salt (a pink-coloured salt available from Asian stores)

Place all the ingredients in a saucepan with 200ml water. Bring to the boil, then simmer for 30 minutes, stirring occasionally. Slacken with more water if needed to give a pouring consistency. Blend and pour through a fine sieve. Leave to cool.

Can be stored in the fridge in a sealed container for a couple of days.

CYRUS AND PERVIN TODIWALA

CAFÉ SPICE NAMASTE

Time Out magazine said: 'If there is a God, the canteen in heaven will be run by Cyrus Todiwala.' Café Spice Namaste is truly unique but you don't have to go as far as heaven to sample Cyrus' food. The restaurant is housed in an imposing Victorian building just a few minutes' walk from The Tower of London. It's a magnet for those searching for remarkable Indian food but also for Parsi food, which is the speciality of chef Cyrus Todiwala and his wife Pervin, herself an able chef and front-of-house manager. This partnership is one of the most successful in the UK restaurant industry. They have a unity that has enabled them to surmount many professional obstacles and yet their celebrity has not coloured their warm approach to customers and staff.

Cyrus was born and, for the most part, brought up in Bombay. He suffered from acute asthma, so he finished his education at a boarding school in Devlali, a hill station 100 miles north-east of Bombay, where the climate and lack of pollution suited him better.

There is no mistaking the origins of Cyrus' love for food: 'You woke up at 5.30 or 6 o'clock to grand-aunt making fresh chapati – a big smear of butter and a sprinkle of sugar, roll it and eat – an amazing experience. On other occasions Mum would start at 4 in the morning to make the toast, which would be ready for breakfast at 6.30. She would toast the bread, butter it, then bake it slowly in the oven. It's to die for, but very dangerous for your health!' Cyrus' mother was a good cook and his inspiration comes from her, with many traditional dishes in the Todiwala repertoire credited to that lady.

Cyrus didn't always want to be a chef. He wanted to do something that involved nature in some way. Food was not far away from that and his sister's friend suggested that he consider her catering college. 'And that was it for me. I didn't know what I was going to do, as there was no career path charted, and I knew nothing about the world of hotels. I was selected from college by the Taj Group, but I didn't have aspirations and didn't think about salary or career, I just worked my socks off, hungry for knowledge.'

Cyrus joined the Taj Group in 1976, and worked in various sections. He was 'fortunate' to have a boss who didn't like him. Well, he thinks of it as lucky now, but at the time

Cyrus was scared of him: 'I would shiver at the sight of the man. He did it deliberately, but he did me a great favour, because his dislike drove him to move me around to various places, and that gave me so much knowledge, and I never regretted it. He says now that he thinks of me as his star pupil, but at the time he said, "As long as I work here you will never be a chef!" He's a much nicer man these days!'

Cyrus worked for the Taj Group for nearly 15 years, rising to Group Executive Chef, Goa. He was charged with opening the new hotel in Kolkata (formerly Calcutta) and to look after the Eastern region, but Pervin and Cyrus wanted to expand their horizons beyond those subcontinental shores.

They arrived in London in 1991 and they exchanged the heat of Poona for the economic and climatic chill of London. They came at the height of the recession, and although Cyrus was voted Best Indian Chef in the UK, debts still forced his employers to close the company. The restaurant was destined to be re-opened by another group; Fay Maschler eventually discovered him and gave a striking and positive review: 'Goan and not to be forgotten' was the headline. But that company, too, was burdened with financial issues. The implication was devastating: if Cyrus was not employed, he would have to leave the country.

Time passed, and Cyrus and Pervin met Michael Gottlieb, owner of Smollensky's. 'He was looking for a chef for a new-concept restaurant chain, and took me on as a partner. We eventually found the present premises (once the offices to which I had come to apply for my National Insurance number!), and the restaurant opened on 14 November 1995. We eventually separated from the group and bought the business ourselves.'

They wanted the design of the dining room to reflect the warmth and vibrancy of the real India: not dark and dim like many Indian restaurants at that time, but bright and colourful, and the concept was created by Steve Thomas. The restaurant displays the more folk-craft element of Indian design rather than Bollywood glitz, with yellows and blues mirroring the tints of the stained-glass windows. They have now added a demonstration area for the popular cookery classes which showcase Cyrus' talents and those of other celebrated international chefs.

'For many the food here does not seem Indian, but it is indeed very Indian. The difference is, we cook for ourselves first, not the British or Asian customer, but us. We use anything and everything that comes with a "British" tag on it, and I will promote British to the best of my ability. The cuisine is *not* fusion, it simply brings British produce into Asian cooking, and that has been going on for many, many years.' His contributions to the promotion of British produce, to education and to the hospitality industry have been recognised with his awards of OBE, DL, an Honorary Professorship at Thames Valley University's prestigious London School of Hospitality, Tourism and Leisure, and an Honorary Doctorate from London Metropolitan University. When Cyrus first started introducing British beef into the

restaurant, there were a lot of Indian chefs who were critical, saying Indians don't eat beef. 'But Indians do eat beef; if you are a Hindu of a particular sect you won't eat it. There are Hindus that won't eat the cow, but they will eat the bull. There are Muslims, Jews, Zoroastrians in India – different people eat different things.'

A lot of game features on the menu. Cyrus' father used to go out hunting, so he grew up eating partridge, quail, pheasant, grouse, deer, mallard and goose. Cyrus sits on Prince Charles' Mutton Renaissance Committee, and mutton features heavily on the menu; he is also promoting veal. 'British veal is probably the best you can get, and we favour rose veal, not white. I spent 8 years in Goa, where they eat pork, and as I eat pork myself, we have pork on the menu.

'I cook for the family at the weekend, if I'm allowed, but I will not get into the bad books of the boss!' jokes Cyrus, and that 'boss' is Pervin, who is the grounding force for the man and the indispensible partner in their restaurant.

Pervin always wanted to be a chef, and she met Cyrus in May 1981 when training at the Dadar catering college in Mumbai. She got a job as a chef at the Taj Group and in 1984 Cyrus and Pervin decided to marry. Cyrus was adamant that they could not work in the same kitchen – he was already Executive Chef at Taj Group in Goa – as he could not envisage being Pervin's supervisor. She moved to the restaurant at the Taj Holiday Village. Their first son was born in Goa, and Pervin stayed at home for a while. They eventually left Taj and moved to Poona to run their own restaurant.

Cyrus had catered for meetings of Commonwealth Heads of Government in Goa, and Bob Hawke (then the Australian PM) had sent him an invitation to come to his home country, but at the same time Cyrus got a job offer in London, which had always seemed like a second home to the couple after earlier visits. Pervin recollects: 'When we had come on holiday in 1985, we discovered that there was no restaurant to be found near the Tower of London. Little did I know that we would be here working in 1991.'

Eventually, in 1995, they opened Café Spice Namaste in Prescot Street, with Michael Gottlieb. He had visited their previous restaurant, and had asked for a meeting with Cyrus and Pervin. Pervin had been able to tell Michael what he had ordered for his meal weeks before, and he was stunned that she could remember, but Pervin explained that she pays attention to what the customer wants because she genuinely cares.

Parsees love their food – they are famed for it – and that includes Pervin. 'I went into catering in order to show my brother that I could beat him at college – and I did! My father loved food, and when he saw anything new in the market he would bring it home to try. Both my mum and my brother are good cooks, as well.

'I don't ever regret not going to Australia. London is my home, and I love it. My younger son is very "British". I still love India, of course, and my elder son lives there, so I'm torn sometimes, and I miss the comforts there, because I'm working harder here than ever before!' That's the price of the very real success of Café Spice Namaste, and its uniquely diverse menu.

Café Spice Namaste
16 Prescot Street, London E1 8AZ
Phone 020 7488 9242 **www.cafespice.co.uk**

KERALA NYAND MASALA

Nyand means crab, and this is Keralan style, taking a little of the local culture and adapting it for our menu, as in India you would not 'pick' the crabmeat, you would eat it straight from the shell – break the shell, cut it into four, crack the claws, throw it into the recipe. Here we serve it with fresh coconut, mustard seeds, white lentils, cumin and curry leaves. The idea emerged from some vegetable dishes that we cooked in the Keralan way. I thought we should apply it to crab, and it worked like magic. It's now on the menu, served with a simple coconut curry and steamed rice – expensive but a great dish.

SERVES 4

300–400g *fresh white crab meat*
2 tablespoons *sunflower oil*
2 teaspoons *black mustard seeds*
1 tablespoon *peeled and finely chopped ginger*
2 *garlic cloves, crushed*
6–8 *fresh curry leaves, finely shredded*
1 *dry red chilli, soaked in water for several hours and finely shredded (optional)*
2 *green chillies, slender types, slit lengthways*
2–3 *small shallots, finely chopped*
150–200g *fresh grated coconut*
$\frac{1}{2}$ teaspoon *red chilli powder*
$\frac{1}{2}$ teaspoon *ground turmeric*
2 *small plum tomatoes, diced and strained of juice*
2 tablespoons *finely chopped coriander leaves*
salt

Measure out all your ingredients in advance. Pick over the crab meat to ensure that there are no hidden pieces of shell or cartilage.

Using a wok or *kadhai* (the Indian version of a wok) or deep frying pan, heat the oil until it forms a haze. Add a couple of mustard seeds to check if they foam and crackle immediately. When the oil is ready, add the mustard seeds and cover the pan with a lid for a few moments to prevent the seeds from flying off in all directions or hitting your face.

As soon as the crackling dies down and there is a roasted aroma, add the ginger, garlic, curry leaves and the red and green chilli. When the garlic turns pale but not deep in colour, add the shallots and continue to sauté for several minutes over a medium heat until they soften. Add the coconut and sauté for 3–4 minutes, then add the red chilli powder and turmeric. Sauté for a minute or two, then add the diced tomato and the fresh coriander. Sauté for about 30 seconds, then add the crab meat, tossing well for about a minute, and check the seasoning.

Serve with some plain rice or thick savoury pancakes – this makes an excellent filler.

LEELI KOLMI NI CURRY

This quite simply translates as green prawn curry. A cultural issue here with Parsee curry: it always was prepared with fish, not prawns, but it works with seafood, or chicken. The reason is that the curry is light and lush. It doesn't like being re-heated as it splits easily. To stabilise the curry I have added cashew nuts to it (which my mother would not do!). A true Zoroastrian would add puréed almonds, but I have used cashew nuts because after soaking in hot water, they purée more easily.

Leeli simply means green, so it's a light green curry, typical of Parsee flavours, not heavily spiced. There is a hint of chilli, but it's not overly noticeable – the flavouring comes from cardamom, cloves and cassia bark. We Indians would love it with onion salad; the British have reservations, but to us raw onions and curry go hand-in-hand, especially red onions.

This dish is adaptable to fish, prawn, chicken, eggs (either poached and slipped into the curry, or soft-boil the eggs, plunge into ice-cold water to make them easy to peel, then simmer in the curry. The yolk will not go black this way.) You can serve this as a starter in a puri, on toast or small pizza bases. A little crab meat can be stretched this way.

SERVES 4

2 tablespoons vegetable oil
4 green cardamom pods, cracked
4 cloves
5-cm piece of cassia bark (Indian cinnamon)
1 onion, finely sliced
3 garlic cloves, crushed
1½ tablespoons peeled and finely chopped ginger
2 green chillies, de-seeded and finely chopped
½ teaspoon ground turmeric
1 teaspoon ground cumin
1 tablespoon ground coriander
1 can (400ml) of coconut milk (or the extract of two coconuts)
100g ground almonds
50g cashew nuts, chopped
5–6 curry leaves
salt
500g raw prawns, shelled, or white fish steaks (we Parsees would settle for white king prawns which we feel give the best flavour, but a good white fish such as sea bass or black tiger prawns work well. Avoid very strongly scented and oily fish, as the curry is delicate and would be easily overpowered. You can use fish fillets or steaks. However, steaks are preferable as they do not disintegrate so easily in the curry – 5–6 fillets are adequate for this recipe.)
a few large cooked prawns, shell on, or 2 tablespoons roughly chopped coriander leaves, to garnish

Add the oil to a casserole over a medium heat. When hot, add the cracked cardamom, cloves and cassia bark, and sauté for a minute. Add the sliced onions and sauté until translucent. Do not allow to brown. Add the garlic, ginger and green chillies and cook for around 5 minutes, again taking care not to brown.
Mix the turmeric, cumin and ground coriander in 100ml of water and add to the casserole.

Blend the coconut milk, the ground almonds and cashew nuts in a blender or processor until you have a smooth paste. Add a little water if required to give it the consistency of single cream.

As soon as the liquid in the casserole begins to dry, add the coconut milk mixture and stir continuously for a minute or two over a medium heat. Add the curry leaves. Bring the contents gently to the boil, stirring slowly. Add salt to taste, and simmer for a minute or two.

Add the fish or prawns. If you are using fish fillets or prawns, I suggest you allow the pan to be on the heat for only 2 minutes, then cover the pan and turn off the heat. The latent heat in the curry will be adequate to cook the fish or prawns through, ready for serving within 5–6 minutes. If using thick-cut steaks, cook for 2–4 minutes and then follow the same procedure. Either way, the fish should not be allowed to overcook.

Garnish with chopped coriander leaves, and serve with fried papads and plain rice or a light cumin pulao.

MASALA NU ROAST GOS

This is a Parsee-style roasted joint of lamb, predominantly made with shank of lamb – British lamb, which is probably the best in the world. Once roasted, the lamb may be sliced and served hot with boiled rice or a light cumin pulao, or cold as a sandwich filler. Parsis will have this with half a ton of deep-fried or crispy-roasted potatoes – don't skimp on these! You marinate the shank with spices, roast it, make the gravy, then simmer the shank in it until the meat literally falls off the bone. I think it works beautifully.

SERVES 4

1 teaspoon cumin seeds
1 tablespoon coriander seeds
50g ginger, roughly chopped
4–6 large cloves garlic, roughly
    chopped
Approximately 12 small potatoes
2–3 tablespoons sunflower oil
4 lamb shanks, medium (trimmed of
    fat and membrane)
Two 3-cm pieces of cinnamon or casia
    bark
3–4 green cardamom pods
2–3 cloves
3–4 peppercorns
3 onions, roughly chopped
200g chopped tomatoes, roughly
    chopped
50ml, or as needed, lamb stock,
    vegetable stock or water
1 teaspoon salt, then to taste
2 tablespoons roughly chopped
    coriander leaves

In a small frying pan dry-roast the cumin and coriander seeds on a low heat until they change colour slightly, and allow to cool.

In a blender, grind together the ginger, garlic and the roasted cumin and coriander to a fine paste with only as much water as is necessary. Set aside.

Peel the potatoes, remove any spots and keep them soaked in water.

Using a casserole big enough to take the shanks of lamb, heat the oil until a light haze forms on the surface. Reduce the heat a little and add the lamb. Brown well on all sides until the meat is well sealed.

If using an oven-proof casserole, preheat the oven to 150°C/Gas Mark 2.

Remove the lamb from the casserole and add the whole spices. Sauté for a minute or so on a low heat until the cloves swell a bit, then deglaze the casserole with a little water and scrape with a wooden spatula to release the residue from the lamb stuck to the base.

Add the chopped onions. Continue cooking until the liquid evaporates and the onions are now being sautéed. Cook for several minutes until the onions are soft, then add the ground ginger and garlic mixture. Rinse out the grinder with a little water to release any stuck masala and add this to the pan as well. Continue cooking for 5–6 minutes, then return the lamb to the casserole.

Coat the lamb well with the ginger and garlic masala, check seasoning and add salt as desired. Lower the heat, cover the pan tightly and continue cooking the lamb.
At this stage if your casserole is ovenproof, transfer the casserole, covered, to the oven. After about 15 minutes, turn the meat. If cooking on the hob, turn the meat after 10 minutes and also check to see that the contents are not burning at the base. In either case, if the contents dry out too much or the onions are burning, add some water or stock to loosen the residue from the bottom of the pan.

In another 15 minutes or so, the lamb should be approximately half cooked. Add the chopped tomatoes and the potatoes and, if necessary, more water or stock, cover and continue cooking for a further 10–15 minutes.

If not using a thermometer, the best way to test the lamb is to note the shrinkage – when the lamb is almost cooked, the muscles at the shin will have retracted and the lamb will feel soft to the touch. If in doubt, insert a thin skewer or a roasting fork and check to see if the juices are running clear. A thermometer inserted into the thickest part should read at least 70°C.

When the shanks are done, remove them and the potatoes from the pan and set aside. Check the gravy and, if necessary, add enough liquid to give a pouring consistency. Finish with the freshly chopped coriander.

Either serve the lamb sliced hot with the gravy and the potatoes, or serve it later by slicing it when cold. Best served with chunks of deep fried par-boiled potato and steamed rice.

MUTTON CANNON NI SEEK BOTI

As a child I grew up eating *Seek Boti* that my Mum used to make. It was the most amazing experience and a special treat (because it was a pain to make, and we used to have to goad Mum into making it once every few months). Back then, we made it with goat, and it's cooked first, then skewered, rolled in flour, dipped in egg and fried. Serve with a raw mango salad – beautiful!

You have to be friendly with your butcher to get cannon of lamb, but you can substitute your favourite cut of lamb. You may like to start the preparation a day before actually cooking it. This will make the meat tender, as well as allow the masala to penetrate. Small wooden skewers used to serve are a little bigger than cocktail sticks and are available in all oriental stores, as well as many supermarkets.

SERVES 4

2 tablespoons ginger-garlic paste
$1/2$ teaspoon ground turmeric
2 teaspoons ground coriander
1 teaspoon ground cumin
1 teaspoon red chilli powder, or to taste
$1/2$ teaspoon garam masala
1 tablespoon lemon juice
salt, to taste
500g cannon of mutton (or your favourite cut of lamb if mutton is not available), cut into 2-cm dice

For frying
vegetable oil (approximately 2cm depth of oil in the pan)
1 large green chilli, finely chopped
1 tablespoon roughly chopped coriander leaves
$1^1/2$ teaspoons very finely chopped ginger
2 garlic cloves, very finely chopped
2 eggs
3–4 tablespoons plain flour

Put the ginger-garlic, turmeric, ground coriander, cumin, chilli powder, garam masala, lemon juice and salt into a non-metallic dish. Add the meat and coat with the spice mix. Cover and set aside at room temperature for 2–3 hours, then transfer to the refrigerator and leave it there for 5–6 hours, or more if possible.

Heat a casserole and add 2 tablespoons of oil. Let the oil heat to almost smoking point.

Pat the meat dry and add to the casserole. (Reserve the marinade if you are using a cut that needs more cooking.) Stir for a few minutes until the meat is well browned – you will find that a residue accumulates at the bottom of the pan.

If using tender meat cuts, simply brown well, remove from the heat. For all other cuts that need more cooking, ensure the pieces are well browned, add one or two tablespoons of water and the juices from the marinade. Scrape the bottom with a wooden spatula, check for seasoning, cover tightly and cook on a low heat, just enough to make the contents bubble gently. When the meat is more than half cooked, uncover the pan and cook until the liquid has almost dried out. When you see a thick coating over the meat, switch off.

Stir in the chopped chilli, coriander, ginger and garlic to coat the pieces of meat. When cool enough to handle, mix once again and start the process of skewering the meat pieces.

Cut the skewers all to an even length. The sticks should be smaller than the pan in which you are to fry them and the bowl which you will use for the beaten eggs. Take four pieces or so per stick if you are offering these as snacks, or more if you are serving as a main course.

Beat the eggs in a bowl, adding a pinch or two of salt, and pour into a wide flat dish. Put the flour on a plate.

Heat the oil in a wide, deep frying pan to a moderate temperature. (If the oil gets too hot, the egg will brown instantly and the kebabs will not heat or cook right through. If you do make this mistake, then place them on a paper towel in a moderate oven for a few minutes before serving.)

Roll each kebab in the flour, dip it in the egg and fry. Do not worry about taking extra egg on the stick as this will help to make the kebabs attractively frilly.

You can serve them with green chutney or a hot ketchup.

OSTRICH TIKKA TOOFAN MAIL

Toofan Mail was India's best-known mail train, thundering from Dehradun in the north to Mumbai on the southwest coast and boasting a very good dining car. Its name came to be used for any fast-moving vehicle or a product that sold fast. *Toofan* also means a storm, a typhoon (from the same Sanskrit word) and I called the ostrich tikka 'Toofan' because I made it really hot, a typhoon in your mouth. I thought ostrich would do extremely well in Indian recipes, because it is easily available, very lean, low in saturated fat and cholesterol, virtually a poultry coloured red.

You should start the preparation the day before, to allow time for marinading.

SERVES 4

500g ostrich, either whole fillet or cut into cubes or thin slices if barbecuing
1 tablespoon salt, or to taste
2 tablespoons sesame or mustard oil
2-cm pieces cinnamon stick
3–4 green cardamom pods
2–3 star anise
1 tablespoon fennel seeds
8–10 garlic cloves, chopped
1 tablespoon finely chopped ginger
2–3 green chillies, chopped
3–4 dried red chillies, torn or snipped into small pieces
250ml Greek-style yoghurt
1 tablespoon lemon juice (juice from about 1/2 lemon)
1 bunch (approximately 100g) of coriander, leaves and stalks separated and roughly chopped

Rub the salt into the ostrich meat and set aside.

Heat the oil in a pan to a medium heat, add all the remaining ingredients except the coriander leaves, yoghurt and lemon juice, and cook gently without colouring. Stir frequently and fry for a couple of minutes, until the heat has penetrated right through and the dried chillies are gently roasting.

Leave to cool, then grind to a smooth paste in a blender with the yoghurt and lemon juice, making sure all the spices are very finely ground. Pass through your finest sieve.

Pat the meat dry with kitchen paper, then rub the paste into the ostrich meat. Place in a clean bowl, cover and leave at room temperature for about 2 hours, then transfer to the refrigerator for 8–10 hours. For a dense meat, such as ostrich, an overnight marinade is essential.

To cook the meat, grill under a high heat or on a barbecue, turning after 3–4 minutes. (If cooking cubed meat on a barbecue, thread onto metal skewers.) Once it is well coloured on both sides, check a piece for tenderness. Be careful not to overcook it.

Sprinkle over the chopped coriander leaves, and serve with a salad and a green pea pulao.

ROHIT KHATTAR AND MANPREET SINGH AHUJA

CHOR BIZARRE

In recent years there has been a trend towards rather anonymous Indian restaurants – contemporary with Asian accents is becoming the norm. There's nothing wrong with that. After all, British restaurants don't have waiters dressed as Beefeaters, and French restaurants don't have sprays of garlic decorating every table. But Chor Bizarre bucks that trend and makes a statement that is undoubtedly Indian. It's a true warehouse of Indian furniture and crafts that we Europeans, and it seems many Indians, find both romantic and exotic.

Rohit Khattar is the owner of this food and fantasy emporium, and it is a reflection of two of his passions. 'I have always had a hobby of collecting junk – I can't throw anything away. My wife Rashmi and I went to various markets around India, gathered together a collection of bric-a-brac, put it all into a restaurant, and called it Chor Bizarre. Bizarre was a pun on "bazaar" and Chor means "thief", so it's a thieves' market! It was great fun: nothing matched, and we bought a four-poster bed, and a vintage Fiat car, some mismatched crockery and cutlery.' Rohit's second passion is, of course, food. 'We did a lot of research on the dishes – we wanted it to be a melting-pot of the best from across the country – and it caught people's imagination.' They opened the original Chor Bizarre in Delhi in 1990 and before they knew it, they had queues of people waiting to sample the food and to admire the 'junk'.

A friend of the family, Mahendra Kaul, OBE, owned the Gaylord restaurant in Mayfair, but used to visit the original Chor Bizarre when in India – he loved it. Mr Kaul was a pioneering restaurateur, not only having opened the chain of Gaylord restaurants in London, Birmingham and Manchester, but was also a broadcaster extraordinaire. So, in 1997, they decided to convert the Gaylord in Albemarle Street into a London version of the Chor Bizarre in India, and Rashmi Khattar designed this. 'Now it has been running for 14 years, very successfully,' says Rohit. 'It is true that you can ask to buy some of the items of furniture and decoration from the restaurant, though that does get difficult, and some of the signature items we would not sell because it's impossible to replace them – it's a nightmare for my wife, who has to try to restock. Some of the cherished items from Delhi have come to London, like the original four-poster bed.'

Yes, there truly is a four-poster bed, as well as ornate window frames made into glass-topped tables, a silver bedhead to act as a sumptuous banquette, marble tables, carved wood chairs, crafts, wrought metal, paintings, tiled floors – they all marry in a harmonious cacophony of subcontinental flamboyance. Rohit describes the furnishings as kitsch, but I would contend that this is kitsch in the very best of furnishing taste.

'The menu in the London Chor Bizarre is very similar to the one in Delhi – regional Indian cuisine, the best from everywhere. We serve some very interesting thalis, or platters: South Indian Tiffin, Maharaja Thali, Kashmiri Tarami. We've kept the character, and some people have been coming to us for over ten years now. We don't need to advertise, it's all by word of mouth.'

Chor Bizarre's Chef Manpreet Singh Ahuja comes from the Punjab. 'My mother played a huge role in instilling value and belief systems. Similarly my father, in saying "Have your own identity; do what you really want to do."' Their son has such a rich and warm singing voice (for which he is still praised) that he could have considered a career in

Bollywood, but evidently he chose not to pursue that avenue.

While in the final year at school, Manpreet applied for a hotel management course. He, unlike most fellow students, had been flicking through the newspaper advertisements for creative career ideas, rather than seeking the more traditional options – medicine or engineering – that were his peers' preferred choices. He saw an advertisement placed by the National Council for Hotel Management and Catering Technology for a three-year course. He liked the sound of hotels – glamorous with the potential for excellent management experience. It seemed to him like a path that offered excitement and the opportunity to do something that was still quite uncommon. 'There was a sense of relief when I passed the entrance test, followed by the interview.' Then came the time to choose a city in which to study. A friend who was a local hotel manager gave Manpreet some advice: 'He told me that if I put my favourite city as my first preference, chances were that I would not get it, so I should put Delhi as number one and my favourite, Mumbai, as number two.' Manpreet's acceptance on to the Mumbai course turned out to be a life-changing moment.

At the end of the course in 1995 Manpreet was interviewed and selected as a management trainee by four hotel companies including the Taj Group. Every year this hotel chain would take on about half the students, so he asked himself what was so special about getting in. Then along came Old World Hospitality, an independent start-up company. They had one small three-star hotel, The Broadway in Delhi; and then there was the managing director, Rohit Khattar, a flamboyant 33-year old who took the whole class of students by storm with his eloquent and persuasive presentation style. He declared, 'I'm looking for ambitious entrepreneurs to help the company grow.' Having recently been awarded the contract to run India's largest conference and convention centre project – Habitat World in Delhi – Rohit's vision and projects looked inspiring and the growth prospects promising. This sounded like the perfect opportunity for the young chef, who chose excitement over security and much to the surprise of his peers, faculty and family he went for it, joining Rohit as a management trainee.

The London branch of Chor Bizarre opened in October 1997 and Manpreet was deputed overseas as part of the management team. Chor Bizarre has stuck to traditional Indian dishes, using authentic ingredients, and presenting a menu that exhibits specialities from all the different regions of India. People are charmed by the ambience. 'I would like to credit Rohit Khattar for his innovation and imagination in bringing together such a great concept – no two tables match, there is a buzz about the place, and like a museum there is always something to look at, to be discovered; one visit is not enough.'

He adds, 'When a customer comes into a restaurant there is typically half an hour or so between the time he comes through the door and the time he sees his first dish – being seated at his four-poster bed or window frame, being offered the menu, taking the drinks order, perusing the menu, placing the order, then waiting for the food. So what are you going to do during that time? Look at blank walls, other customers? At Chor Bizarre, you are constantly gazing around and discovering new things. The Kashmiri corner, for instance, resembles the interior of a houseboat in the Dal Lake – wood panelled, a small bed, a little window onto the lake.' The décor is striking, but it's equally the memory of Chor Bizarre's authentic cuisine that will linger.

'The "old-world" hospitality of the company's name chimes with the values instilled in me by my family, who always extended the warmest hospitality to guests and relatives who would visit home. I don't know if it was just coincidence that I joined a company with that name, but I naturally bought into that philosophy, and we at Chor Bizarre aim to provide just that. It's a complete dining experience. I like to have a rapport with my customers and give them what they want. I try to be flexible, so if they want me to do an event that is unique I tweak the menu and improvise to make it a bespoke occasion – I don't insist that there is only one way to do it.'

Chor Bizarre is a testament to the company name. The restaurant is warm, intimate and welcoming. Guests, for indeed that's what you are considered here, enjoy some of the best Indian food from across the subcontinent. You relax and soak up the scene. On leaving, ladies are offered a bangle or two as a souvenir of their evening. I now have a good collection of bangles and there will be more in future.

Chor Bizarre
16 Albemarle Street, Mayfair, London W1S 4HW
Phone 020 7629 9802 **www.chorbizarre.com**

BHARWAN SEENA, KESARI ANGUR RAS
(STUFFED CHICKEN BREASTS WITH A SAFFRON SAUCE AND GRAPES)

I may have digressed here towards a western European style, as stuffed chicken is not common in traditional Indian cuisine. But Indian food is not the same any more, is it? People are adventurous, and want to see what they can do differently with ingredients. This recipe was inspired by the first chef I worked for in Old World Hospitality, whose name is Chef Anand. He was passionate about European food, and he used to do a divine chicken breast stuffed with spinach and prunes served with jus. Here I have made a heartier stuffing, and have used saffron in the sauce – I love the colour and the unique flavour of that spice. This is a rich and substantial main course. It may take a while to prepare but the end product is really exquisite in terms of taste, textures, flavours and presentation.

SERVES 4

4 chicken breasts, skinless, with wing
  bone attached
pinch of salt
pinch of ground white pepper
vegetable oil, for grilling

For the stuffing
150g chicken mince
75g onions, finely chopped
20g pistachios, roughly chopped
20g almonds, blanched, slivered
20g water chestnuts, roughly chopped
1 teaspoon chopped fresh ginger
1 teaspoon finely chopped coriander
  leaves
salt and ground white pepper

For the sauce
4–5 stigmas saffron
50ml milk
50ml sunflower oil
200g onions, finely chopped
5–6 green cardamom pods
7-cm piece of cinnamon stick
2–3 fresh bay leaves
15g ginger paste
15g garlic paste
50g whole cashew nuts, lightly fried
1 tomato, chopped
1/4 teaspoon ground turmeric
1/2 teaspoon Kashmiri red chilli powder
1/2 teaspoon ground coriander
1/4 teaspoon ground cumin
75ml yoghurt
50ml single cream
8 grapes, seedless, red or green, halved

For the garnish
12 grapes, seedless, red or green,
  carefully halved with a sharp knife
few pistachio nuts, roughly chopped
few stigmas of saffron (optional)

Soak the saffron for the sauce in the milk and leave while you continue with the other steps.

Combine all the ingredients for the stuffing and season with salt.

Slit open each chicken breast lengthways to create a flat heart-shaped sheet; season with salt and pepper. Place the stuffing in the chicken breasts, roll them up tightly and secure using a trussing needle and string.

Pre-heat the oven to 170°C/ Gas Mark 3½.

Continue with the sauce. Heat the oil in a saucepan, add the chopped onions, and stir over a medium heat for a few minutes until they become translucent. Add the cardamom, cinnamon and bay leaves, and cook for a few minutes on a medium heat. When the onions turn light golden colour, add the ginger and garlic pastes and the cashew nuts. Cook until the onions turn light brown, then add the tomato, followed by the ground spices, and cook for another 10 minutes. Add the yoghurt and cook for 5–10 minutes.

Remove the sauce from the heat and leave to cool. Remove the cinnamon sticks and bay leaves; process the sauce until smooth using a blender, and strain.

Grill the stuffed chicken breasts on a ridged non-stick pan, coated with a little oil, for 5–7 minutes, then transfer to the pre-heated oven for around 30 minutes or until cooked through.

Remove the string around each chicken breast and thickly slice each breast diagonally. Keep warm.

Return the sauce to a low heat, bring to a simmer, add the cream and adjust the seasoning. Gently reduce the sauce to a thick consistency, add the soaked saffron and milk, and remove from the heat. Stir the 8 halved grapes into the sauce to warm through.

To serve, ladle the sauce onto the plate, place the sliced chicken breasts on the sauce and serve hot garnished with the remaining grapes, the pistachio nuts and the saffron, if using. Serve with rice or Indian bread.

BHEIN AUR LAUKI TIKKIS
(MARROW AND LOTUS ROOT PATTIES)

Marrow and lotus root are both cheap and easy to find in India, but they are quite bland, so you need to add lots of flavour. When you boil the lotus root it still retains some bite, compared to the marrow which becomes soft. I wash and deseed the chillies, then wash them again, but you can retain the seeds if you want more punch. I love the explosion of the pomegranate seeds when you bite into the patty. Enjoy these with a really hot cup of masala tea.

SERVES 4

For the patty mixture
250g marrow (lauki or doodhi)
salt
250g lotus root
50g chana dal, boiled until soft (20–30 minutes) and mashed
100g potatoes, boiled and grated
1/2 teaspoon cumin seeds, toasted in a dry pan and crushed
1/2 teaspoon crushed garlic, fried until golden
1 teaspoon chaat masala

For the stuffing
30ml vegetable oil
1/2 teaspoon cumin seeds
1/2 teaspoon finely chopped ginger
1 tablespoon green peas, blanched
pinch of ground turmeric
1/2 teaspoon finely chopped green chillies
about 50 fresh pomegranate seeds, 4 seeds per patty
pinch of salt

Peel the marrow, cut lengthwise, deseed and grate it into a non-metallic dish. Sprinkle about 1 teaspoon of salt over and stir it in, set aside for 10 minutes, then squeeze out excess moisture using a muslin cloth.

Peel the lotus root and boil in salted water for 35–40 minutes, then drain, cool and grate.

Combine the marrow and lotus root together in a mixing bowl with the chana dal, potatoes, cumin, garlic and chaat masala, and add salt to taste. Divide the mixture into 12 equal portions, and press each one with moistened hands to make a compact ball.

To make the stuffing, heat the oil in a small pan, add the cumin seeds and allow to crackle, and add the ginger and peas. Add the turmeric, stir and remove from the heat; allow to cool. Combine the green chillies and pomegranate seeds with the pea mixture; adjust the seasoning. Flatten each ball and make an indentation in the centre. Put a one-twelfth portion of the stuffing into the indentation, fold the sides over to form a ball again, and flatten evenly into a square shape.

Heat more oil in a non-stick pan over a medium heat and fry the patties for a few minutes on one side until light golden. Turn the patties and repeat on the other side. Drain on kitchen paper and serve hot on a decorative plate with a chutney of your choice – I prefer sweet tamarind chutney.

MANGO AND MINT SMOKED SALMON WITH KACHUMBER SALAD

I fell in love with this particular creation almost by accident. I was cooking for a charity event at Old Billingsgate serving 600 people, which was the biggest outdoor catering event that Chor Bizarre had ever undertaken. The biggest challenge was that we couldn't cook 'live' at the event, so we had to pre-cook. I used a smoking chamber to get the smoky flavour infused into the salmon. This was a great success, and the coriander, mint and green mango helped create a very light and fresh-tasting dish. This recipe gives the normally heavy and oily salmon a tangy kick and a lightness that tickles the tastebuds and builds your appetite for the rest of your meal. Serve as a starter or as a second course before mains.

SERVES 4

450g salmon fillets, skinned and pin-boned

For the first marinade
2 teaspoons finely chopped garlic
1 teaspoon lemon juice
1/2 teaspoon salt, or to taste
1 teaspoon finely chopped coriander stalks
1/2 teaspoon royal cumin seeds (black caraway)

For the paste or second marinade
30g coriander leaves
30g mint leaves
30g raw mango (a small green mango used only for cooking, and labelled as 'raw'), peeled and stone removed
1 tablespoon lemon juice
2 tablespoons roughly chopped ginger
2 garlic cloves, roughly chopped
1–2 green chillies, de-seeded
1 tablespoon rapeseed oil

2–3 tablespoons Greek yoghurt

For the kachumber
50g cucumber, finely chopped
1 tomato, deseeded and finely chopped
30g pink onions or shallots, finely chopped
1–2 long, thin, green chillies, deseeded and finely chopped
salt
a few drops of lemon juice
1 teaspoon finely chopped mint leaves
1 teaspoon finely chopped coriander leaves
1/2 teaspoon cumin seeds, toasted in a dry pan and ground

For smoking
8-cm piece burning charcoal
2–3 cloves
1/2 teaspoon butter

1 tablespoon rapeseed oil for cooking/grilling
a few banana leaves, cut into circles, for serving
fresh mint sprigs, to garnish

Cut the salmon into 8-cm square pieces (or 4 equal pieces from the fillet), wash and pat dry. You may cut into 8 even-sized pieces if you prefer.

Combine all the ingredients for the first marinade in a non-metallic bowl, add the salmon, stir to coat and marinate for 5–10 minutes. Remove the fish to a clean plate and pat dry with kitchen paper. Set aside.

Prepare the second marinade by processing all the ingredients except the yoghurt in a blender to a smooth paste. Combine the yoghurt and the paste in a mixing bowl and whisk together. Add this to the salmon pieces and refrigerate for around 15 minutes.

For the kachumber, combine the finely chopped cucumber, tomatoes, onions, chillies and salt. Hang in a muslin cloth over a bowl for about 5 minutes to allow excess moisture to drip through. Tip the drained cucumber mixture into a bowl, add the lemon juice, chopped herbs and toasted cumin, and refrigerate.

To smoke the fish, place a small stainless steel bowl in the centre of a larger mixing bowl. Place the marinated salmon in the bigger bowl, around the small bowl. Prepare an aluminium foil sheet large enough to cover and seal the large bowl. Put the hot charcoal in the small bowl, place the cloves and butter on the charcoal and immediately seal the mixing bowl with foil to retain the smoke. Keep covered for 15 minutes, then transfer the salmon pieces onto a non-stick ridged griddle pan.

Ensure that the marinade is lightly, but evenly distributed over the surface of the fish, and brush with a little oil. Grill the salmon pieces for about 2–3 minutes then turn, brush that side with a little oil, and grill for another 2–3 minutes.

Place the banana leaves on serving plates, spoon the kachumber salad into the centre and gently place the hot and smoked salmon on the salad; garnish with sprigs of mint.

MAKAI, BHINDI AUR HARE PYAAZ KI SABZI
OKRA WITH BABY CORN AND SPRING ONION

This is one of my favourite dishes – I absolutely love the colours, textures and flavours. I'm very fond of vegetables, and I think they are so much more interesting than meat which usually needs the addition of vegetables and herbs to give it a lift. This recipe is dedicated to my paternal grandmother who is a fantastic, strictly vegetarian cook – everything she makes has such sweetness, which comes from the TLC she puts into every dish.

The recipe is very simple and combines ingredients of different textures that complement each other to create a colourful and tasteful dish. Serve as an accompaniment on your lunch or dinner table. You can use corn kernels instead of baby corn, and it works just as well.

SERVES 4

400g okra
100g baby corn
$\frac{1}{4}$ teaspoon, plus a pinch of ground turmeric
2 tablespoons sunflower oil
30g fresh ginger, thinly sliced
salt
$\frac{1}{2}$ teaspoon dry mango powder (amchur powder)
2 long, thin green chillies, halved, seeds removed, thinly sliced
4–5 spring onions, finely sliced diagonally
50g cherry tomatoes

For the garnish
$\frac{1}{2}$ teaspoon crushed coriander seeds
a few coriander leaves

Wash the okra well and soak in cold water for 2–3 minutes to remove the grit. Drain and pat dry. Trim off the heads and the small tapered ends. Cut the okra into 5-cm pieces.

Cut the baby corn diagonally into 5-cm pieces. Blanch in salted boiling water infused with a pinch of turmeric for about 2 minutes, drain and cool.

In a wok or kadai (an Indian wok) or deep frying pan, heat the oil, add the ginger and cook for a few seconds. Add the okra and stir frequently, but gently on high heat (okra releases its stickiness in this process, but this stops by itself after a while). At that point, reduce the heat and add salt, $\frac{1}{4}$ teaspoon of turmeric and a little water. Add the mango powder and green chillies, stir gently and add more water if necessary so that the contents do not stick to the bottom of the pan. Cover with a perforated lid for 2–3 minutes (this ensures that the okra does not discolour or lose its green hue).

When the okra is tender, add the baby corn and spring onions and combine gently ensuring the okra is not mashed. Add the cherry tomatoes and switch off the heat.

Transfer into a flat white or glass serving dish and serve hot, garnished with crushed coriander seeds and fresh coriander leaves.

CHENA SEB SANDWICHES AUR STRAWBERRY RABRI

(STEWED APPLES SANDWICHED WITH SOFT CHEESE, WITH STRAWBERRY-FLAVOURED INDIAN CUSTARD)

This is something that I really wanted to incorporate in Chor Bizarre's menu this year – the idea was to have a sweet sandwich. The inspiration came from a very dear friend, Brinder Narula of Star of India, who brought me a lot of beautiful green apples from his garden. The stuffing came about when I was trying to demonstrate a Ras Malai recipe (an Indian milk dessert) to my wife, and we had some of the mixture left over. Cinnamon has long been used as the spice to complement the tanginess of apples. I suggest Pink Lady apples as they are the sweetest, but you could use Cox's or Braeburn because they have a good texture, but don't use Granny Smith's.

SERVES 4

3 Pink Lady apples, peeled and cored
   and sliced into thick rounds
cloves, for securing sandwiches
cinnamon powder, for dusting
strawberries, for garnish
milk chocolate shavings

For the cinnamon syrup
100g sugar
200ml water
8-cm cinnamon stick

For the rabri
1 litre full-fat milk
250g strawberries, hulled
30g sugar

For the chena
1 litre full-fat milk
30ml lemon juice
30g caster sugar
1/4 teaspoon ground cardamom

To make the cinnamon syrup, combine the sugar, water and cinnamon stick in a small saucepan, bring to the boil, stirring frequently, and simmer until slightly reduced.

To prepare the rabri, boil the milk in a non-stick saucepan and then transfer to another non-stick saucepan (a second pan is needed because the sides of the first pan will become coated with cooked milk which would be liable to burn), return this to the heat and simmer over a low heat, stirring frequently and ensuring it does not stick to the bottom, until the milk has reduced to approximately half its original volume. Stir in the chopped strawberries and cook for a minute or so. Remove from the heat, allow to cool, then chill.

For the chena, boil the milk and allow to cool to around 85°C. Slowly add the lemon juice and stir thoroughly until the curds and whey separate, then pass through a muslin cloth. While still in the muslin cloth, rinse the cheese well to rid it of any acidity. Squeeze out any excess moisture, then tip into a bowl and combine with the caster sugar and cardamom.

Place the apple rounds into the cinnamon syrup and stew for around 2 minutes. Remove the apples from the syrup and place in a strainer to drain. Place some chena in between three apple slices (like a club sandwich); continue with the remaining slices to make the rest of the sandwiches.

Place strawberry slices in the centre of each plate. Spoon the rabri over the strawberries. Place the apple sandwiches (one three-storey sandwich per plate) on the rabri. Sprinkle ground cinnamon onto the apples and the plate. Serve garnished with strawberry fans and with a biscuit curl or milk chocolate shavings on the sandwich.

HARI NAGARAJ

CINNAMON CLUB

Cinnamon Club is just a short stroll from some of Westminster's most iconic and prominent sites, including the Houses of Parliament, the London Eye and Westminster Abbey. It's housed in the former Westminster Library, which was first opened to the public in 1893. It was thoughtfully converted into The Cinnamon Club, and this Grade II listed building still retains its Victorian charm and character.

There is no mistaking the pedigree of the building even before you enter the main restaurant. Warm wood and leaded windows remind the visitor of days past, when even a library was used as a canvas for craftsmanship. The bar lounge still sports bookshelves, but these days they are mostly filled with bottles of wine and decanters rather than *Grey's Elegy and The Rise and Fall of the Roman Empire*. The main dining room is an elegant space which displays many original architectural features, including a gallery of bookshelves, domed skylights and the mezzanine floor.

A hint of marble, the shimmer of Victorian glass, tan leather and suede, high-backed banquettes and dark wood contrive to offer the guest a haven from the rigours of Westminster. Those clients number amongst them the powerful and the posers, the celebrated and the celebrating, and anyone who wants a unique and thoroughly engaging culinary experience. Think fine French dining with an Indian vibrancy – an unbeatable marriage when those two elements are thoughtfully combined.

The Cinnamon Club was opened in 2001 after years of planning by Iqbal Wahhab, the former editor of *Tandoori* magazine. He employed chef Vivek Singh (see page 77) from the start, and Hari Nagaraj joined the team shortly after. Hari's passion for learning and food runs high, and he epitomises The Cinnamon Club's philosophy of 'beyond authenticity'.

It should have opened in 2000 and the reasons for the delay are a catalogue of building and financial horror – money trickles too slowly, builders down tools, builders find other work, money arrives, builders are otherwise occupied, and bits of building fall off. A lesser man than entrepreneur Iqbal Wahhab would have thrown in the oven glove.

The very fabric of the new Cinnamon Club kitchen was almost a catastrophe. The stoves – and they are always handy in a restaurant kitchen – arrived late, and when they were installed the kitchen was still minus a couple of vital components: gas and electricity. Enter one youthful and talented chef from India, Vivek Singh, who saved the day by suggesting that the opening cocktail party could be salvaged if the brand new tandoors could be commissioned.

Hari Nagaraj was born in Hyderabad in the south of India. His parents originated from a town in Kerala called Palakkad, near the border with Tamil Nadu. Hari remembers summer holidays back home in India. He and his two sisters were each allocated jobs in the house and kitchen. In Hyderabad there are so many culinary specialities from all the cultures – although it's mainly Muslim, there are Hindus, and people from other parts of the country settling there. Hari loved omelettes which he couldn't have at home as the family was vegetarian. So Hari would buy the eggs, give them to his neighbour to cook,

and Hari would go there to eat! 'My grandmother especially was very conservative, and disapproved of my cooking meat when I became a chef, but despite that, I was still her favourite grandson!'

Both sets of Hari's grandparents had experience in hotels and bed-and-breakfast hospitality. His father's generation took a break from catering and worked in education or administration, but hospitality was in his genes: 'Once I got into this profession, I loved it – I had the option of going into the service section or front-of-house, but I chose the kitchen from day one, and I've been learning ever since and these days I oversee both kitchen and restaurant. I landed up doing a hotel management course in Bangalore, and joined a group called Country Club India. After three months in Hyderabad with them, they opened a large club in Bangalore, and I helped them with that.'

At that time Oberoi's were opening a number of properties, and in 1998 Hari joined their Rajvilas Hotel where he worked for four years. That's where he met Vivek, who was to have such an impact on his career. Vivek had the opportunity to come to London to open Cinnamon Club, and Hari followed about six months later. 'I moved up the ladder from chef de partie to sous-chef to head chef, a position I have held for the past four years. I also have responsibility as Operations Manager for front-of-house, too, although it's the Head Chef part that I love best. I am very passionate about cooking.

'Before coming to Britain, the only other country I had been to was Hong Kong, so I was expecting huge buildings here, too, and as our staff accommodation was close to Canary Wharf, that was the "Hong Kong" connection for me! But, as I explored other parts of London, I saw the parallels with

Mumbai – the Victoria rail terminus, the double-decker buses and so on. I was living in an area with quite a large Bangladeshi community, so things didn't seem so different, and I didn't miss home too much. My first shock was when I actually had to make an appointment to go to a barber's shop for a haircut!' Most barbers in India, it seems, have a strictly 'walk-in' policy!

But Hari found the food was appalling, with curry-houses calling themselves 'Indian', but serving food that he didn't recognise. It motivated him to recreate what they were doing in India, but in a modern way. 'It's important to me to serve authentic food, but I want to break the barrier and educate people in modern Indian dishes. The best thing about this city is the access to the freshest of ingredients – seafood deliveries twice a day, the best of lamb. In India you can really only get mutton, so at Oberoi we used to import frozen New Zealand lamb. Here it's fresh, and aged, a concept not found in India. And I had not heard of so many different varieties of fish until I came to London.'

After 15 years working with Vivek, they now think alike. Both are great team players, and that's an important strength. 'There are 18 of us in the kitchen team now, with 10 or 11 working at any one time. We are open for breakfast, serving some Anglo-Indian specialities, as well as traditional English breakfasts. We needed someone here in the morning to receive deliveries, and someone to set up for lunch, so it seemed a good idea to combine that with a breakfast service.'

Cinnamon Club is famed for its meat dishes. Pigeon is a signature dish, either as a starter or main course, and is on the menu most of the year, except when game is in season, when they can give more prominence to partridge and pheasant. Red deer is also very popular, and they sometimes change the cooking style, the marination or the sauces, to give it a new twist. In 2005, the deer with pickling spices and aloo methi won *Restaurant* magazine's Best Curry Dish, and in 2009 with different accompaniments it won Best Game Dish. Since 1947 there has been a game-hunting ban in India, and the newer generations of chefs have little knowledge of game cooking. So when Hari got his hands on game, he was inspired to add grouse with pickling spices to the menu.

At home, both Hari and his wife cook, and perhaps once every two months they have a proper South Indian meal – a feast. 'My wife's from Mumbai, she's a good cook and

loves baked vegetables, pasta and Indian street food. If we go out to eat, I like to explore new openings. I don't have any preference for cuisine, though I enjoy Thai, Italian, Japanese, and French – Eric Chavot at The Capital was good, and Gordon Ramsay in Hospital Road.'

Hari is evidently fascinated by culinary innovation, and that is admirably reflected in Cinnamon Club's ever-changing seasonal menu. The restaurant has become a magnet for those with discerning palates; those who tread the corridors of power are regulars here, but its accessible charm attracts anyone with an appreciation of deft Indian spicing.

The Cinnamon Club
The Old Westminster Library, 30–32 Great Smith Street, London SW1P 3BU **Phone** 020 7222 2555
www.cinnamonclub.com

HERB-CRUSTED BLACK BREAM WITH JERUSALEM ARTICHOKE 'PODIMAS' AND TOMATO LEMON SAUCE

This is a traditional Keralan dish. If you can get a banana leaf, wrap the fish in that, or use parchment paper, to hold in all the moisture and it will be hard to overcook the fish. You can also use tilapia, sea bass or plaice. Podimas is a crushed vegetable dish, and this is a particularly delicate version, with Jerusalem artichokes giving a nutty taste.

SERVES 4

4 bream fillets, pin-boned
1/4 teaspoon fennel seeds
1/4 teaspoon black onion seeds
1/4 teaspoon ground turmeric
1/4 teaspoon salt, or to taste
1 teaspoon Dijon mustard

For the spice crust
4 slices of white bread
leaves from 1/2 bunch (approximately 50g) of coriander, roughly chopped
6 curry leaves
1/2 teaspoon chilli flakes

For the sauce
2 tablespoons ghee or clarified butter
1 bay leaf
8 ripe tomatoes, boiled in a little water until tender, then pushed through a sieve to make a purée
1 teaspoon ginger paste
1 teaspoon garlic paste
1 teaspoon red chilli powder, or to taste
1 teaspoon ground cumin
300ml coconut milk
1 lemongrass stalk, lightly crushed
2 lime leaves
1 1/4 teaspoons salt, or to taste
1/2 teaspoon sugar

For the Jerusalem artichoke podimas
200g Jerusalem artichoke, peeled and cut into 3–4cm chunks
1/4 teaspoon ground turmeric
2 teaspoons salt
1 tablespoon vegetable oil
1/4 teaspoon black mustard seeds
1 dried red chilli, broken in half
1 teaspoon chana dal, roasted in a dry pan
5–6 curry leaves
1 small onion, sliced
1 tablespoon finely chopped ginger
2 tablespoons finely chopped coriander leaves
juice of 1/2 lemon

To make the spice crust, chop the bread, coriander leaves and curry leaves in a processor to make a crumb, mix in the chilli flakes; lay out on a baking sheet and set to dry in a warm area or a very low oven.

Put the fish in a non-metallic dish and coat with the fennel seeds, onion seeds, turmeric, salt and the mustard; cover with clingfilm and put in the fridge or somewhere cool while you continue with the other steps.

To make the sauce, heat the ghee or butter in a wide non-stick frying pan, add the bay leaf and sieved tomatoes and simmer for 5 minutes. In a bowl, mix the ginger and garlic pastes, red chilli powder and cumin with a little water to make a smooth paste. Add the mixture to the pan and simmer for 5 minutes, stirring occasionally to prevent sticking. If the purée is very thick, you can thin it using some water or fish stock.

Stir in the coconut milk and simmer for 3–4 minutes, then add the crushed lemongrass and lime leaves. Cook for a few minutes until the sauce turns glossy. Add salt and sugar, simmer for another 3–4 minutes, until the sauce is infused with the lemon flavour. The sauce should have a pouring consistency. Discard the bay leaf, lemongrass and the lime leaf. Keep the sauce warm.

To make the podimas, boil the Jerusalem artichokes in 1 litre of water with the turmeric and salt for 10–15 minutes until tender but not disintegrating , then drain.

Heat the oil in a pan over a medium heat. Add the mustard seeds; when they crackle add the dried red chilli and the roasted chana dal. When they turn golden, add the curry leaves and sliced onion, and sauté until the onions are translucent. Crush the artichoke and toss this in the spice mix to combine; add the ginger. Sprinkle in the coriander leaves and lemon juice and mix well. Keep the podimas warm.

Preheat the oven to 180°C/Gas Mark 4. To cook the bream, heat a non-stick pan and sear the fish, skin side down, for a minute until the skin is crisp, then transfer to a baking tray and place in the preheated oven for 3–4 minutes. (Alternatively you can dispense with searing the fish, and just roast in the oven for 5–6 minutes.)

To finish the bream before serving, top the skin side with a generous layer of the herbed crust and grill it for a few minutes under a hot grill until it turns golden.

To serve, spoon the podimas on the centre of the plate, place the crisp bream on top and spoon the sauce around.

RAJASTHANI ROAST RUMP OF LAMB WITH CORN SAUCE

The best bit about this recipe is you can cook it in the tandoor if you have one, the way we do it, or you can roast it with a marinade. Rump cooked well and rested well can be wonderful. We have tried more expensive cuts, but rump is the best bet.

SERVES 4

4 lamb rump steaks, fat trimmed off
$\frac{1}{2}$ teaspoon salt, or to taste
20ml corn oil
$\frac{1}{2}$ teaspoon red chilli powder, or to taste
4 cloves

For the sauce
100ml ghee or clarified butter
8 cloves
2 large black cardamom pods
1 bay leaf
2 onions, finely chopped
$\frac{1}{2}$ teaspoon ground turmeric
1 teaspoon salt, or to taste
1 tablespoon garlic paste
100g lamb, finely diced
200g corn kernels (tinned or fresh)
2 tablespoons yoghurt
150ml lamb stock or boiling water
3 tablespoons finely chopped ginger
50g coriander leaves, finely chopped
juice of 1 lemon

Put the rump steaks in a non-metallic dish, coat with the salt, oil and red chilli powder, cover with clingfilm and put in the fridge or somewhere cool for 20–30 minutes.

To make the sauce, heat the ghee or clarified butter in a heavy-bottomed pan. Add the cloves, cardamom and bay leaf; when they start to crackle add the onions and cook over a medium heat until they start to change colour. Add the turmeric and salt and sauté briskly for a minute, taking care that the dry spice does not start to burn, then add the garlic and stir for a further couple of minutes.

As soon as the fat starts to separate, add the diced lamb and cook until the meat turns slightly brown and begins to sear on the outside – this takes 4–5 minutes. Add three-quarters of the corn and all the yoghurt, and cook over a low heat for around 30 minutes until the corn is softened and the sauce starts to become very thick.

Meanwhile, preheat the oven to 150°C/Gas Mark 2.

To cook the rump, heat a heavy pan with a little oil. Add the cloves and let them crackle and pop. Now add the rump and sear over a medium heat for 4 minutes. Turn it over and cook for a further 4 minutes. Finish cooking the lamb in the oven for 6–7 minutes, then rest the meat for 3–4 minutes.

Add the lamb stock or water to the sauce. Bring back to the boil, add the chopped ginger, coriander and the remaining corn (these will add texture) and reduce to a medium heat for a further 10 minutes. Check for seasoning and finish with a squeeze of lemon juice.

Slice the lamb evenly. Pour the sauce on to a serving dish and arrange the lamb on top. Serve with pilau rice.

SMOKED VENISON SADDLE WITH ONION SAUCE

We used to get red deer from Ireland, though there are now other sources in the UK, and it's a signature dish at Cinnamon Club. We marinated it in Rajasthani spices, cooked it in the tandoor and served it with pickling spices, and this is what earned us Best Curry Dish 2006. Before then it was not considered a curry, or even an Indian dish. We change the recipe a little from time to time, and it's still on the menu.

SERVES 4

1kg saddle of venison, trimmed and cut into 4 steaks
2 tablespoons vegetable oil, for frying

For smoking
10-cm piece of smouldering charcoal or wood
3 cloves
1 tablespoon ghee or butter

For the marinade
1/2 teaspoon salt, or to taste
1/2 teaspoon red chilli powder, or to taste
1/2 teaspoon ginger paste
1/2 teaspoon garlic paste
1 tablespoon corn or vegetable oil

For the sauce
30g whole cashew nuts, dry-fried until golden
50g onion, sliced and fried until golden in a little vegetable oil
100ml yoghurt
1 tablespoon vegetable oil
1 cinnamon stick
1 teaspoon royal cumin (or caraway)
1 teaspoon ginger paste
1 teaspoon garlic paste
1/2–11/4 teaspoons red chilli powder, or to taste
1/4 teaspoon ground turmeric
8 tomatoes, boiled and puréed, then passed through a sieve
1/2 teaspoon salt, or to taste
1/4 teaspoon garam masala

Mix all the ingredients for the marinade in a non-metallic bowl. Rub the marinade over the steaks, cover and set aside in the fridge or a cool place for 1–2 hours.

Arrange the steaks on a baking tray which can be covered by a lid. Place a smouldering piece of charcoal or wood in the centre of the tray, add the cloves and ghee or butter and cover immediately with the lid, ensuring that none of the smoke escapes. Leave for at least 8–10 minutes to impart a good smoky flavour.

Pre-heat the oven to 200°C/gas mark 6.

To prepare the sauce, blend the cashew, fried onions and yoghurt to a fine paste. Heat the oil in a heavy-based pan and add the cinnamon and royal cumin; when they begin to crackle, add the ginger and garlic pastes and sauté for a minute. Add the chilli powder, turmeric and cashew paste and cook over a low heat for 5–7 minutes, making sure it does not stick to the bottom of the pan. When the oil starts to come to the surface, pour in the tomato purée and bring to the boil. If the sauce gets thicker, thin it down with a little water or stock. Simmer for a further 5 minutes over a low heat, then add the salt and garam masala. Keep the sauce warm.

To cook the meat, heat the oil in a large frying pan. Add the meat and sear over a medium heat for 2–3 minutes, turning until browned all over. Transfer to an ovenproof dish and roast in the oven for 6–8 minutes if you like your meat pink, longer if you like it cooked more. Remove from the oven and rest it for 3–4 minutes before you serve.

Divide the sauce between the serving plates and place the steak on top. You can serve the meat sliced or as steaks, depending upon preference. Serve with pilau rice or a potato dish on the side.

TANDOORI-STYLE CHICKEN TERRINE

This terrine is very dramatic and resembles the work of an impressionist painter! Each layer of chicken is flavoured with different spices, divided by different colours of roasted peppers. It took us a while to perfect this dish – it's very difficult to make a cold starter from an Indian taste perspective. You can also serve it with baby watercress.

SERVES 4

8 skinless, boneless chicken breasts
1 teaspoon salt, or to taste
2 tablespoons ginger paste
2 tablespoons garlic paste
juice of ½ lemon
1–2 teaspoons red chilli powder, or to taste
1 teaspoon chilli flakes, or to taste
1 teaspoon ground turmeric
1 teaspoon black onion seeds
1 tablespoon coriander chutney (see recipe, right)
1 teaspoon dried fenugreek leaves (kasoori methi)
1 teaspoon coriander seeds, roasted in a dry pan and crushed
1 egg white
1 red pepper, roasted, skinned and deseeded, cut into strips

For the mince
10 chicken thighs, skinned and boned
2 teaspoons roughly chopped ginger
2 green chillies
3 garlic cloves, roughly chopped
1 teaspoon red chilli powder, or to taste
1 tablespoon chopped coriander stalks
1 teaspoon salt, or to taste
2 teaspoons pineapple juice
¼ teaspoon garam masala
¼ teaspoon dried fenugreek (kasoori methi) powder

Cut each chicken breast lengthways into four strips. Mix together the salt, ginger paste, garlic paste and lemon juice in a non-metallic bowl, coat the chicken with the marinade, cover with clingfilm and put in the fridge or somewhere cool for 20 minutes.

Divide the marinated chicken strips into three separate bowls. Coat the chicken in one bowl with chilli powder and chilli flakes, the chicken in another bowl with turmeric and black onion seeds, and the chicken in the final bowl with coriander chutney, fenugreek leaves and coriander seeds. Cover each bowl with clingfilm and put in the fridge or somewhere cool while you continue with the recipe.

For the chicken mince, mix all the ingredients and put in a food processor or pass through a mincer to achieve a fine consistency.

In a terrine mould or 450-g loaf tin lined with oiled foil, place a layer of one flavour of chicken breast, making sure the chicken pieces overlap and there are no gaps. Spread some of the chicken mince evenly over the chicken, then brush with egg white.

Layer the roasted red pepper and a second flavour of chicken breast, followed by a layer of chicken mince, and egg white, continuing similarly with the third layer, finishing with a layer of mince, so have three distinct layers. Press the terrine with a tight lid or weight and refrigerate for 3–4 hours.

Preheat the oven to 220°C/Gas Mark 7.

Place the terrine in a deep baking tray. Fill the tray with hot water to come halfway up the sides of the terrine and cook for 25–30 minutes. Insert a metal skewer after this time to check that the meat is cooked: the juices should run clear and the skewer should feel hot to the touch.

Allow to cool, then cover with clingfilm and refrigerate the terrine.

To serve, turn the terrine out on to a plate and slice. Serve with salad and a sweet chutney of your choice; honey and mustard dressing is another alternative.

CORIANDER CHUTNEY

½ bunch (approximately 50g) coriander, finely chopped
½–1 green chilli, or to taste, de-seeded and roughly chopped
juice of ½ lemon
pinch of salt

Blend all the ingredients to a fine paste. Keep covered in the fridge and use within a few days.

WILD MUSHROOM RAVIOLI WITH TRUFFLE TOMATO SAUCE

When working in India, a few other chefs and I used to cook a kind of 'fusion' food – pasta cooked in Indian sauces – and this recipe is inspired by one of those. When in season we can get all sorts of wild mushrooms, and we cook them in pickling spices. Our customers really love them made into ravioli and served with a creamy tomato and truffle oil sauce.

You can make the pasta dough for the ravioli as described here, or for a simple shortcut, use Chinese wonton wrappers.

SERVES 4

For the ravioli pasta dough
550g plain flour
generous pinch of salt
4 eggs
6 egg yolks
2 tablespoons olive oil

For the tomato truffle sauce
6 large tomatoes, halved
75ml water
2 garlic cloves, crushed
1 tablespoon crushed ginger
3 green cardamom pods
5 cloves
1 bay leaf
½–1 teaspoon red chilli powder, or to taste
50g butter
50ml single cream
½ teaspoon salt, or to taste
¼ teaspoon garam masala
1 teaspoon truffle pâté (available from specialist delicatessens)

For the wild mushroom stuffing
2 tablespoons mustard oil
¼ teaspoon fenugreek seeds
½ teaspoon black onion seeds
½ teaspoon cumin seeds
½ teaspoon fennel seeds
1 small onion, chopped
150g assorted wild mushrooms, cleaned and roughly chopped
¼–½ teaspoon chilli powder
¼ teaspoon ground turmeric
1 teaspoon finely chopped ginger
salt
1 teaspoon finely chopped coriander leaves
1 teaspoon truffle oil

For the garnish
truffle oil
truffle shavings

To make the pasta dough, sift the flour and salt together into a large mixing bowl. Make a well, add the eggs, yolks and oil. Work the dough slowly, first with a knife and then with your hands, until the mixture starts to come together in coarse crumbs. Knead well until you have a smooth, firm ball of dough. It should feel soft, but not sticky. If the mixture is too wet add a little more flour. (You can use a dough kneader if you wish.) Wrap the dough in clingfilm and rest in the fridge or a cool place for an hour or two.

Divide the dough ball into eight equal pieces and knead each piece again until smooth; work on one ball at a time, keeping the others covered with clingfilm. Roll out each one in turn on a lightly floured board until you have a rectangle about 5mm thick, and narrow enough to go through your pasta machine.

Feed each rectangle of dough through the pasta machine several times, starting with the mechanism adjusted to the thickest setting (i.e. with the rollers widest apart) and adjusting the setting by one notch each time, finishing with the thinnest setting. (If you do not have a pasta machine, continue rolling with a rolling pin until the dough is the thickness of a sheet of lasagne.) Cover with a damp cloth or clingfilm. When all the dough has been processed in this way, you are ready to cut, fill and shape your pasta.

To make the sauce, place the tomatoes in a pan over a medium heat and cook gently. As they soften, add the water, garlic, crushed ginger and the whole spices. Bring to the boil and cook until the tomatoes are cooked through and soft.

Pass the tomatoes through a sieve to get a fine tomato purée. Return the purée to the saucepan, bring back to the boil and add the chilli powder. When the purée thickens, add the butter bit by bit, stirring constantly. When the butter emulsifies and the sauce turns glossy, stir in the cream and simmer for 2–3 minutes. Add salt to taste, the garam masala and the truffle pâté, and stir well.

To make the mushroom stuffing, heat the oil in a wide non-stick frying pan over a medium heat, add all the seeds and cook until they begin to pop. Add the onion and cook over a low heat until the colour starts to change, then add the chopped mushrooms and sauté, adding the chilli and turmeric. Increase the heat. The mushrooms will expel water at this stage, so cook until the mixture is dry, then add the ginger and salt. Finish by stirring in the coriander and truffle oil. Allow to cool.

Continued on page 74

Continued from page 72

Once the stuffing mixture is cold, lay
out four of the pasta sheets. You can
make the ravioli to any shape you like,
rectangular, square or round – either
one large ravioli per person, or several
smaller ones. Cut the pasta sheets as
desired, divide the stuffing to give one
portion per ravioli, and place this in
the centre of each shape. Cut the
remaining four sheets of pasta to the
same size and shape as your filled
bases. Brush the edges of the bases
with water, cover with the second
pieces of pasta and crimp the sides
with a fork to seal.

When the ravioli are all made, blanch
them in boiling salted water for
2 minutes before draining and serving.
Meanwhile, gently reheat the sauce.

Serve the ravioli on a plate, with the
sauce spooned around and topped
with a drizzle of truffle oil and a
sprinkling of truffle shavings.

VIVEK SINGH

CINNAMON KITCHEN

Vivek Singh was born in Bengal, 200km west of Kolkata, in a coal-mining region – his father was a mining engineer. It was a small, safe and close-knit community, with many festivals and celebrations to which everyone was invited.

Weddings were, and always have been, a very important part of the Indian way of life. 'Some of my earliest memories go back to attending Bengali weddings. In fact, I had something of a reputation for attending them! There were times when an event was organised, and perhaps an invited friend could not go along. I would always ask to go in their place, and because it was a small community it was always safe for me to be there alone. My parents would give me a 5-rupee note in an envelope labelled "With best wishes from the Singhs", I'd pop along to the wedding, hand it over to the bride and groom, and go and sit down and enjoy the food! I was probably only 9 or 10 years old.'

Growing up in his community was very much about food and eating well, but it was still unusual to see boys in the kitchen. Vivek's first experience of cooking was when he was 14 or 15 years old. He and a friend tried their hands at roasting some food: 'We attempted to prepare a tandoori chicken, but I had far too much spice on it and put it directly on the coals, so it was a disaster!'

Typical of most boys, he hadn't cooked with his mother, nor helped her in the kitchen at all; his path to a cooking career came about by chance. He was introduced to hotel management through friends of his older sister. They had followed this career path and told him it was a three-year picnic – no coursework, no project to submit, no books to read, just a dream course. So if you hadn't gone into engineering or medicine, as most parents would want, and if you didn't fancy three years studying for a career in administration, hotel management was the new thing, and Vivek thought he'd have a go – a brave move at a time when careers in this sector were relatively unheard of.

'I got into the best hotel school (probably it was not as competitive as it is now!) and studied for three years in Delhi – food and beverage production, service, front office, housekeeping and so on. I knew I could cook as well as anybody else, but I had not given it a thought as a career. When the Oberoi came in to interview for kitchen trainees, I was invited along, and got the job – out of 2,500 applicants for 12 positions. When I started work I realised

how little I knew, and how much more there was to learn.

'I worked for a couple of years at the Oberoi Delhi, part training and part work experience, then for a year at Oberoi Flight Services. It was not my preferred type of kitchen, but it was a time of intense learning for me. We produced about 5500 meals a day for British Airways, KLM and other airlines to very stringent standards. It was a steep learning curve and an extremely good grounding. After that, I moved to the Oberoi Grand, Kolkata, where I gained more experience with fine dining and running restaurants.

'I ran that kitchen for a year, and then Mr Oberoi asked me to move to the Rajvilas, Jaipur – 72 rooms set in 32 acres of grounds, $650 per night... We had access to the best salmon, black cod, monkfish, New Zealand lamb, Angus beef and so on. We spent good money buying imported

vegetables, meat and fish; but none of this was for the Indian kitchen – after all "it was just a curry!" I thought, "We've got all these ingredients, why not use them?" But the hotel wouldn't let me do that. I had a very good relationship with the owners, but there came a time when I felt I couldn't progress much further.

Remember those weddings that Vivek used to attend as a boy? Well, there was going to be another one that would change his life, and it wasn't even his own wedding. 'It happened that Iqbal Wahhab was attending a wedding at the hotel, for which I was cooking. We found that we were both on the same wavelength with our ideas about the direction that Indian cooking might take. I had previously been approached by restaurants in London, but I had always asked myself, "Why come to London to do just the same thing as I'm doing in India?" So it would only be worth it if I were going to do something unique. That's where Cinnamon Club came in – it was a departure from what was happening in India, and very different from the rest of the UK. It's been 10 years now, and it doesn't feel like that.'

In coming to Cinnamon Club (see page 63), Vivek was not thinking of the potential for commercial success, but of the creative process. Joy of joys, the commercial success came, and they serve 100,000 people a year. But that cuisine doesn't have to remain the prerogative of the rich and famous, the very successful. Vivek and his team wanted to make it available to a wider audience, and that's how Cinnamon Kitchen came about.

Opened in 2008, this is a striking and contemporary restaurant housed in a sympathetically refurbished warehouse complex at the eastern edge of the City, not far from Liverpool Street station. There are features of the original building which remain; there is an outside covered terrace which extends the short British al-fresco dining season. Cinnamon Kitchen boasts its own characterful bar – Anise sports an array of filigree metal lamps offering dappled and muted light to a space that has become popular for pre-dinner drinks, and is equally the haunt of the 'smart set' looking for chic conviviality garnished with spicy signature cocktails.

The restaurant itself is a wash of subtle brown, and taupe hues are accented by bricks and bottles, creating an ambiance of big-city buzz. Cinnamon Kitchen offers modern Indian food to a crowd of regulars who might be slightly younger than the Cinnamon Club habitués, but who expect the same high standard of ingredients and presentation. The truly open grill station allows diners within (almost) spattering distance of the sharp end of food preparation. A melange of drama and delicious char awaits those who want a more intimate relationship with their next course.

Cinnamon Kitchen offers a fine dining menu at more moderate prices and in a slightly more casual fashion than in most venues across the city. From the menu, Scottish Lobster Momos, Tomato and Curry Leaf, or perhaps Barramundi, Mussel and Shrimp 'Doi Maach' Style are memorable, but Caramelised Ox Cheek, Date and Apricot Sauce is daring and takes advantage of a cut of meat that would seldom be seen in the chill room of any other Indian restaurant. Vivek once again shows his excitement at having access to ingredients that are outside the traditional 'curry' norm.

It's still about seasonality, creativity, innovation and quality ingredients. It does not necessarily translate to very high prices, nor is it the exclusive domain of Cinnamon-clubby people. 'The concept is still real Indian dining, combining the best of both worlds: authentic Indian spicing and cooking techniques, with very good quality, local, seasonal produce, and deconstructing recipes to create layers of flavours and textures. What's changed is the ambiance, the informality of the experience, the price point, appealing to a different clientele – it's more accessible. It's not about re-educating you: that was needed then, when we were establishing Cinnamon Club. What's exciting, inspiring and encouraging is that so many new Indian restaurants are appearing with that kind of ethos: seasonal, light, fresh, relevant to the audience – and it's not just at the high end, which can be a bit exclusive, but at every level.'

Cinnamon Kitchen
9 Devonshire Square, London EC2M 4YL
Phone 020 7626 5000 **www.cinnamon-kitchen.com**

GRILLED SALMON WITH DILL AND MUSTARD, GREEN PEA RELISH

One of our favourites, this frequently features on the menu. In the restaurant we use Kasundi Indian mustard paste from Bengal. Dill, mustard and salmon go really well together, as in gravad lax. We make a home-cured salmon alongside tandoori salmon to make a starter, and we serve it with green pea relish – it's almost like wasabi. This is my Mum's recipe, and it's excellent with salmon or any similar fish, as filling for wraps, and as a dipping sauce too!

SERVES 4

4 salmon fillets, each 175g

For the first marinade
1/2 teaspoon ground turmeric
1 tablespoon ginger-garlic paste
1 green chilli, finely chopped
1/2 teaspoon salt, or to taste
juice from 1/4 a lemon
2 teaspoons vegetable oil

For the second marinade
1 teaspoon ground mustard (black mustard seeds soaked for a couple of hours in warm water and vinegar, then ground to a paste; alternatively use 1 tablespoon wholegrain mustard)
1 teaspoon chopped dill leaves
1 teaspoon sugar
1 tablespoon yoghurt
2 teaspoons mustard oil

For the green pea relish
2 cups green peas, shelled
1 tablespoon roughly chopped ginger
3 garlic cloves, roughly chopped
3 green chillies, roughly chopped
1/2 teaspoon salt, or to taste
1/2 teaspoon sugar
1 1/2 tablespoons mustard oil
juice from 1/2 a lime

Green leaves, to garnish

Mix all the ingredients for the first marinade in a non-metallic bowl, rub them over the fish and set aside to marinate while you prepare the second marinade.

Mix all the ingredients for the second marinade, coat the fish with this second preparation, cover with clingfilm and place in the refrigerator or cool place for 30 minutes.

Pre-heat the oven to 180°C/Gas Mark 4.

Place the salmon on a greased roasting tray and bake in the oven for 10–12 minutes.

To make the relish, put the green peas, ginger, garlic, chillies, salt, sugar and 1 tablespoon of the mustard oil in an electric blender and make a fine purée. Check the seasoning and finish with lime juice, then fold in the rest of the mustard oil. Serve cold.

To serve, put a portion of green pea relish on each plate, with a piece of hot salmon next to it or on top. Garnish with your choice of green leaves.

TANDOORI BREAST OF SQUAB PIGEON

We serve pigeon breasts marinated and cooked in the tandoor or seared. The mince is made from the thigh, heart and liver, finely chopped beetroot, onions, mint, garam masala, ginger, green chillies – it is almost like a burger pattie. This was one of the highlights of our tenth anniversary dinner at The Cinnamon Club. It's an amazing-looking plate with lots of colour.

SERVES 4

2 pigeons, breasts boned, but with the skin on; the leg, liver and heart minced together

For the first marinade
1 teaspoon ginger paste
1 teaspoon garlic paste
$^1/_2$ teaspoon salt, or to taste
$^1/_2$–1 teaspoon red chilli powder
juice of $^1/_2$ a lemon

For the second marinade
$^1/_2$ onion, chopped, fried until golden and blended into a paste
1 tablespoon yoghurt
$^1/_2$ teaspoon garam masala
$^1/_2$ teaspoon salt, or to taste
1 tablespoon vegetable oil

For the kebabs
1 tablespoon vegetable oil
$^1/_4$ teaspoon Royal cumin (caraway)
1 onion, finely chopped
1 small beetroot, boiled, peeled and finely chopped
$^1/_4$ teaspoon red chilli powder
$^1/_4$ teaspoon cumin seeds, roasted in a dry pan and ground
$^1/_2$ tablespoon finely chopped ginger
2 green chillies, chopped
1 sprig of mint, shredded
$^1/_2$ teaspoon salt, or to taste
$^1/_4$ teaspoon garam masala
1 egg
breadcrumbs, to coat
vegetable oil, for deep-frying

First make the kebabs. Heat the oil in a pan, add the royal cumin seeds and when they crackle, add the chopped onions and sauté until golden brown. Add the minced pigeon and beetroot and sauté for 3 minutes, then add the chilli powder and cumin and cook until the mixture is almost dry.

Add the ginger, green chilli, mint, salt and garam masala. Set aside to allow the mixture to cool.

In a small bowl mix the ingredients for the first marinade. Pat the pigeon breasts dry with kitchen paper, put in a non-metallic dish and coat with the first marinade; cover with clingfilm and put in the fridge or somewhere cool for 20 minutes.

In a small bowl mix the ingredients for the second marinade, and set aside.

Preheat the oven to 200°C/Gas Mark 6.

Heat an ovenproof pan over a high heat. Remove the breasts from the marinade and put directly into the hot pan and sear for 2 minutes on each side, skin side first.

Spoon the second marinade over the pigeon breasts and finish in the oven for 5 minutes, or until just done.

Take the cooled kebab mixture and blend to a smooth texture. Shape the mince into four cakes. Dip them in beaten egg, then roll them in breadcrumbs. In a deep pan, wok or fryer, heat the oil over a high heat, to shimmering. Deep-fry the kebabs for just a minute or two, until golden brown.

Serve the breast on top of the kebab cake. You can also serve a little mint chutney and raita alongside if you like.

GRILLED AUBERGINE WITH PEANUT, TAMARIND AND CHILLI

We were pondering what we could cook on the grill at Cinnamon Kitchen, and this is one of several recipes we created. The mixed grilled platter is popular, selling 60–80 a day – duck, prawns, fat chillies stuffed with paneer and mince, yoghurt kebab, and these aubergines. This a true Hyderabadi combination of sesame, peanut and tamarind. It's almost a deconstructed version of bagara baingan. You can also add dessicated coconut to the crust, if you wish. Grill the aubergine just enough to be cooked through.

SERVES 4

4 firm Japanese or Bengali aubergines (long, narrow variety), halved lengthways
1 tablespoon vegetable or corn oil
½ teaspoon salt, or to taste
½ teaspoon red chilli powder, or to taste
½ teaspoon ground turmeric
¼ teaspoon carom seeds
¼ teaspoon black onion seeds
¼ teaspoon fennel seeds
melted butter or oil, for brushing

For the spice crust
50g peanuts, roasted or fried in a dry pan, cooled and coarsely crushed
1 tablespoon white sesame seeds, lightly roasted in a dry pan
2 teaspoons jaggery or brown sugar
1 teaspoon garlic, chopped and fried crisp (or dried granules)
½ teaspoon red chilli powder, or to taste
½ teaspoon dried fenugreek leaves, crushed
1 teaspoon chaat masala

For the tamarind chutney
6 tablespoons tamarind concentrate
pinch of red chilli powder
2 tablespoons jaggery or molasses
120ml water

Score the aubergines across the flesh side, put them into a non-metallic dish and marinate with the oil, salt, chilli powder, turmeric and carom, onion and fennel seeds for 3–4 minutes.

Meanwhile, combine all the ingredients for the spice crust to obtain a spicy nut mix. Check seasoning and set aside.

Place the cut side of the aubergines on a hot grill or non-stick pan and sear for 2 minutes. Brush the skin side with butter or oil, turn over and cook for about 3 minutes or until cooked through. Alternatively, you could do this under a very hot grill or on a barbecue.

To make the tamarind chutney, simply mix all the ingredients together in a small pan and heat gently until the jaggery dissolves.

Place the aubergines on a plate, flat side uppermost. Spread a smear of tamarind chutney on the aubergines, sprinkle the spicy peanut crust on them and serve hot with a green salad.

PEAR SORBET

Sorbet makes an excellent sweet and a refreshing end to any Indian meal. This pear sorbet is delicate and light, and is elevated when served with jewels of saffron jelly (see page 85). It can also be used as a palate-cleanser between courses. This couldn't be simpler to prepare, especially if you have an ice-cream maker.

SERVES 4

500g pear purée
125ml water
juice of ½ a lemon
25g sugar
30g liquid glucose (this is a form of sugar which keeps the sorbet moist and reduces crystallisation. If you cannot get hold of it, use double the quantity of sugar)

Put all the ingredients in a mixing bowl and stir to combine. Tip into an ice-cream maker, then churn and freeze to the manufacturer's instructions.

Chef's Tip
If you don't have an ice-cream maker you can make a pear granita instead of a sorbet. Fill a shallow plastic tub with the liquid and place in the freezer. Check every few hours, and use a fork to stir in the frozen crystals from the edge of the container. You will eventually have a fluffy, granular and delicious granita.

SAFFRON-POACHED PEARS WITH SAFFRON JELLY

Poached Pear has been on the menu for 10 years, since we opened. This is one of the latest variations, and different from the more common poached pears in red wine. We generally use the Williams pear as it is nice and stout, poached in a sugar syrup with saffron for about 20 minutes. The pear is sweet and the sharpness of the yoghurt cuts through that sweetness. During autumn this works really well.

SERVES 4

For the saffron-poached pears
4 Williams pears, not too ripe, peeled
300g sugar
large pinch of saffron

For the saffron jelly
3 gelatine leaves

For the yoghurt mixture
100ml Greek yoghurt
1 tablespoon raisins, chopped
1 teaspoon finely chopped coriander
   leaves

Place the pears in a deep pan and cover with water, add the sugar and saffron. Bring to the boil and simmer uncovered until the pears are just tender but still firm – up to 20 minutes.

Leave in the syrup off the heat for another 5 minutes until the pears are soft, then remove the pears from the syrup and refrigerate them to cool.

Measure out 500ml of poaching liquid (add water if you have less than this volume) and bring it back to the boil. Soak the gelatine leaves in cold water for 5–6 minutes, strain them, and add them to the simmering liquid, whisking well until they dissolve.

Choose a tray big enough to give a depth of jelly of about 1cm. Take the liquid off the heat, pour it into the tray, cover with clingfilm and refrigerate to set. When ready to serve, tip the jelly out of the tray and chop into small dice.

When the pears have cooled, cut them in half from top to bottom and use a melon baller to scoop out the cores.

Mix the yoghurt, raisins and coriander leaves together and spoon into a piping bag. Put a generous spoon of the yoghurt mixture onto the plate, sit the pear on top and chill until ready to serve.

Serve the pears on chilled plates with dices of saffron jelly, sprinkled with some chopped coriander leaves.

SHAMIL THAKRAR
AND NAVED NASIR

DISHOOM

Dishoom is the new kid on the block – a fresh concept for Indian dining, which opened in 2010. A café, but not your regular greasy spoon breakfast venue that we all love for its fried breakfast, and far from your American-themed coffee-house with blackboards emblazoned with 'tall, skinny something-or-others'. Dishoom is in the style of the fast-vanishing Bombay cafés of yore, which were originally opened by immigrants from Persia. The people who run these cafés in Mumbai are really Parsi, but everyone refers to them as 'Irani' to distinguish them from the much earlier wave of immigration a thousand years ago.

Dishoom takes its name from the sound of a speeding bullet or the draught from a flying fist, as depicted in Bollywood movies – the equivalent of an English 'whoosh'; but somehow the word 'dishoom' has a bit more stage presence.

Shamil Thakrar, who started Dishoom with his cousin Kavi and family friends Amar and Adarsh Radia, is a devotee of this little-known element of Indian culinary culture. 'Sadly in Mumbai these cafés are dying out, and the community itself is dwindling. The children of the people who used to own these cafés quite reasonably want to be bankers and lawyers, which is fine, but it means that modern "plastic" replacements are taking over, and there are now only 20 or 30 cafés left, where there once used to be 400. They reflect the iconic design characteristics of the 1920s and 30s in which they were built. They are evocative spaces with marble tables, bentwood chairs, slowly-turning ceiling fans, pendulum lights, wood panelling, pictures and mirrors, and we have paid homage to that. We decided to dig deeper into that tradition to capture that essence and transplant it to London. What's fun is that we don't sit in the curry-house tradition, we are a café from Bombay, an Irani café.'

Shamil was born in Africa, but his family is Gujarati, from north of Mumbai, and he has many happy memories of spending holidays in that city with his grandmother. 'We had already been considering the place of Indian food in British society, when we began to develop Dishoom. The fact is that in the UK we are so used to Indian food that we take it for granted. We thought that it was time for a fresh look at it. We all cherish the curry-house tradition, but the institution is a uniquely British one, and would not be recognised in India. There is this rich seam of heritage in the Irani cafés of Mumbai, set up by immigrants from Iran

in the early 20th century. They established these wonderful and very democratic eating, meeting, drinking places. We were inspired by them, and asked ourselves how we could propagate that culture.'

It was always their intention to have an open kitchen. Shamil worried that Indian food has a reputation for opacity: 'It's covered in sauce, the kitchen is in the back, you're not quite sure how it's been prepared. There's a transparency about what we're doing – you can see right into the kitchen, it is grilled food and it's honest on the plate, not a lot of sauce. This is part of our philosophy, we love sharing, and we want people to see what we're doing. We want to celebrate how beautiful the process is.'

In design as well as in cuisine, Shamil and the Dishoom team want to display a seriousness of purpose, but they don't take themselves too seriously. They are businesslike, but there is good humour in both concept and execution. They collected and hung pictures of their own grandparents, and reference that heritage with the rest of the decor throughout the café, but at the same time they also have whimsical 60s pop-art on the walls. The basement restrooms are similarly adorned with iconic and archaic packaging for soaps and shampoos. They do, however, take their biryani and their dal seriously, but the chilli cheese toast, which most Indian restaurants would not put on the menu, raises a smile. 'That's not a bastardisation of an English favourite, it's comfort food in cafés all over India! It's OK to adopt some fun piece of tradition, it doesn't all have to be serious. We have a lot of people who come in very regularly – some even every day – for lunch. A lovely mix of South Asians and English: older, for the nostalgia, and younger, who think it's quite funky.'

Head chef Naved Nasir gave up a prestigious job in India to join Dishoom. He was inspired by the commitment the team had to their unique project, and the evident passion to build an Irani café in London. 'I had been working in Mumbai for the previous six years and I had grown up on that food. I fell in love with the concept and it didn't take much time to say "yes". We all put our hearts into this, rather than it being just a business.' The team had already found the premises when Naved arrived, so he was able to influence the design of the kitchen, the layout, the flow, where the tandoor and the roomali dome should go. This hot-plate resembles an upturned wok, heated from below, and is used for cooking the soft, paper-thin handkerchief bread called roomali.

His father was a doctor, and he encouraged Naved to follow in his career footsteps. His son wanted to be a chef, but to his father a chef was just a cook, and he hated the idea. But Naved joined a catering college in Delhi, and after completing a three-year degree in hospitality management, was picked by ITC Hotels. They own Bukhara, the restaurant at the ITC Maurya hotel in New Delhi. 'It had been my dream to work there, and now I was training there! After a year I moved to Mumbai, and I fell in love with the city, the culture, the food.'

As the youngest Executive Chef in India, Naved was promoted to another ITC property, the WelcomHotel

Aurangabad, and while there he was invited to come to Dishoom. 'It was a big decision to come to London, but a really quick one to take. I had had offers from places like the Gulf and other parts of the UK, but the idea of a Bombay café in London? I thought they were crazy!' But evidently crazy in a good way.

The team at Dishoom undertook a lot of food development. 'Bombay food can be quite tricky, and it caught me off-guard sometimes! Take a Biryani cooked "dum" (in a sealed pot), the traditional Kacche Gosht ki Biryani, for example – the meat is raw, and it's cooked together with the rice, so you have to judge it carefully so that the rice and the meat are finished at the same time. Somebody not familiar with it will be struggling to get it right.'

Dishoom's most popular dishes include Black Daal – bread and lentils make a typical meal everywhere in India. 'It's at the core of so many Indian meals and if you can't get that

right, you're not on the right track. And biryani – I've been to some restaurants making pan and dum biryanis, and they don't even get close to ours!

'It's very important to know your ingredients – in Dishoom the emphasis is on authenticity, which has to be there, you really can't compromise. At the same time you have to be sure the ingredients are absolutely fresh: lime, coriander, mint, ginger, chillies, you can really taste that freshness. I'm still looking for yellow chilli powder here, though – it's hot and it's so amazing. In India we used to do a tandoori salad, and with a marinade of yellow chillies it makes such a lovely dish.'

Naved gives a history of Indian food: 'The Indian food in the UK has a very royal heritage. In the 16th century, in the reign of Akbar, India was peaceful for the first time, and there was a flourishing of the arts, including the culinary arts, and what we think of as Mughlai cuisine comes from that period; similarly Nawabi cuisine, from the area around Lucknow. These are the cuisines of the royalty, and it's very much about the richer flavours: cardamom, almonds, saffron, cinnamon, dried fruits; creamy and sweet. The food in most traditional Indian restaurants owes its heritage to that. Ours is not like that, it's more the working man's food: ginger, garlic, green chilli, mint, coriander, lime – much more earthy and rustic. Even the biryani, which became royal, owes a lot more to its origins as just food in a pot, stewed up!

'Every chef has his own recipe mix for garam masala, and ours is freshly ground in-house, so different. We cook just two curries a day, so the flavour is authentic. Indian food has its own intricacies, its own techniques, but it's cooking food, man – come on!'

Dishoom
12 Upper St Martin's Lane, London WC2H 9FB
Phone 020 7420 9320 **www.dishoom.com**

The Dishoom family, left to right: Amar Radia, Adarsh Radia, Shamil Thakrar and Kavi Thakrar.

SPICY LAMB CHOPS

The recipe was inspired by Bademiya –
a food stall in the area just behind the
Taj Hotel in Mumbai. They start
serving at around 8 in the evening,
when the traffic has died down, and
there's no menu – you know by heart
what is good. We use a prime cut of
lamb, dry marinated, no oil.

SERVES 4

12 lamb chops, French cut, best end,
    single rib, 100g each
1 tablespoon garam masala
2 teaspoons ground black pepper
1 teaspoon ground cloves
1 teaspoon ground coriander seeds
1 teaspoon ground cumin
salt, to taste
20g jaggery or brown sugar
2 tablespoons lime juice
4 red chillies, or to taste, coarsely
    chopped
60g coriander stalks, coarsely chopped
60g garlic paste
60g ginger paste
20ml vegetable oil

For the garnish
4 lime wedges
50g fresh pomegranate seeds
a few leaves of mint, shredded

Remove any extra back fat from the
chops, and flatten the chops with a
meat mallet.

Combine all the dry spices and salt
in a large non-metallic bowl.

Put the jaggery, lime juice, chillies
and coriander stalks into the bowl of
a blender, and process for 5 seconds.
Mix this into the bowl of spices and
stir in the ginger and garlic pastes and
the oil. Add the lamb chops to the
bowl and spread the marinade evenly
over meat. Cover with clingfilm and
marinate in the refrigerator for
8 hours.

Preheat the grill to its highest heat
setting. Put the chops on a wire grid
and grill for 3–4 minutes on each
side, until cooked through and well-
coloured. Serve hot with a lime
wedge and garnished with fresh
pomegranate seeds and the mint.

PAU BHAJI

Pau Bhaji *is* Mumbai, and this recipe is just as it would be found there, not tweaked for London. This can be found on any street or in any café. It is very healthy, and many poor people live on it – we knew that it would sell. The Pau is a basic fluffy European-type bread roll. A meal for anybody and everybody.

SERVES 4

50ml vegetable oil
75g onions, finely chopped
½ teaspoon Kashmiri red chilli powder, or to taste
½ teaspoon ground turmeric
1 tablespoon ground cumin
2 teaspoons pau bhaji masala, or to taste (available at Indian supermarkets)
75g tinned tomatoes, chopped
1 teaspoon sugar (optional)
70g potatoes, cut into small dice
30g green pepper, cut into small dice
20g cauliflower, cut into small florets
30g carrots, cut into small dice
20g French beans, roughly chopped
20g green peas
25g butter, plus extra for spreading
4 pau (burger-type bread rolls)
salt, to taste

To garnish
100g red onions, finely chopped
handful of coriander leaves, roughly chopped
4 lime wedges

Heat the oil in a large frying pan or wok over a medium heat. Add the chopped onion and sauté until lightly browned.

Add the dry spices and cook for a minute. Sprinkle a little water over, add the tomatoes (and sugar if needed) and cook until they are soft and the oil separates.

Parboil or microwave all the vegetables until *al dente* and add to the pan. Cook over a low heat until they soften and begin to break down, then mash with a potato masher, over a medium heat. Add half the butter and continue cooking until the vegetables are almost mashed. Season to taste. Add the remaining butter just before serving.

Split the pau in half and grill the cut sides on a hot-plate or under the grill, spread with butter and serve with the bhaji in individual bowls, topped with chopped onions, coriander and a lime wedge.

CHICKEN BERRY BIRYANI

This recipe is inspired by the Berry Pulao from the Britannia Café in Mumbai – I used to frequent that café when I was at college. I love that place and hope the Kohinoor family keeps running it. The building was designed by George Wittet, architect of the Gateway of India, and it's been there since 1923.

SERVES 6

50ml vegetable oil
100g shallots, finely sliced
200ml yoghurt
40g ginger paste
30g garlic paste
1 teaspoon Kashmiri red chilli powder, or to taste
4 teaspoons ground cumin
2 teaspoons salt, or to taste
1 tablespoon lime juice
20g coriander, finely chopped, plus a sprig or two for garnish
20g fresh ginger, cut into juliennes
30g barberries or dried cranberries, plus a handful for garnish
1–5 green chillies, to taste, sliced
1kg chicken legs or thighs, boneless and skinless
50ml single cream
a good pinch of saffron
500g basmati rice

Heat half the oil in a pan over a high heat, add half the shallots and fry for a few minutes until brown and crispy.

Put the the crispy fried shallots, yoghurt, ginger, garlic, all dry spices, half the salt, lime juice, coriander, ginger juliennes, barberries or cranberries and green chillies into a non-metallic bowl and stir to combine. Add the chicken and coat with the marinade, cover with clingfilm, and rest in the fridge or a cool place for 2 hours.

Put the cream in a small bowl, add the saffron and allow to infuse for at least 30 minutes.

Preheat the oven to 250ºC/Gas Mark 9, or the maximum on your oven.

Cook the rice in plenty of boiling water, with the remaining salt, until it is 60% cooked (approximately 4–5 minutes), and drain it.

Put a layer of chicken in a heavy-based ovenproof pan or casserole, cover it with a layer of rice and sprinkle with some saffron cream. Continue in this way until you have used up all the chicken, and finish with a layer of rice and cream. Seal the pot with a tight-fitting lid or kitchen foil, leaving no space for steam to escape.

Turn the oven down to 200ºC/ Gas Mark 6. Cook the biryani for 1 hour in the oven, then allow to stand, without removing the lid, for 15 minutes. Check that the chicken is thoroughly cooked.

In a small frying pan, heat the rest of the oil over medium heat and fry the remainder of the shallots for a few minutes until crisp.

Serve the biryani sprinkled with some chopped coriander, barberries or cranberries and the crispy shallots.

MURGH MALAI

I've been cooking this dish for years and it's never been changed – a simple marination with yoghurt and cheese. The meat is leg meat because this is the most moist – the end result is much better than using breast meat.

SERVES 4

4 chicken legs or thighs, boneless, skinless, 280–300g each
90g Greek yoghurt
60g cream cheese
30g mild Cheddar cheese, finely grated
2 teaspoons ground ginger
2 teaspoons ground white pepper
2 teaspoons salt, or to taste
1 tablespoon green chilli paste, or to taste
1½ teaspoons vegetable oil
25g ginger paste
25g garlic paste
juice of ½ a lime
1 egg
melted butter, for basting

Cut each chicken piece into 6 pieces, each 5cm long, following the natural meat fibres. Pat dry with kitchen paper.

Place the yoghurt in a non-metallic bowl, add the cream cheese and Cheddar cheese, and mix to make a smooth paste. Add all the remaining ingredients apart from the melted butter, and mix well.

Add the chicken pieces and coat them with the marinade. Cover with clingfilm and place in the fridge to marinate for 8 hours or overnight.

Preheat the grill to medium-high. Skewer the chicken pieces 2cm apart and grill for 5–6 minutes on one side. Baste with melted butter, and continue grilling on the other side for another 3–4 minutes. The kebabs should be well charred and cooked through.

PINEAPPLE CRUMBLE

Crumble may not be Indian, but pineapple certainly is. It's found on fruit stalls and hand-carts laden with ice and you can buy pieces of pineapple sprinkled with sugar.
We want our English guests to eat this crumble and think of India. This has a magnificent topping of seeds, coconut and oats, with just a suspicion of black pepper – a simple yet exotic dish.

SERVES 4

300g pineapple, cut into 1-cm pieces
40ml sugar syrup (made by heating and dissolving 40g sugar in 40ml water)
seeds scraped from 1 pod vanilla seeds
$\frac{1}{2}$–1 teaspoon crushed black pepper
4 scoops of cinnamon or vanilla ice cream, to serve

For the topping
50g rolled oats
12g pumpkin seeds
12g sunflower seeds
25g ground almonds
5g sesame seeds
15g desiccated coconut
25g brown sugar, plus more to sprinkle on top
30g butter, melted
$\frac{1}{2}$–1 teaspoon crushed black pepper

Put the pineapple pieces in a non-metallic bowl and coat with the sugar syrup, vanilla seeds and pepper, cover with clingfilm, put in the fridge and marinate for 2 hours.

Preheat the oven to 180°C/Gas Mark 4.

For the topping, simply mix all the remaining ingredients together. Layer the pineapple mix on the bottom of a baking dish, and sprinkle the crumble mix on top. Sprinkle brown sugar over.

Bake in the oven for 7–8 minutes, or until the top begins to look toasted.

Serve topped with cinnamon or vanilla ice cream.

NAVIN BHATIA

DOCKMASTER'S HOUSE

London's Docklands can boast a long history of vibrant activity. For centuries it bustled with stevedores hauling produce arriving from the four corners of the Empire (the pink bits on old maps, over which the sun was said never to set), and now it throngs with big business and those looking to pass a convivial evening with stunning food.

Dockmaster's House brings together those disparate threads in a striking fashion. The building that houses this increasingly celebrated restaurant is a listed three-storey Georgian edifice in the heart of the newly-gentrified Docklands. This imposing building was erected 200 years ago by The West India Dock Company, and Dockmaster's House was once the Excise House for the these docks. In 1846, Joseph Montague converted the building into the Jamaica Tavern – there was evidently more profit in a pub than in a tax office! However, the hotel's licence was not renewed in 1925 due to its colourful reputation. Police were taking steps to eradicate the local opium trade, which was the scourge of ports worldwide. In 1926 the building became the offices for the Dock Superintendent and his staff, and continued in that capacity until 1980. It then changed its name to Dockmaster's House, and changed its function to that of a standard Indian restaurant.

Chef Navin Bhatia is perhaps an unfamiliar name. You don't find him gracing the small screen, but he is one of the most respected chefs in high-end Indian restaurant circles in Britain. He has worked tirelessly to elevate the standard of staff in British Indian restaurants.

Navin was born in India, in the northern town of Lucknow, regarded by many as the food capital of India and celebrated for its phenomenal food. India has sophisticated and advanced cuisines which developed in the Nawabs' and Maharajahs' palaces in Lucknow and in Hyderabad. Navin explains: 'Lucknow's cuisine is considered superior to that of Hyderabad, because Hyderabad relies on a lot of hot dishes that take advantage of the chillies grown in that region. Lucknow's food became refined to such an extent that it reached the notice of the Moghul Empire, and that's how mughlai cuisine developed.'

Navin's close relationship with food stems from the family business. His family runs grocery stores, and he has lived with the 'raw materials' of his trade all his life. When he was a small child, many friends did not know what a prune

was, for example, or about the different kinds of raisins, but he knew because he would see all those things in the shop. His grandfather had established the business in 1932, and it's still there. It was famous even amongst the British, who used to do their shopping there, and his family used to stock Christmas puddings just for those ex-pats!

Navin started making cakes at home and discovered a passion for cooking, so he took his diploma at the Institute of Hotel Management. From there he progressed to the prestigious Oberoi School of Hotel Management (it has changed its name since then, and is now known as The Oberoi Centre of Learning and Development), and that was the start of his professional culinary journey.

'It took a little time to decide on my career. By the time I finished my three years in catering school I was pretty sure what I wanted to do. I know so many who started the

training but left because, I think, they were not passionate about it – it's a way of life, a long-term commitment, and you have to be true to it. Let's face it, if the food is no good, nobody's going to come to your restaurant!

'I initially went into operations, but very soon got back into the training school as a trainer myself, and stayed there about three years. I have trained some of the best-known chefs, such as Michelin-starred Atul Kochhar (see page 11), who now work in London and around the world.'

Navin came to London in 1998 to become Group Executive Chef for Café Lazeez Group to develop their chain of restaurants. That company did very well, and won contracts to provide catering at such venues as Lord's Cricket Ground, Brands Hatch race track and Twickenham Rugby Stadium.

'When I arrived in Britain, I came from a 5-star deluxe background, and when I was told that the kitchen was down in the basement, I thought I would be working in a dungeon. When I saw the kitchen, I thought I might turn around, say "thank you" to the owner and walk out. But within a week I was down on my hands and knees preparing for our first inspection, and slowly built it up from there to a group of five restaurants and an outdoor catering business. That experience gave me the confidence and ability to design this restaurant – I knew exactly what I wanted to do here.

'I got the opportunity in 2006 to come to Dockmaster's and redevelop the place from its previous existence as a curry house. It's now called The Dockmaster's House Restaurant and Bar – modern food, contemporary and traditional dishes presented in a more sophisticated manner. Indian food is not just "curry", it's much more than that, and we want to take the customer to all the regions of India. In Britain we are so lucky to have so many different raw materials – all kinds of meat and game, marvellous fresh fish – and we play with those ingredients and Indian spices to create something new.'

When Navin took over the building, he discovered all sorts of practical issues, and with a listed building there is little one can do. Nevertheless, they were able to remove virtually everything from inside, leaving just the shell, and start again with the interior. It's now a light and airy restaurant, with evidence of original brickwork and a conservatory that is a chic and stylish backdrop for Navin's handiwork.

Navin is concerned about the future of Indian restaurants in the UK: 'I fear that the quality of Indian food in Britain is going to deteriorate because of the difficulty of finding the staff. Cyrus Todiwala (see page 37) and I tried to find government funds to set up a culinary school to train people in Asian and Indian cookery, on a commercial basis, but there was no interest – probably because there has until now always been a ready supply of labour to the industry. The immigration rules having recently changed and the prospects for training in the UK may now be different.'

There is also a need to educate the palate of the British diner, says Navin. 'So many people have become used to

the curry-house style of food, which bears no relationship to true Indian cooking. When they come to this restaurant, if they ask me for Beef Madras or Chicken Tikka Masala I offer them something of my own, and they are always pleasantly surprised!'

The food at Dockmaster's House can be described as mainly from northern India. 'I have taken nuances from many areas. The flavours from the south, the west and the east are phenomenal, so I use a few items from everywhere. You can't just stick to the food from one region. But if I started producing just the true food from Lucknow, I would lose all my British customers. They would just not relate to it. The aromas are so strong and robust that they would think it's off! The food uses unusual floral scents, which would not suit the European palate. Like our eight fingers and two thumbs, everyone is different, and everyone's palate is different. So everyone cooks differently, and every family cooks differently, and they are all "right". I choose dishes that offer authenticity and taste. I prepare lamb shanks with spices I buy directly from a particular shop in Delhi. It's his proprietary blend; I know the ingredients, but I don't know the proportions, but I use it because it gives a different dimension to my sauce.

'I "demoted" myself to come to Britain to get back to cooking, and although it's been tough, it's also been a great pleasure, as I am cooking with my own two hands. I'm here for all the services, and I have the right kind of people in the kitchen and front-of-house to enable us to offer a memorable dining experience.'

Dockmaster's House
1 Hertsmere Road, London E14 8JJ
Phone 020 7345 0345 **www.dockmastershouse.com**

BAKED TAMARIND HALIBUT

This is actually a take on what the Japanese do. I go to Japanese restaurants from time to time, and have been inspired by miso-marinated black cod. Instead of miso paste, we make a glaze with tamarind and a few spices – star anise, garlic, chilli. We marinate the fish and then bake it in a hot oven so you get a brown glossy exterior with white flaky fish inside. This would work with cod and any chunky fish. I like to use what's available over here as this is what modern Indian food is all about. Indian cuisine is changing and adapting, and taking advantage of new ingredients and cooking methods.

SERVES 4

4 halibut steaks, skin on, 180g each
vegetable oil, for frying
4 pieces of banana leaf, for serving

For the tamarind marinade
100g dry tamarind (from a block of
    pressed tamarind)
5 star anise
2 garlic cloves, crushed
1–2 teaspoons chilli powder
150g sugar
500ml water
salt

For the apricot sauce
50g dried yellow apricots
10g green chilli paste, or to taste
150ml water

To make the tamarind marinade, place all the ingredients in a heavy-based pan and slowly bring to the boil, stirring occasionally. Continue for 15–20 minutes, until the liquid thickens and coats the back of a spoon; strain and cool.

Place the fish in a non-metallic bowl, pour over the marinade and cover with clingfilm. Put the bowl in the fridge or somewhere cool for at least 4 hours.

To make the apricot sauce, slowly cook all the ingredients in a small pan for about 10 minutes, until the apricots are soft and pulpy, adding a little water if the mixture becomes too thick. Use a handheld blender or a counter-top blender to purée the sauce, then strain and keep warm.

Preheat the oven to 200°C/Gas Mark 6.

Heat a little oil in an ovenproof pan and pan-fry the marinated steaks to seal the fish. Coat the fried fish with a little more of the marinade, then bake in the oven for 7 minutes.

Serve the fish on a sheet of banana leaf, with the apricot sauce.

COCONUT CHILLI BEEF

Beef isn't commonly used in India –
any restaurants offering beef on their
menus will usually substitute buffalo,
which is, in fact, very tender. This is a
recipe from the Christian community
and they, unlike Hindus, can eat beef.
A whole community of Bengali
Christians came to India and they
were predominantly chefs. One who
worked with me used to make a
delicious quick beef stir-fry. I have
used that as my inspiration and
incorporated a little coconut, because
British people like the taste.

SERVES 4

600g beef rump, cut into finger-sized
    pieces
1 large red onion, sliced
1 tablespoon crushed ginger
5 garlic cloves, chopped
2 green chillies, deseeded and finely
    sliced
¼ teaspoon red chilli powder
¼ teaspoon ground turmeric
¼ teaspoon ground coriander
¼ teaspoon garam masala
salt
75ml vegetable oil
½ teaspoon black mustard seeds
5 curry leaves
2 tomatoes, chopped
100ml coconut milk

For the garnish
2 teaspoons coarsely chopped
    coriander leaves
50g fresh coconut, thinly shaved
1 red chilli, sliced (optional)
1 green chilli, sliced (optional)

Mix the sliced beef in a large bowl
with the onion, ginger, garlic, green
chillies, all the ground spices and salt
to taste. Stir to coat the meat.

Heat the oil in a large heavy-based
pan. Add the mustard seeds and after
a few seconds, when they start to
crackle, add the curry leaves and the
marinated beef. Cook over a high heat
for 5–6 minutes to brown the meat
uniformly.

Add the chopped tomatoes and
coconut milk. Cook for a few more
minutes until the tomatoes have
softened and are incorporated into
the beef mixture. Check that the beef
is cooked through and adjust the
seasoning.

Serve garnished with coriander and
coconut shavings and the chillies, if
using.

Chef's Tip
To remove the hard shell of the
coconut, soak the whole coconut in
boiling water for 3–4 minutes, then
break with hammer; insert a short,
blunt knife between the shell and
white flesh and turn.

BANANA ORANGE YOGHURT RAITA

This is my mother-in-law's recipe. My wife, Sapna, learned it from her, and she passed it on to me – I had it on my first menu. Indian food can sometimes be oily and spicy, and this yoghurt and fruit-based dish cuts through that. The sweetness comes from the banana, but you add segments of orange at the end, so you get little bursts of refreshing citrus. It's versatile and works as a foil for so many rich dishes.

SERVES 4

1 ripe banana
500ml thick Greek yoghurt
¼ teaspoon cumin seeds, roasted in a dry pan and ground
50g orange segments, membrane removed
salt

Using a fork, mash the banana to make a thick purée. Mix the purée with the yoghurt, then season with salt and ground cumin seeds. Gently stir the orange segments into the yoghurt mix.

The raita should be served chilled.

ROASTED AUBERGINE SOUP

This isn't a traditional dish. I got the idea when I was working at the Oberoi Hotel, where we used to experiment. The inspiration came from the very traditional Baigan Ka Bharta – tandoori-roasted aubergines mixed with spices and garlic – which is adored in India. I have blended the aubergine flesh with stock to create a soup with a hint of garlic, which comes from the cloves with which the aubergine was studded before roasting. It's finished with cream, and served with crisp naan.

SERVES 4

2 large purple aubergines
5 garlic cloves, cut in half longways
30g butter
1 small onion, chopped
200ml chicken stock or vegetable
   stock
pinch of ground nutmeg
25ml double cream
salt and pepper
a few chives, chopped, for garnish

Preheat the oven to 200°C/Gas Mark 6.

Make a few cuts into the aubergines and fill each slit with half a garlic clove. Place the aubergines on a baking tray and roast the aubergines in the oven until the skin chars – 30 minutes or so.

Allow to cool for 10–15 minutes so that you can handle them. Remove the charred skin and chop the flesh, incorporating the roasted garlic.

Melt the butter in a pan and sauté the onions until golden, then add the aubergine and the stock, adjust the seasoning and bring to the boil.

Remove from the heat, purée the mixture using a handheld blender, or in the goblet of a counter-top blender, then stir in the ground nutmeg and double cream. Check the seasoning. Reheat the soup if necessary.

Serve garnished with chives accompanied by crusty bread or crispy naan.

KHUBANI KA MEETHA
(STEWED WHITE APRICOTS)

We use the hard white apricots from Iran rather than the Mediterranean ones. The stone inside forms part of the recipe and the kernel has a bitter almond taste – in fact, some of these are too bitter, so it's wise to try just a little piece of each one before you use them. This is delicious with fresh cream.

A simple yet famous recipe, from the Nawabs of Hyderabad, the finished dish resembles an apricot compote. Generally served at room temperature or cold, depending on what you want to serve it with – room temperature with ice cream, cold with cream.

SERVES 4

400g dried white apricots with stones
150g sugar
double cream or vanilla ice cream, to serve

Soak the fruit in a bowl of luke-warm water for at least 6 hours. This will soften the fruit to enable you remove the stone more easily.

Drain the apricots, saving the soaking water.

Cut the fruit into chunks and remove the stones (save them, as you will need these later).

Put the apricots in a heavy-based pan, add the water in which the fruit was soaked and cook over a low heat until the mix starts to boil. Add the sugar and cook for at least 45 minutes, until a jam consistency is reached, but do not let the apricots disintegrate – some of the fruit should still be in chunks.

Break open the reserved stones with a nutcracker, or tap with a hammer, to extract the kernels. It's important not to use the bitterest kernels, so take just a tiny sliver off each and taste; discard the most bitter. Flake or crush the remainder and stir into the stewed fruit.

Serve chilled with double cream, or at room temperature poured over vanilla ice cream.

CLAIRE FISHER

There are a few neighbourhoods in London that are synonymous with good Indian food. Brick Lane in East London is celebrated for its concentration of variable eateries, Southall has a good collection of decent restaurants, cafes and sweetshops, and then there is Peckham.

Even Londoners will be forgiven for not realising that Peckham is the home of a noteworthy Indian restaurant that is unique in many regards. Ganapati isn't in the middle of a predominantly Asian area, it isn't on a bustling high street, the restaurant doesn't have your predictable decor, the owner/chef is a woman, and she is European and called Claire Fisher. A whole raft of 'firsts' there.

Ganapati is the south Indian name for the elephant-headed god more usually addressed as Ganesh. He is the best-known god and most widely worshipped in the Hindu pantheon. He is revered as the Remover of Obstacles and is depicted carrying sweets. An elephant after my own heart!

Ganapati offers casual and convivial dining. The small restaurant is furnished with communal tables, and has a loyal following of both locals and, increasingly, those from further afield, who return for the predictably good food. At least a brace of recognisable Indian chefs are also known to periodically grace those aforementioned tables – another accolade for Claire and her unique restaurant. It's never boring, even for those regulars, as the kitchen makes frequent changes to the menu.

Claire was designing furniture, self-employed, and cooking in tapas restaurants in the evenings to make some extra money. She and a Spanish friend with whom she was working both very much wanted to visit India, so they decided to save up some cash and go. They went off with their backpacks, and tried to visit as much of the country as they could in three months. Claire muses, 'It was a very foolish thing to try to do, but you don't have any idea how big the country is until you get there! But we even made it to Nepal.'

Her eyes were opened to the richness of the culture: 'I knew there was something there for me already, but the colours, the smells, the openness of the people, the vibrancy of the place ignited something in me. I came back wanting to bring those things into my daily life – not only the food,

but also pattern and colour and texture for my furniture designs.'

The budding chef started cooking the street snacks that she had tasted in India. She particularly liked the south, and found the food there to be so different, with flavours she had never experienced before – tamarind, curry leaves, the way the spices were put together, Claire found it all fascinating.

'So I made it into a social thing – I started a curry night at our local bar, taking over the kitchen for the evening, and making a thali once a week. I had very little experience but lots of enthusiasm, and that's what drove me forward.

I bought lots of Indian cookbooks and made different dishes each week.'

Claire found a job working in an Indian restaurant. The place she really wanted to get into was Rasa. 'Despite my lack of professional training, I knew I had the dedication, and I was prepared to do whatever it took. Chef Das Sreedharan was opening a new restaurant, Rasa Samudra, in Charlotte Street; I got the job and I didn't know what had hit me. It was a big kitchen: there was a separate dosa chef, a seafood chef, a vegetarian chef, a starters chef, so I picked up a lot, and I used to go home and write notes on ingredients.'

So that was Claire's initiation into the Indian restaurant scene, and there was no going back – her life had changed. She worked in Rasa for a year and a half, long enough to learn more about traditional cooking, but she really wanted to do something herself. One of the Rasa chefs had had his own restaurant in Kerala, and he too wanted to do his own thing, so they looked for a venture together. They found a pub named the King's Head in Islington, that Claire describes as an eccentric old theatre-pub. They initially offered only European food, but gradually introduced Indian meals.

After travelling some more in south India, Claire found the building that was to become Ganapati. It had been a French restaurant. 'The Ganapati staff and I did the fitting out ourselves and opened just as soon as we could. That was seven years ago. The essential atmosphere and what we are trying to achieve has remained true to our initial concept, but I think we have become more accomplished with our cooking, and our service and presentation. We have learned on our feet, and being in the kitchen full-time from the start has been a valuable experience, but as the business has grown it has become necessary to spend periods of time overseeing other aspects. We remain a very close team, and the chefs are like family. We have reached a maximum capacity here, but we don't want to move, so we have been exploring ways of developing it further.

'We did a demo recently at Books for Cooks [the well-known bookstore in Notting Hill], and that kind of work is something we have to become familiar with. It's not like just talking through some recipes. We tried to prepare a complete banana-leaf thali of about 12 dishes to make up

a South Indian meal, in the space of two hours – and we managed it. The participants' heads were spinning afterwards, but they did enjoy the food very much!

'Indian food is such a vast subject that I sometimes feel I will never get to the end of it, which makes it so very exciting: there is always more to learn, new stories, new flavours. When I go to India I tend to go to Kerala and Tamil Nadu, and their cooking styles have similarities, but every family has got something very different to show me.'

Ganapati still occasionally gets asked for Chicken Tikka Masala, and has to let the customer down gently! People eating at Ganapati for the first time have an experience that they were not expecting at all. Most people have now woken up to the idea that there are different types of Indian cooking out there. A lot of people are taking holidays in Kerala these days, and their palates are changed by the experience. 'Using a particular spice as a starting point, we explore all the different applications, because a lot of the same spices are used in savoury and sweet dishes – they are so versatile. We are re-learning about food in this country – it's so different in India, where food has always been a central part of everyday life.'

Claire employs several students from Goldsmiths College (part of University of London, just down the road in New Cross), and a mixture of full-time and part-time staff for front-of-house led with great warmth and dedication by manager Adrienne Woods. 'Everyone who works here loves the food and knows a lot about it, and that enables them to pass that on to the customers. The service here is very informal, but efficient: some staff have a professional background in service and they have brought their skills with them. That has moulded us into a cohesive team. We have online booking now, and that has really brought us a bigger audience – we could never have known that, but it's one of the best things we have ever done, and the feedback that those customers leave has helped build our reputation.'

Claire makes changes to the menu every six weeks or so. All the kitchen staff get together to try out new things, to take advantage of seasonal produce like green mangoes, and to come up with lighter dishes for summer, heartier ones in the colder months. They do like to experiment, to push themselves to try new ideas. That is good, too, for the customers, who get to sample an array of ever-changing dishes. 'Although we are led by authenticity, we do like to present twists on the classics sometimes. We do a Brussels sprout kofta curry dish in December which is very popular. It is not a South Indian dish at all, but why not? It's fun! And we do an ice cream of Kesar mango with ginger and green chilli, and a white chocolate and cardamom ice cream – you can do anything with desserts.' Well, Ganapati does love his sweets, after all.

Ganapati
38 Holly Grove, London SE15 5DF
Phone 020 7277 2928 **www.ganapatirestaurant.com**

IDIAPPAM

Also known as string hoppers in Sri Lanka, these little nests of rice vermicelli are made by putting rice dough through a sev-maker or idiappam press (see below) and steaming. They are traditionally eaten at breakfast with sweetened coconut milk, and they make a charming visual and textural alternative to rice.

SERVES 4

450ml water
75ml coconut milk
½ teaspoon salt, or to taste
450g rice flour
25g fresh grated coconut to sprinkle
    in the moulds

Utensils
An idli steamer or large vessel for
    steaming.
An idiappam press (wooden or brass,
    a tubular vessel which extrudes
    noodles under pressure). Some
    presses require you to turn a handle,
    others use manual pressure or a
    trigger action. The brass ones with
    a handle are easier to use.
Both these items are available in good
    South Indian shops selling cooking
    equipment. (Try Little India, 191
    Upper Tooting Road, London SW17
    7TG, phone: 020 8696 1016, or
    Swathi Cash and Carry, 306–308
    High Street North, London E12
    6SA, phone: 020 8586 7648).

Put the water, coconut milk and salt in a saucepan and bring to the boil. Simmer for a couple of minutes. Add the rice flour and briskly mix in using a wooden spoon. You will have a stiff dough the texture of play-dough – add a little more rice flour if the dough is too wet.

Remove from the heat and turn out onto a work surface. Press the dough into a slab and allow it to cool a little before continuing. While still hot, knead the dough a little to make sure it is mixed well.

Meanwhile, put water on to boil in the steamer. If you have an idli steamer, remove the trays and sprinkle a little coconut in the bottom of each mould. This will prevent the idiappam from sticking. You could smear a little oil in each mould instead if you do not wish to use coconut.

It is easiest to make the idiappam before the dough cools too much. Fill the idiappam press with portions of the dough so that it is nearly full and compact inside the tube. Attach the lid and, working in a circular motion, make nests of the rice noodles in the moulds. The idiappam should be heaped up to a height of 3–4cm. When you have your heap ready, break the noodles at the base of the press with your forefinger, then move onto the next mould. You will need to refill the press about three times to make about 12 nests.

When you have a batch ready, place it in the steamer, close the lid, and steam cook on full heat for 7 minutes. Then reduce the heat to low and finish for 3 minutes. Remove the tray from the steamer and allow to sit for a few minutes, then carefully remove the idiappam with a spoon. Keep warm until you are ready to serve. Repeat the process until the dough is finished.

As an alternative to an idli steamer, you could use an oiled saucer or plate, fitting as many idiappams as you can with a little space between each. The plate or saucer could then be put in a bamboo steamer or similar contraption. The ideal size for each idiappam is about 7cm diameter.

Serve hot with Vegetable Istoo (see page 119). Idiappams are also enjoyed with meat curries.

They can be stored in the fridge for a few days, and microwaved in a covered container to reheat.

VEGETABLE ISTOO

A Kerala 'stew', this is usually made with meat or vegetables, cooked lightly in coconut milk without the use of a rich masala, but gently flavoured with a few cloves, cardamom pods, cinnamon and curry leaves. It is a festive dish, but also wonderfully comforting, and light on the stomach.

SERVES 4

4 tablespoons vegetable oil
10 cloves
10 green cardamom pods, cracked with the back of a knife
5-cm stick of cinnamon, broken into 4 pieces
$\frac{1}{2}$-1 teaspoon ground black pepper
2 onions, peeled, halved and finely sliced
2 tablespoons finely chopped ginger
2 green chillies, slit lengthways
handful of curry leaves
$\frac{2}{3}$ teaspoon ground turmeric
$\frac{3}{4}$ teaspoon salt, or to taste
2 small or 1 large tomato, halved and sliced
2 medium or 3 small potatoes, peeled and cut into slightly larger cubes or chunks
2 carrots, peeled and cut into 2-cm cubes
300ml water
400ml coconut milk
1 small head of broccoli, cut into florets
75g frozen peas (a couple of handfuls)
handful of coriander leaves, chopped
salt

Heat the oil in a medium-sized saucepan. When hot, add the cloves, cardamom, cinnamon and black pepper, and let the aromas release for a few moments. Add the onions, ginger, chillies and curry leaves. Sweat the onions on a medium heat until translucent, then stir in the turmeric and salt.

Add the tomatoes and cook down for a few minutes. Add the potatoes and carrots and sauté for 5 minutes, stirring to prevent sticking. (You could speed the process by par-cooking the potatoes and carrots beforehand, if you wish.)

Add 100ml water. Cover the pan and leave to cook gently on a low heat for a further 5–10 minutes, or until the vegetables are partially cooked, but still firm to the bite.

Add the coconut milk and a further 200ml water. Bring to the boil. Add the broccoli and simmer until almost *al dente*. Add the peas and cook for 3 more minutes. Stir in the coriander leaves, and season.

Serve with Idiappam (see page 116).

KADALUNDI SEAFOOD CURRY WITH COCONUT RICE

This curry is from our head chef Aboo, whose family lives on the Malabari coast just below Calicut. His brothers work in the fishing industry there, and the whole family have a love and respect for all things from the sea. Nearby Tellicherry is famous for its black pepper and mussels.

Coconut rice has a wonderful rich savouriness which comes from the fenugreek seeds and curry leaves, and a touch of sweetness from coconut milk. These elements really complement the chilli and pepper spice in the Kadalundi curry, the sweetness of the prawns and mussels, and the sour note from the tamarind.

SERVES 4

For the seafood
150g cleaned fish cut into bite-sized pieces (eg kingfish, sea bass or snapper fillets)
8 king prawns, shelled and de-veined, leaving tail piece on
700g fresh mussels, cleaned (allow about 8 per person, or more if small)
4 whole baby squid, cleaned, tentacles removed

For the stuffing for the baby squid
1 tablespoon rice, washed and soaked in water for 30 minutes, then drained
2–3 small Indian shallots, peeled and finely chopped, or ½ tablespoon finely chopped red onion
3–4 curry leaves, finely chopped
1 teaspoon finely chopped ginger
1 tablespoon freshly grated coconut
the tentacles from the squid, finely chopped

For the masala
1 teaspoon black peppercorns
¾ teaspoon fenugreek seeds

For the sauce
4 tablespoons vegetable oil
2 white onions, finely chopped
1 red onion, finely chopped
3 cloves garlic, finely chopped
1 tablespoon finely chopped ginger
2 green chillies, finely chopped
¼ teaspoon ground turmeric
½ teaspoon red chilli powder
1½ teaspoons ground coriander
3 small or 2 large tomatoes, finely chopped
1 teaspoon tomato purée
35g dried tamarind block, soaked in 150ml hot water for 15–20 minutes
salt
100ml coconut milk
handful chopped fresh coriander leaves and stalks
10 curry leaves

To prepare the baby squid, mix all the stuffing ingredients together in a small bowl and stuff the squids, securing the ends with a toothpick. Set aside.

For the masala, roast the peppercorns and fenugreek seeds together in a small pan over a low heat until the fenugreek turns a nutty brown colour (but do not burn). Cool and grind to a fine powder in a spice or coffee grinder. Set aside.

Barely cover the base of a saucepan (large enough to hold all the seafood) with oil (about 3–4 tablespoons) over a medium heat. When the oil is hot, add the white and red onions, garlic, ginger and chillies, and sweat for 4–5 minutes until soft but not coloured. Add the turmeric, chilli powder and ground coriander, stirring in. Then add the tomatoes and the tomato purée.

Mash the soaked tamarind with your fingers or a spoon, and push through a sieve to extract the juice. Discard the fibres and seeds. Add this juice to the pan and cook for 5–6 minutes until the tomatoes break down, stirring from time to time. Stir in the roasted pepper-and-fenugreek masala and a teaspoon of salt, or to taste.

Add 350ml water and bring to the boil. Put the baby squid in the saucepan, bring back to the boil, then simmer for 5 minutes. Add the fish pieces, prawns and mussels, and cover the pan. Cook over a brisk heat until all the mussels open (no more than 10 minutes) and discard any that remain closed. By this time all the other seafood will also be cooked through.

Add the coconut milk and the fresh coriander and curry leaves, and check the seasoning. Stir carefully, and serve immediately with rice. Remove the toothpicks from the squid before plating up.

Continued on page 122

Continued from page 120

COCONUT RICE

SERVES 4

200g basmati rice
2–3 tablespoons vegetable oil
¹/₂ teaspoon fenugreek seeds
2 garlic cloves, sliced lengthways 3 or
    4 times
¹/₂ onion, halved and finely sliced
small handful of curry leaves (about 8)
250ml coconut milk
250ml water
¹/₂ teaspoon salt, or to taste

Wash the rice in 3–4 changes of warm water, then leave to soak in clean water for 30 minutes.

Heat the vegetable oil in a saucepan which has a tight-fitting lid. Add the fenugreek seeds and allow to turn a shade darker, then add the garlic, onion and curry leaves. Sauté over a low-medium heat until the onions are soft and starting to turn golden at the edges.

Strain the rice and add it to the pan along with the coconut milk, water and salt. Stir and bring to the boil. Immediately turn the heat to the lowest possible setting and cover the pan.

Check the rice after 10 minutes. On a very low heat it should be ready within 15 minutes. The liquid will have been absorbed by the rice.

OKRA AND
GREEN MANGO CURRY

This is a Ganapati recipe built around the wonderful fragrant and tart green, or raw, mangoes, which are at their best from around March to May, before the arrival of the sweet Indian mangoes. Look out for the large Rajpuri green mango which is a revelation in itself. Otherwise they tend to be small, and should be hard and vivid green. This is a hot dish, with clean flavours, onions slowly cooked and sweet, the tomatoes adding acidity, mangoes fragrance and sourness, fennel marrying all. Finally, the okra should be cooked until just *al dente*, adding its fresh flavour to the mix.

SERVES 4

1 *fresh raw mango (size of a lemon)
   or 2–3 small ones (a small green
   mango used only for cooking, and
   labelled as 'raw')*
4 *tablespoons vegetable oil*
3 *onions, finely chopped*
2 *green chillies, slit lengthways*
1 *tablespoon peeled and finely
   chopped ginger*
1/2 *teaspoon fennels seeds, ground to a
   powder*
1/2 *teaspoon ground turmeric*
3/4 *teaspoon chilli powder, or to taste*
1 *teaspoon ground coriander*
1 *teaspoon tomato paste*
2 *large or 3 medium tomatoes, finely
   chopped*
350ml *water*
handful of curry leaves
300g *okra (the Asian variety which are
   longer, more slender and a deeper
   green)*
salt

Halve and stone the mangoes, then cut into thick wedges, leaving the skin on. Heat the oil in a saucepan. Add the onions and green chillies, and stir briskly over a high heat for 4–5 minutes. Add salt and turn the heat down to low, cover the pan and sweat the onions until they start to melt down. This will take about 15 minutes; ensure they do not brown.

Add the ginger and ground spices and stir well, then add the tomato paste and tomatoes. Cook until the tomatoes break down and start to melt into the onions. This will take about 8–10 minutes over a moderate heat. Keep stirring.

Trim the stalk-ends of the okra into a point, but do not cut into the hollow part of the vegetable. Rinse in water and pat dry.

Add the water to the pan and bring to the boil, add the curry leaves and mango pieces and boil for a couple of minutes, then add the okra. Bring back to the boil, and simmer until okra is *al dente*, about 5–7 minutes. They should be a vivid green colour. Check the seasoning.

Serve with chappatis, paratha or basmati rice.

PINEAPPLE MORU

Kerala is home to some wonderful dishes and curries made with yoghurt. They work brilliantly at cooling the body and are often eaten towards the end of a meal. By adding seasonal fruit to these sour savoury preparations, they are taken to a different level. Here we use pineapple. The riper the fruit, the better the contrast with sourness of the yoghurt and the savouriness of the curry leaves, fenugreek and mustard seeds. This is a treat for the taste buds and the stomach all in one.

SERVES 4

4 tablespoons vegetable oil
$\frac{1}{2}$ teaspoon brown or black mustard seeds
$\frac{1}{2}$ teaspoon fenugreek seeds
4 dried red chillies (the large dark red variety)
2 tablespoons finely chopped ginger
handful of curry leaves
2 green chillies, slit lengthways
2 red onions, peeled and thinly sliced
1 teaspoon salt, or to taste
1 teaspoon asafoetida powder
1 small or half a medium to large juicy pineapple, peeled, cored and cut into bite-sized chunks
$\frac{1}{2}$ teaspoon ground turmeric
2 tomatoes, each cut into 6 pieces
600ml yoghurt (not Greek set or strained yoghurt, but ordinary natural yoghurt), whisked

Heat the vegetable oil in a medium-sized saucepan, over a medium heat. When hot, add the mustard seeds, and as they pop, add the fenugreek seeds. Cook until they become a shade darker, then add the dried chillies, ginger, curry leaves and green chillies, the onions and salt. Stir over a medium heat, sweating the onions, but not browning.

Add the asafoetida and pineapple pieces, and stir for 5 minutes until the pineapple juices start to release. Stir in the turmeric and finally add the tomatoes. Heat them through, stirring from time to time.

Remove the pan from the heat. Pour in the whisked yoghurt and fold in gently. Place the pan back over a very low heat until the yoghurt is warmed through. Take care at this stage to keep stirring and not to let the yoghurt boil, as it will curdle. Check the seasoning.

Serve with a fluffy rice, some pickle and poppadoms.

RAJESH SURI AND SAMIR SADEKAR

Imli is a ground-breaker. Yes, in many ways it's a conventional Indian restaurant, but it offers something a little different from that you might find elsewhere. Its location between Soho and Oxford Street is vibrant, with an eclectic mix of Italian pâtisseries, Caribbean cafés and Middle-Eastern fast-food outlets. It's a magnet for shoppers, tourists and office workers who want a tapas-style meal from a broad menu of subcontinental favourites whilst on the run. Those who have time to linger will just order more of those curries and tikkas.

Rajesh Suri is CEO at the Tamarind Group (*Imli* means tamarind in Hindi), but he didn't always have a clear vision of his future. After completing his education, Rajesh started searching for possible career opportunities. 'A friend of mine was going into the hospitality industry. In those days it wasn't a popular path – most Indian families would favour their sons becoming doctors or engineers. In my family, my brothers were Masters of Economics, Masters of this science or that, but to be honest I was not very academic, and the hospitality industry was attractive. Without telling anyone, I joined the course, and graduated from Pusa Catering College in Delhi.'

Rajesh joined the Maurya Sheraton as a kitchen trainee under a French chef. Unfortunately his career in the kitchen didn't last very long – he was assigned to the saucier section. The room had five massive kettles, and all day long he boiled bones to make the stocks. 'You were living and breathing in that steam, and eventually your body begins to smell. I hated it, so that was the end of becoming a chef!'

Luckily Oberoi Hotels came to the rescue: they were recruiting management trainees at that time, and Rajesh had the opportunity to join as an apprentice. A little later, another group was recruiting for a post in the Middle East and Rajesh got the job. He became the Assistant Manager in the coffee shop at The Gulf Hotel, Bahrain, a night-shift job. 'I quickly saw that there were ways in which I could improve the service standard and increase the revenue, and I asked the manager if I could try my ideas. Within a week I had tripled the sales!

'I met my wife while I was in Bahrain. She was from the UK, and that's where we eventually decided to settle. We arrived in June 1987 and I joined Bailey's Hotel as food and beverage manager. During 1989 I was part of the opening team at The Washington Hotel, also as food and beverage manager. I was looking for new challenges, and wanted to create and run the outstanding Indian restaurant of which I had always dreamt.'

A restaurant called Tamarind (see page 241) had opened in Mayfair. It is one of the restaurants that broke the mould of Indian food presentation, introducing the fine-dining concept to the UK for the first time. In September 1998 Rajesh was invited to become its General Manager. 'Within 18 months we felt confident enough to ask Michelin to consider us for their Guide. In January 2001 we gained our first Michelin star.

'We looked at opening a "Tamarind 2" with a different concept, giving the customer tastes that they had not met

before, in an effort to convince them that Indian street food was something special. This is where the idea of Indian "tapas" was born, and we opened Imli in December 2005 on that basis.'

Executive Chef Samir Sadekar was born in Goa. His mother was a very good cook, and Samir loved eating, but was never fond of cooking. It was only later, when he was 13 or 14, that he began to help out in the kitchen, making

chapatis, making tea, and so on. He realised that cooking was as enjoyable as eating, although he didn't think of it as a possible career at that time.

There was a catering college just a kilometre from their house, and there were lots of students lodging in the area. Samir got to know some of them, and heard about the curriculum. 'I thought this was something I would love to study. I spent three years there, training in 5-star hotels owned by the Taj and Oberoi groups. Even during my holidays, instead of going home I used to spend the time in training placements. That was of great benefit to me. At the end of the three years the colleges held their All-India Chefs Competition. I and two others from Mumbai competed, and we won, which was quite a feather in the cap.

'Once we graduated there were the on-campus interviews, including ITC Hotels. I was more interested in Indian rather than other cuisines (not that I don't like French, Italian and so on), so I decided to remain an Indian-speciality chef, and joined ITC.'

They had a two-year training programme: theoretical training, as well as practical training in their flagship hotel, the Maurya Sheraton. After that Samir was posted to Chennai, and that's where he met Alfred Prasad (see page 241), who had been a fellow-student.

Alfred got the chance to come to London, and when he became head chef at Tamarind, he invited Samir to join as sous-chef. Samir worked there for three years, and looked after the outdoor catering as well as the restaurant. The owners began to consider a 'mid-market' outlet. At that time there were either curry houses or fine-dining Indian venues. Slowly the idea began to develop: 'I came in to help devise the menu. It was to be Indian street food, light, not too many curries, but not drastically different from other types of Indian food available in Britain. Quality, consistency and presentation would be key and, of course, value for money. So we had a lot of trials before deciding on the menu. We call it Indian tapas, but there are several dishes of slightly larger portions, to suit those customers who just want a single dish for a light lunch.

'Dishes like Pani Puri, Bhel Puri and Papdi Chaat are found everywhere in India at street stalls, and that's where people will congregate. Those vendors sell Dosa, Uttapams, Idli,

Samosa Chaat, Aloo Tikki on railway stations. These casual dishes are what has made us popular, rather than the curries. We wanted to make this restaurant a place where anyone could come and eat, or come and learn to cook. Customers were asking for naan and parathas, so we decided to introduce the tandoor last year, to provide breads and kebabs.'

One thing that caught everyone's attention was that concept of Indian tapas. 'The Spanish have little dishes to share, and Indians have always had the same. Just because we didn't have a term for it didn't mean we didn't have the notion. You have to have something different to set yourself apart from other restaurants, and I think it's been our strength.

'At home, because I'm a chef I don't cook for just a single meal – I tend to cook for five meals at a time! But when I'm here in the restaurant my greatest pleasure is seeing our customers enjoying this very different face of Indian food.'

Imli represents a style of eating that is becoming more popular worldwide. It is particularly sought by those who want Indian food, but a lighter option at lunchtime, or a grazing menu for the evening. Its small plates still offer the spice and flavour of the subcontinent, but are more accessible and affordable for those who want just a bite rather than a feast.

Size of plate and gold-leaf covered walls are all that separate Imli from the most celebrated of fine-dining establishments. Its wood carvings of Indian gods evidently mark this as an Indian restaurant, but it has the air of a smart contemporary European brasserie. It attracts a young clientele with discerning tastes.

Imli is a bright and modern restaurant with windows offering views over Wardour Street. If you are a film buff, then you will recognise the name: it was the hub of the British film industry, with the big production and distribution companies having their headquarters in the street. That industry is ailing, but Imli is very much alive and looking to the future.

Imli
167–168 Wardour Street, London W1F 8WR
Phone 020 7287 4243 **www.imli.co.uk**

POTATO AND PEA CAKES

A staple of India, this is typical street food and very simple to make. Made on the tava, you find it on the streets of Mumbai, Delhi and all over. It goes very well with tamarind chutney or (as in our ragda potato dish) with boiled chickpeas cooked with onion, tomato and spices. Garnish with chopped coriander and raw onions.

SERVES 4

300g potatoes, boiled
100g peas, fresh or frozen, cooked
1 teaspoon chopped coriander leaves
15g fresh ginger, finely chopped
1–2 green chillies, or to taste, finely
    chopped
80ml vegetable oil
salt

To serve
tamarind chutney
4 parsley sprigs
2 cherry tomatoes, halved

Grate the potatoes into a bowl. Mash the peas, and add to the bowl with all the ingredients, except the oil. Divide into 12 portions and flatten them to form cakes, using damp hands so the mixture doesn't stick.

Heat the oil in a non-stick pan over a medium heat and slide in the cakes; fry for 3–4 minutes, and when they brown, turn them over and brown the other side.

Serve with tamarind chutney and garnish with a sprig of parsley and a half of cherry tomato.

MASALA GRILLED CHICKEN

This combination of mashed potato and grilled chicken has been on our menu right from the start. There's a similar dish called Jeera Aloo (cumin potatoes, which is made with cubed potato), but here we have mashed them, so they have the same flavour, but with a different texture. The grilled chicken recipe works just as well with fish. The avocado chutney is our Indian version of a salsa, and it looks good on the plate.

SERVES 4

4 chicken breasts, boneless, skinless
2 tablespoons vegetable oil

For the marinade
1 tablespoon vegetable oil
1–2 green chillies, roughly chopped
1 teaspoon tamarind concentrate
1 teaspoon fresh ginger, chopped
3 large garlic cloves, crushed
salt

For the chutney
1/2 an avocado, peeled and stone
    removed
1/4 bunch (approximately 25g) of
    coriander, leaves and stems
20g raw mango (a small green mango
    used only for cooking, and labelled
    as 'raw'), peeled and stone removed
20ml yoghurt
3 large garlic cloves, crushed
1 teaspoon sugar
1 green chilli, roughly chopped
salt

For the mash
1 tablespoon vegetable oil
1 teaspoon cumin seeds
1 green chilli, chopped
1/2 teaspoon ground turmeric
400g potatoes, boiled and mashed
1 teaspoon lemon juice
15g butter
15ml single cream
1/2 bunch (approximately 50g)
    coriander leaves, finely chopped
11/2 teaspoons chaat masala
salt

For the garnish
4 parsley sprigs
1 red chilli, chopped

Cut each chicken breast across into three sections, and place in a non-metallic bowl. Combine all the ingredients for the marinade in a blender or mini-processor to make a paste and coat the meat. Cover with clingfilm and marinate for 2 hours in the fridge.

Blend all the ingredients for the chutney to a chunky consistency (smoother if preferred), transfer to a serving bowl and keep covered.

For the mash, heat the oil in a non-stick frying pan over a medium heat, add the cumin seeds and when they crackle add the chilli and turmeric. Stir-fry for a minute

Add potato, lemon juice, butter, cream, coriander and chaat masala. Mix well and cook over a medium heat until the potato has warmed through, stirring occasionally. Add salt to taste.

Heat the oil in a pan and fry the chicken over a medium heat until just done (no pink flesh).

To serve, put a portion of mash on the plate and top with three chicken slices. Garnish with a parsley sprig and a few pieces of chilli, and serve with the avocado chutney.

GRILLED STUFFED PANEER

Stuffed paneer is very popular in the north of India, and is liked by vegetarians for its protein content. Every restaurant has their own version of this. I like the difference in textures and flavours – the spice of the chillies, the crunch of the cashew nuts, the sweetness of the raisins. The diners are impressed by this!

SERVES 4

500g block of paneer
80ml vegetable oil, for frying
mint chutney, to serve

For the stuffing
300g potatoes
2 tablespoons finely chopped
  coriander
15g fresh ginger, chopped
20g whole cashew nuts, toasted in
  a dry pan and crushed
1 tablespoon pistachio flakes
1 tablespoon chopped raisins
2 teaspoons chaat masala
1 teaspoon Kashmiri chilli powder
1 teaspoon mango powder (amchur
  powder)
salt

For the coating
1 tablespoon vegetable oil
1 teaspoon salt, or to taste
1/2 teaspoon Kashmiri chilli powder

Boil the potatoes in plenty of salted water until soft, then drain and mash. Mix with the remainder of the stuffing ingredients.

Cut the paneer block into 10-cm squares. Stand the block on edge and slice into 1-cm thick squares, then cut each slice part-way through so that you get two slices of paneer joined at one end.

For the coating, mix the oil, salt and chilli powder in a bowl. Add the paneer and turn gently to coat.

Open out each pair of joined slices and spoon in the stuffing. Press firmly to close.

Heat the oil in a non-stick pan and cook the stuffed paneer over a low heat, taking care that the paneer does not get burnt. Turn over after 2 minutes and cook the other side for a further 2 minutes. Drain on kitchen paper.

Serve with mint chutney.

PAN-FRIED LAMB CAKES

Lamb cakes are very popular in the north of India – it's a Muslim dish. Some take the mince, mould it on skewers and cook in the tandoor. They also use the mince to make into patties and cook them on the grill – not the ordinary barbecue or tandoor griddle, because the mince would fall through, but the tava hotplate. You put the lamb cake in the centre and a very little oil, and then fry, so they cook in their own flavourful fat. Unlike the shaami kebab, you don't need to cook the mince beforehand, and with the herbs, ginger and onion it gives you a very fresh taste.

SERVES 4

500g lamb mince
10g chopped ginger
2 tablespoons chopped coriander
   leaves
1 teaspoon red chilli powder
bunch of mint, chopped
40g onion, finely chopped
1½ teaspoons ground cardamom
salt
80ml vegetable oil
mint chutney, to serve

Mix all ingredients with 20ml of the oil. Divide into 12 balls and, using damp hands so the mixture doesn't stick, flatten them into patties.

Heat the remaining oil in a pan and add the lamb cakes, cook over medium heat for 3 minutes, turn the patties over and cook the other side for a further 3 minutes. Drain on kitchen paper.

Serve with mint chutney.

GRILLED FISH WITH GREENS

This is not an Indian dish, but a fusion invention. We were looking for something that wasn't spicy, so we adapted Euorpean recipes by 'Indianising' them with coriander and spices to make them exotic.

SERVES 4

600g firm white fish fillets, such as
    sea bass or haddock
30ml vegetable oil

For the marinade
1 tablespoon finely chopped basil
$1/2$ teaspoon ground turmeric
2 teaspoons cumin seeds, roasted in
    a dry pan and crushed
1 teaspoon crushed black pepper
40ml vegetable oil
2 teaspoons rice flour
20ml lime juice
salt

For the pine nut sauce
4–6 large garlic cloves, roughly
    chopped
10g fresh ginger, roughly chopped
2 teaspoons cumin seeds, roasted in
    a dry pan
70g pine nuts
large handful of coriander leaves,
    finely chopped
3 tablespoons vegetable oil
1 teaspoon crushed black pepper, or
    to taste
10g baby spinach
1 tablespoon lime juice
salt

For the vegetable base
100g broccoli florets
80g fine beans, cut to 2.5-cm lengths
60g baby sweetcorn, cut in half
$1^1/2$ teaspoons vegetable oil
60g red peppers, diced

Mix all the ingredients for the marinade in a non-metallic bowl. Coat the fish with the marinade, cover with clingfilm and leave to marinate in the fridge for 30 minutes.

Put all the sauce ingredients in a blender and process until smooth.

For the vegetable base, bring a pan of water to the boil and add the broccoli, fine beans and sweetcorn. Cook for 4–6 minutes until *al dente*, then strain. Add the oil to a small frying pan over a medium heat and sauté the red peppers for a few minutes until just tender; mix into the cooked vegetables. Keep aside.

Heat the oil for frying the fish in a large frying pan, add the fish and cook over a medium heat for 3 minutes, When the first side is lightly browned, turn and cook the other side for a further 3 minutes.

Either serve with the vegetables and sauce separately, or mix the sauce with the vegetables, put a portion on the plate, then top with the fish.

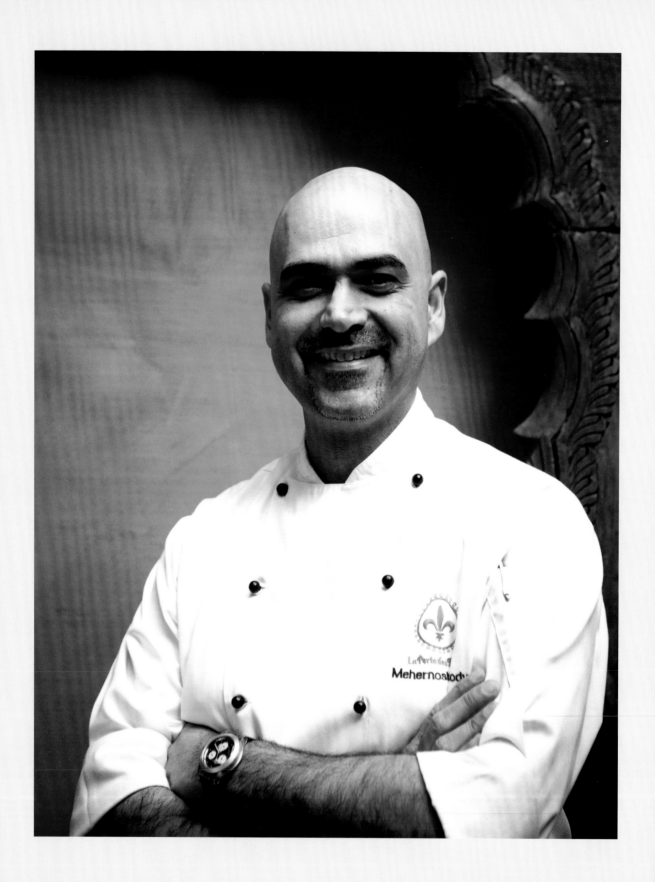

MEHERNOSH MODY

LA PORTE DES INDES

Mehernosh Mody was born in Mumbai, and spent most of his early childhood there. His father was an automotive engineer and Mehernosh inherited his love of tinkering with machines from him. 'So I studied engineering, and at one time considered joining the merchant navy. I'm still a great DIY enthusiast today.'

His father moved around between the east coast and the west coast, but the family finally settled down in Pune, close to Mumbai. 'The beauty of living in Mumbai was that it is a very cosmopolitan city, and I was exposed to all sorts of different cultures. From an early age I was very open-minded. This has held me in good stead today, because I understand more about the diverse Indian influences.'

Chef Mody was drawn to the glamour of the hospitality industry, and liked the sound of the 'all-India' entrance exam to catering college. 'I knew I would have to be good to succeed, as there were only four colleges in the whole of India at that time (Delhi, Mumbai, Kolkata and Chennai). I was surprised to be shortlisted, to be invited for interview, and then to pass that.'

When the hotel groups came recruiting, he was selected by the Taj Group to be a trainee chef. 'It was a very tough, but "beautifully tough" for the first five years there. They put us through the mill. When you leave college you have a diploma in your pocket and you think you are top dog, but they tell you to forget all that – this is the real world and you are starting again on the lowest rung of the ladder.' His first three months were spent in the main banqueting kitchen, catering for hundreds and thousands of covers at an event. For a trainee chef, wanting to prove yourself, you have to work hard! Then came the bakery, then the French kitchen. People advised him that if he was to succeed, he should specialise in just one aspect, but Mehernosh disagreed. 'That broad spectrum has helped me so much – it has opened my mind to so many things, which I can now bring into my own cuisine. It's like cycling or swimming: once you have the knack you can go back and pick it up again years later.'

In 1991 a vacancy arose for a chef at the Blue Elephant group in Brussels. This was for the Belgian version of La Porte des Indes. Mehernosh and his wife Sherin, also a professional chef, decided to leave India and go to Belgium to head their kitchen. After five years there, the company put together a project to open in London. They arrived in 1996, and got involved in every detail of planning and renovating the dilapidated building.

'All I knew of London was what I'd learned playing Monopoly! But I felt so at home when I arrived – the station names were the same as in Mumbai, the Victorian buildings, the double-decker buses – it was a cleaner, less-polluted Mumbai. This was great, I loved this city!' He did lots of market research, and quickly realised that there was no beef or pork on the menus of Indian restaurants here. When he asked the reason, he was told, 'Indians don't eat beef.' '"Wow, perhaps I'm not Indian!", I thought. This was ridiculous, and I made up my mind to bring in beef and pork dishes. The best pork dish is Pork Vindaloo, from Goa, made with belly pork – delicious! And I'm doing a stir-fried beef dish from southern India, and we sell a lot of portions. In the same way I introduced scallops and squid to the restaurant.'

Mehernosh didn't realise the identity problems to be faced by a Belgian company in London, speaking French, with a French-named restaurant serving Indian food! The first few months were tough, but they rose to the challenge, and over the years established their position in the market. The well-known Belgian architect Yves Burton designed the restaurant, travelling frequently to India to take in architecturally 'what India was about'. He commissioned the pink marble and sandstone panels direct from Jaipur, and the team had fun assembling the staircase 'jigsaw puzzle' when the parts all arrived. There were some worries that perhaps some of the pieces might have been lost in transit, or might not fit. Rather difficult to take it back and complain!

The chef was on the crest of a learning curve. He knew every nook and cranny of the place, and his technical background helped him a great deal when trouble-shooting the kitchen equipment. The restaurant didn't have the back-up to be found in a big hotel. 'That is a protected environment, where the chef is there just to cook and run the kitchen. If something goes wrong you pick up the phone and call maintenance. Here, if you are head of the kitchen you are everything. I love it, and it would be too boring if it all worked too smoothly all the time.'

They were a team of four, including Sherin, putting the menus together, and they were all fascinated by the French-influenced food still to be found in the former French colonies in India, principally Pondicherry (now Puducherry), and they spent some months researching. That is one unique aspect of the menu at La Porte des Indes, but it's an 'Indian' restaurant so Mehernosh draws on his wider knowledge of Indian food for other dishes. 'We don't change the menu significantly, but from time to time we might change 10 to 20 per cent. We also put on a themed food festival occasionally, and our team of chefs is good at coming up with new things. We learn a lot, and I make a point of being in the kitchen most evenings – it's my escape route, my comfort zone.'

The restaurant has a very large percentage of customers coming by recommendation. La Porte des Indes has its regular private customers as well as lots of corporate clients. The location in central London makes this former ballroom ideal for functions – an entire floor can be given over to weddings and large or small events. The décor is stunning, giving an ambiance of exotic and palm-laden charm, with a Jungle Bar that sets a more casual tone.

Mehernosh says that at one time in India culinary horizons were somewhat limited: 'When I was training, we used to think of European chefs as doing things that we could only dream of, but this wasn't true at all. The talent was there, but no one told us that we had talent! We had great chefs who taught us, but at that time we were limited to local ingredients. When I had access to different ingredients, I used them. For example, in India our Parsee Fish dish is always made with pomfret; in London I could only get frozen pomfret, so I experimented and found lemon sole worked perfectly in the dish, so that's what I serve. In the same way, I use scallops here, which you can't get back home.'

With two trained chefs in the family, one wonders who cooks at home. 'My wife cooks. We eat all kinds of food – sometimes it's comfort food, dishes from childhood that my Mum used to make, and that my wife's Mum used to make. We come from very different cultural backgrounds: she is a Syrian Christian from Kerala, I am Zoroastrian, and we love foods from each other's repertoire. I learnt that there is no fixed recipe for a certain dish: Kerala Stew, for example, is a term used very loosely, and it changes dramatically from house to house, Hindu, Muslim, whatever. You can't say, "This is the way to cook Dal." I can show you a thousand different dals, every home does it differently. Your palate is used to the taste you grew up with, but in our profession you can't just present your family favourites. I love food, and discovering new tastes, and your palate learns to accept new things.

'Food is an integral part of life – you need food, in whichever form you eat it, and you should enjoy it. You might as well taste everything there is to taste, because you only live once.'

La Porte des Indes
32 Bryanston Street, London W1H 7EG
Phone 020 7224 0055 **www.laportedesindes.com**

CHARD AND WATERCHESTNUT PAKORAS

Quintessentially a pakora but using chard which is not common in India. I find it reminiscent of spinach, and the leaves blend in well as a pakora with the spices. For crunch, I added water chestnuts which are Indian. The caraway seeds heighten the flavour and work well with the chard.

SERVES 4

75g *Swiss chard*
75g *red chard*
50g *water chestnuts (fresh or tinned), diced*
40g *gram flour*
10g *cornflour*
1/4 *teaspoon ground turmeric*
1/2 *teaspoon ground cumin*
1/2 *teaspoon caraway seeds, lightly crushed*
1/2 *teaspoon red chilli powder*
salt, to taste
vegetable oil, for deep frying
1 *teaspoon chaat masala*

Remove the stalks from the two chards and shred the leaves very finely with a knife.

Put the chard in a bowl and add all the remaining ingredients except the oil and chaat masala, mixing them together and adding a few tablespoons of water to form a thick mixture. Using moistened hands, form 12 golf-ball-sized balls of the mixture.

Heat the oil to 180°C in a deep pan or wok. Lower the pakoras into the pan and deep fry for 1–2 minutes. Remove and drain. Place the balls between two sheets of kitchen paper and press lightly to flatten into round cakes.

Return the cakes to the oil and deep fry again for a further 1–2 minutes until crisp. Drain on kitchen paper.

Sprinkle with the chaat masala and serve hot.

CREVETTE ASSADH

A lightly sauced and mild dish typical of the old French colonies in India, indeed unique to that area. I claim no credit for this one – we were taught this recipe by an old lady who was born and brought up in Puducherry (formerly Pondicherry). The recipe works equally well with fish.

SERVES 4

2–3 tablespoons vegetable oil
1 teaspoon black mustard seeds
1 sprig of curry leaves
1/2 onion, chopped
2 green chillies, deseeded and cut into julienne strips (small matchsticks)
2–3 garlic cloves, finely chopped
1/2 teaspoon ground turmeric
400ml coconut milk
16 prawns, shelled, heads removed, deveined
1/2 raw mango (a small green mango used only for cooking, and labelled as 'raw'), cut into julienne strips
salt
juice of 1/2 lime

For the garnish
handful of curry leaves, fried in a little oil until crisp

Heat the oil in a large frying pan over a medium heat, add the mustard seeds and cook for a few seconds until they crackle. Strip the curry leaves from the stem, then add the leaves to the pan, followed by the onion and chillies. Sauté for a few minutes until the onion becomes translucent. Add the chopped garlic and sauté for a further minute.

Lower the heat and add the turmeric, followed by the coconut milk, prawns and mango juliennes. Add salt to taste and cook gently for 3–4 minutes, then add the lime juice.

Serve garnished with fried curry leaves.

GREEN PAPAYA AND CARROT THORAN

Thoran is a Keralan stir-fry dish, and this one is unusual. Normally they would use carrot, cabbage and spinach, but this version has green papaya which creates a great combination of crunchy textures.

SERVES 4

1 teaspoon cumin seeds
2–3 dry red chillies, whole
1 green chilli, roughly chopped
2 garlic cloves, roughly chopped
60g grated coconut
¼ teaspoon ground turmeric
2 teaspoons vegetable oil
1 teaspoon black mustard seeds
½ teaspoon urad dal
1 sprig of curry leaves
200g red onions, chopped
500g green papaya, cut into julienne strips (small matchsticks)
500g carrot, cut into julienne strips
½ teaspoon salt, or to taste

Put the cumin, chillies, garlic, coconut and turmeric in a spice grinder and process to a powder, and keep aside.

Heat the oil in a large frying pan or wok over a medium heat and sauté the mustard seeds for a few seconds until they start to pop. Add the urad dal and the curry leaves, and stir for a few seconds.

Add the onions and sauté for a few minutes until lightly brown. Add the ground spices and cook for 1–2 minutes. Toss in the green papaya and carrot and cook for 3–4 minutes. Season and serve.

TANDOORI BROCCOLI

This marinade for broccoli uses lemongrass, along with traditional Indian ingredients. The lemongrass heightens the flavour of the other spices, and the addition of cream cheese balances the dish. The vivid green of the broccoli is contrasted with the white of the cheese mixture. This makes a marvellous spicy side dish for Thai, Indian or European meals.

SERVES 4

1 head of broccoli, cut into large
  florets
180ml thick Greek yoghurt
3 stalks of lemongrass, crushed
zest and juice of 1 lime
70g cream cheese
1 teaspoon green chilli paste
1 teaspoon ginger-garlic paste
$^1/_2$ teaspoon ground white pepper
a pinch of ground mace
salt

Blanch the broccoli in boiling salted water for 45 seconds, drain and pat dry.

Place the yoghurt in a bowl, then add all the remaining ingredients. Mix well, taste and adjust the seasoning, and allow to stand for 30 minutes for the flavours to infuse.

Mix the broccoli into the marinade and set aside for 30 minutes.

Preheat the grill to high heat.

Skewer the broccoli florets and grill them for 3–4 minutes, turning once, until the coating begins to brown and the broccoli is cooked, but still *al dente*.

GULABI PHIRNEE
(RIZ AU LAIT AU CONFIT DE ROSES)

Phirnee is a classic dessert from Maharashtra in the west of India. It is simply rice pudding flavoured with sugar and cardamom, and sometimes with mango. I thought rose would work well too, so we use rose jelly to add richness (this can be found in both Indian and European specialist supermarkets). We sometimes add raspberry pieces as well, but you must allow the pudding to cool before carefully stirring them in.

SERVES 4

1 litre full-fat milk
50g basmati rice, crushed into fine
    granules
50g sugar
2 tablespoons rose syrup
100ml double cream
60g confit de roses (rose jelly)
rose petals, to garnish

Reserve 100ml of the milk and bring the remaining milk to a boil in a heavy-based, preferably non-stick, pan.

Pour the reserved milk into a blender or mini-processor, add the crushed rice and blend to a paste. Tip this mixture into the boiling milk. Stir continuously and cook until it thickens – this will take 15–20 minutes.

Add the sugar and bring back to a boil. Add the rose syrup and cook for a few minutes. Stir in the cream and confit de roses and remove from the heat. Continue stirring until the confit has dissolved.

Transfer to serving ramekins and allow to cool before covering and transferring to the fridge. Serve garnished with rose petals.

SUSHMA AND DEEPAK KAPOOR

MA GOA

Leafy Putney, in south-west London, has a diverse selection of shops and eateries but Ma Goa is a destination in its own right. It might not be the first restaurant to come to mind when one thinks of Indian culinary excellence in the UK, but it holds its head high in London – an unsung hero of the capital's neighbourhood restaurant scene.

It's one of those rare family restaurants. Yes, truly a restaurant that is owned, managed, catered and inspired by the mother-and-son team of Sushma and Deepak Kapoor. Mrs Kapoor is the eponymous 'Ma' and is fondly called 'Mum' by all of us who know this attractive lady. The food isn't uniquely Goan, but it is indeed a reflection of this family's heritage.

Sushma grew up in Goa, after spending her first years in Mumbai. Her parents had a house in Goa, and used to stay there from time to time. Her father was in the film business and used to do some shooting in Goa. Young Sushma had a lady (an *ayah*) to look after her and she was Goan. Her mother was from an area close to Goa, in the Konkan region, with a very similar cuisine, so they ate a lot of seafood and fish curries. Sushma's recipes come from her own mother, aunts and her ayah.

'From the age of nine or ten I have loved cooking. Normally we would never go into the kitchen – there were chefs to prepare the food – but I used to ask mother, "Teach me how to cook this, or that!" and the chefs would show me how to make my favourites. Then my father, seeing how fond I was of cooking, made it a rule that once a week I was to cook and he would eat only the food that I made. He used to praise it so much, and that gave me a lot of confidence at an early age. I liked making him Fish Caldin, Prawn Balchao and Goan lamb curries. My father had specially built a tandoor in the garden because he loved tandoori dishes – quails, fish, prawns, even chapatis and rotis were cooked outside.' Sushma married a man from the North, so she learnt a lot about Punjabi and other regional foods – it's very different from Goan, so she puts some of those dishes on the menu from time to time.

The family came to London in 1969. They had not intended to come to London, but Sushma's father-in-law, who worked in the catering business in India, Pakistan and the USA, suffered a heart attack while on a work visit to

Pakistan. While his son and wife went to Pakistan to help him, the India-Pakistan war broke out and they were stranded. They couldn't go back to India, so they decided to migrate to the UK, for a few years at any rate. Mrs Kapoor's family is Muslim and Mr Kapoor's Hindu, so they felt they were almost 'on the run' from certain factions.

Deepak remembers: 'We started here in 1993, but as kids we were constantly in restaurants. The restaurant business is a unique way of life, and if the whole family is not behind it, it can be very difficult. So we were always involved in Dad's restaurant, Shezan in Knightsbridge. I started working there, and then, while I was at college, I worked in some other restaurants. I developed this passion for food so, although I was studying sound engineering, it was in my blood to work with food. So we

said, "Let's open a restaurant together, as a family. We can do this – we've got Mum as a fantastic cook." We were so driven to have a place where we could show off Mum's cooking!'

It was going to be a big departure for all the Kapoors, but as Deepak says, 'We knew it was a going to be a change for us. Gone were the evenings at home, inviting friends or family round for dinner, and so on, but we decided not to open on a Monday for the family's sake.' Sushma adds, 'But the family come here and we can sit and chat in the evenings, and the kiddies (her grandchildren) have been coming here since they were babies, and now they have the passion as well, and want to help!' Looks like there will be three generations of Kapoors involved in Ma Goa one of these days.

Passion for food is pivotal to the success of Ma Goa. Deepak smiles, 'Whenever we were thinking of going out somewhere, the first question my father asked was: "What are we taking to eat?"' The family have a video of a little portable stove set up in a bus shelter somewhere in Scotland: 'How embarrassing! Making parathas, chicken, boiled eggs and goodness knows what else, with about 12 aunties around.' Sushma laughs, 'It was so windy, I remember, we had to use our saris as windshields!'

The Kapoor family opened their little nine-table restaurant, furnished with secondhand chairs and tables; Sushma cooked and even made the tablecloths and laundered them at home. Unfortunately Mr Kapoor Senior has passed away, but Ma Goa continues as he started it, in terms of business ethics and regard for their customers and staff.

Sushma says: 'I didn't want to know anything about the finance, just give me the kitchen! I cook different meals for the staff, things that they haven't eaten for a while. I say, "Oh, come on, let's make that." We have meals together, we have staff parties, play cards together.' Deepak agrees and adds 'It's important to maintain standards and keep to the rules, but I tell the staff, "You are all adults, we are not going to hound you every day. That's not the way I want to work. You know what we expect." We are very passionate, and the staff knows that. Nothing sub-standard must be served to a table, and if I have to send something back to the kitchen they know that it's not worth the hassle – just do it right first time!'

Many diners at Ma Goa are Indian and are curious about the restaurant's array of dishes. 'So many of my childhood favourites are on our menu,' says Deepak, 'but some of our biggest critics are Goan guests, and I always say, "I can't compete with your mother! This is what we had at home."' When they started, their menu was strictly Goan, but they learned quickly that if they were to make a success of the restaurant, they would have to be a bit more flexible.

'Indian food is about sharing. We tried "plating", stacking the food, and all that stuff, but it didn't work. My father said, "That's not Indian food." So we always advise couples to order not just one dish, but two different dishes so you can share and enjoy some variety. When we go to a restaurant, the first thing we do is to scour the menu for new and unusual things, we analyse what's on offer – it's exciting.' But, by contrast, there are some customers who are not interested in the menu, they chat and chat and take ages to get around to ordering their food. Then there are those who say, 'No, I don't need a menu, I'll just have Chicken Tikka Masala.' But Ma Goa doesn't do Chicken Tikka Masala!

Of course, there are Portuguese influences in Goan food: Ma Goa has a dish called Feijoada, which they make with black-eyed beans. There are names of dishes, like Lamb Borrego, that remain, but in terms of cooking there is little in common. But the restaurant does play Portuguese and Brazilian music, it's quite popular in Goa; some customers recognise the Portuguese tunes as traditionally Goan.

There are several styles of cooking in Goa: the Hindu is quite different from the Christian style, let alone the differences from house to house. 'We've done a lot of research to compare dishes and find recipes that are authentic and will be loved by our customers.'

Ma Goa represents the ideal neighbourhood restaurant – a standard of cooking every bit as good as you will find in celebrated central London establishments – with a casual ambiance that appeals to the locals as well as those discerning folks in the know. They know it's a place to find vibrant, diverse and delicious Indian food. A high-street restaurant, but a million miles from a curry house.

Ma Goa
242–244 Upper Richmond Road, London SW15 6TG
Phone 020 8780 1767 **www.ma-goa.com**

GOAN PORK VINDALOO

In Goan cookery, you keep some fat on the meat because it adds so much to the flavour. Marinating in the vinegar and spices overnight is very important, followed by a quick braise to cook the spices, then slow cooking until tender. Adjust the seasoning just before serving, as the intensity of the spices changes during cooking. It is not supposed to be searingly hot, but to have a vinegar-chilli kick, plus the roasted spices. This is best the next day, because this is a pickling process.

SERVES 4

500g pork shoulder, cubed
vegetable oil, for frying
2 onions, finely sliced
1 tablespoon grated ginger
160g tomatoes, chopped
salt

For the vindaloo spice paste
1 teaspoon black peppercorns
1 teaspoon whole cloves
6 garlic cloves, roughly chopped
1 teaspoon yellow mustard seeds
4 black cardamom pods, seeds only
2 x 5-cm cinnamon sticks
8–10 dried Kashmiri chillies
   (or 5 regular dried red chillies)
1 teaspoon sugar
2 teaspoons paprika
1/2 teaspoon ground turmeric
120ml white wine vinegar
salt

Soak the ingredients for the spice paste in the vinegar in a large non-metallic bowl and set aside for 2–3 hours, then transfer to a blender or spice grinder and grind to a smooth paste. Return the spice paste to the bowl, add the pork, stir to coat in the marinade, then cover and refrigerate overnight.

Add oil to a large flameproof casserole dish, using enough to cover the base. Add the onions and fry over a medium heat for 4–5 minutes until they are soft and light brown in colour. Add the grated ginger. Cook over a medium heat for 5 minutes.

Add the pork and the spice paste and fry in the oil, stirring frequently until the oil separates from the spice mixture. This should take about 8–10 minutes. You can add splashes of water to the dish if the spices begin to burn, but be careful with the quantity as you don't want to boil the spices – they should be fried.

Add the chopped tomatoes and cook for a further 5 minutes. Add 240ml boiling water, cover and cook over a medium heat for 45 minutes; check and stir every 15 minutes.

Adjust the salt, chilli and vinegar if necessary. Cook, uncovered, for another 5–10 minutes until the sauce thickens and the pork is tender.

Serve with plain boiled rice.

This is even better reheated the next day – add a dash of vinegar to give the flavour a bit of an edge. For a variation, garnish with roasted cashew nuts and more fried onions.

STUFFED POPPADUMS

Mum introduced this to the restaurant, and there is a knack to it. The key is to have the filling dry – prawns, crab, pork or minced lamb – and fry it with less oil than you would normally, and make sure that the envelope is well closed, so nothing spills out.

It's our version of a dosa; it's not quite the same, but it's a lovely snack to have with tea in the evening.

SERVES 4

3 white potatoes, cut into pieces
1 teaspoon lemon juice
1 teaspoon ground cumin
vegetable oil, for frying
$\frac{1}{2}$ teaspoon black mustard seeds
$\frac{1}{2}$ teaspoon cumin seeds
pinch of red chilli powder
6 curry leaves
$\frac{1}{4}$ teaspoon ground turmeric
6 plain 'raw' poppadums (or 10 small ones) – these are the 'unpuffed' poppadums available in many supermarkets and all Asian stores
salt

Place the potato pieces in a pan of salted water, bring to the boil and cook for 10–15 minutes, or until tender. Drain well and mash. Add the lemon juice and ground cumin and stir until well combined. Season to taste with salt.

Heat 1 tablespoon of the oil in a frying pan over a medium heat. When the oil is smoking, add the mustard seeds, cumin seeds, chilli powder, curry leaves and turmeric, stir well and fry for 15–20 seconds until the seeds start to pop. (Hold the pan well away from your eyes and face as the seeds may pop out of the pan.) Stir the spices and oil from the pan into the potatoes, and mix well.

Soak each poppadum in very hot water for 10 seconds to soften. Place each poppadum onto a clean surface and place a tablespoon of the potato mixture into the centre of each. Carefully fold the poppadums into parcels. (If a poppadum breaks, seal with a little flour-and-water paste.)

Heat enough oil to deep-fry in a deep heavy-based saucepan, until a bread cube sizzles and turns brown when dropped into it. Carefully lower the stuffed poppadums into the hot oil, one at a time, and fry for 30–45 seconds on each side, or until pale golden-brown on both sides. Remove with a slotted spoon and drain on kitchen paper.

To serve, place the stuffed poppadums onto a large serving plate and serve your favourite chutneys in dipping bowls alongside.

BUND GOBI
(SIMPLE, CRUNCHY, STIR-FRIED SHREDDED CABBAGE)

This is something we have as a side dish instead of a salad. The idea is to toss it in the pan for 30 seconds, so it cooks in the residual heat and doesn't become soft, but stays crunchy. It should be served right away. An important ingredient is the ginger, which flavours the oil.

Serve it garnished with coconut, or you can mix in some split lentils, cooked separately. We sometimes serve it with green peppers and carrots tossed in at the end. Goes well with robust vindaloo and shacuti curries.

Heat the oil in a wok or large shallow pan and add the ginger. Follow 30 seconds later with the rest of the tarka spices. Once they begin to pop and splutter (but not burn!), add the cabbage and the carrot batons. Stir-fry for a minute or so. Add salt to taste and the lemon juice

For a variation, boil some split lentils until soft in turmeric-flavoured water, drain and add at the end.

SERVES 4

2 tablespoons vegetable oil
1/2 head of white cabbage, very finely shredded
2 carrots, cut into thin batons
salt
1 teaspoon lemon juice

For the tarka spices
1 teaspoon grated ginger
1/2 teaspoon cumin seeds
1/4 teaspoon ground turmeric
1/2 teaspoon black mustard seeds
1/4 teaspoon crushed red chilli
1 1/2 teaspoons dessicated coconut
8 curry leaves

LOBIA BLACK-EYED BEANS

Make sure you soak the beans before you use them. You can substitute chickpeas or any other beans. You can use more or less chilli, maybe some tamarind, and the garnish should be lots of fresh ginger and coriander or mint. A really comforting dish.

SERVES 4

250g black-eyed beans
4 tablespoons vegetable oil
1 tablespoon grated ginger
1 teaspoon finely chopped garlic
1 onion, finely chopped
3 dried kokum (or the juice of ½ lime)
salt

For the spice paste
2 tablespoons ground cumin
2 tablespoons ground coriander
1 teaspoon garam masala
¼ teaspoon chilli powder
¼ teaspoon ground turmeric
125ml water

For the garnish
juliennes of green chilli and ginger
chopped fresh mint and coriander

Soak the black-eyed beans in 500ml water overnight.

Next day, drain and rinse the beans in cold water. Place the beans in a large pan of salted water and bring to the boil. Reduce the heat, cover and simmer for 30 minutes until the beans are soft. Drain and set aside.

Blend the spices and water to a paste.

Heat the oil in a deep pan over a medium heat and add the ginger, garlic and onion. Fry for 5 minutes until they soften and begin to change colour. Add the spice paste and fry for a further 5 minutes until the oil begins to separate from the spices – this tells you your spices are cooked.

Add the beans and 2–3 tablespoons of water and the kokum or lime juice. Check the seasoning. Cook for a further 5–8 minutes, stirring continuously and adding more water if needed to make a creamy consistency.

Serve garnished with juliennes of green chilli, ginger, and chopped fresh mint and coriander. Enjoy with rice or roti.

For a variation, add some diced boiled potato at the same time as the beans.

CHILLED SPICED COFFEE

Indians drink a lot of tea (or *chai*) as it's the national beverage. It's consumed hot, milky and very often spiced. This practice translates very well to coffee: this recipe for icy-cold spiced coffee is simple, and can be prepared in advance for a dinner party and just assembled when you're ready to enjoy it. It's a lovely refreshing drink for a summer afternoon in the sun.

SERVES 4

14 star anise
4 cups strong-brewed black coffee
2 cinnamon sticks, about 7cm each
6–8 green cardamom pods
400ml sweetened condensed milk
16 ice cubes
4 scoops of coffee or coffee liqueur ice cream (optional)
4 chocolate-covered coffee beans (optional)

Place a star anise in each of 12 compartments of an ice-cube tray, fill with water and freeze.

Pour the coffee into a pan, add the remaining 2 star anise, the cinnamon and cardamom and simmer for 5 minutes; strain out the spices, then set aside to cool.

Place the spiced coffee in a blender with the condensed milk and plain ice cubes (not the star anise cubes). Blend for 30 seconds.

To serve, pour into 4 tall glasses, each filled with 3 star anise ice cubes. As an option, top with a scoop of coffee or coffee liqueur ice-cream, and a chocolate-covered coffee bean.

SANJAY ANAND

MADHU'S

Madhu's is a Southall institution. It's one of the most popular restaurants in a neighbourhood full of Indian eateries, cafés and sweetshops. The Anand family has founded a dynasty that has spanned two centuries, several generations and three continents. This unassuming and contemporary restaurant has risen from a devastating fire like a culinary phoenix, to continue its restaurant and catering celebrity.

Sanjay Anand was born in Nairobi, where his family had worked in the hospitality industry since 1930. They were originally from Jammu, Kashmir, right on the border between India and Pakistan, and to this day Madhu's dishes still retain a strong Pakistani influence, with a twist of Kenya in the ingredients.

Sanjay's grandfather had moved to Kenya in 1930, establishing a restaurant in the capital, Nairobi. He was so successful that he then opened a hotel, followed by a night club – in fact he was the first night-club owner in Kenya. However, in 1974 all businesses in Kenya were nationalised and the family was given three months to leave; Britain was to be their next home.

In 1975 Sanjay's uncles opened their restaurant in Southall. It's still just down the road, and is called the 'Brilliant'. It is one of the most iconic Asian restaurants in all of London. Sanjay's father was doing some outside catering from home at the time, and as soon as Sanjay left school he and his brother decided to open up their own restaurant – Madhu's. It was originally called 'Madhu's Brilliant': 'Madhu' was his father's nickname – in Hindi it means 'honey' or 'sweet' – and 'Brilliant' was the name of his grandfather's night club and hotel in Nairobi. Because they were such a well-known family there, they knew that if they put 'Madhu's Brilliant' on the board outside they would at least be remembered by all the people who had known them in Nairobi!

Sanjay's father put up his house as the security for the restaurant – an amazing show of confidence in the younger generation. After all, Sanjay was only 17 years old, and his brother just 16. That was 30 years ago, and they haven't looked back, going from strength to strength in the restaurant and also becoming the most prestigious Asian caterers in the area. Madhu's is famed for its wedding and celebration catering, as well as its function catering for such events as the World Food Awards.

Sanjay recalls 'I think my background in food gave me the confidence to do this – from the age of 13 I was helping Dad with the outside catering, and by the age of 16 he would leave me with an event of 200 or 300 people, and let me run it. At 17, I remember going to 21 different banks looking for a loan. These days, if I had a project I might go to two or three banks and, if they rejected my ideas, I might say, "This is not a viable project, let's shelve it!" But I was very enthusiastic, full of energy. We opened a tiny 36-seater restaurant; my brother was in the kitchen with my Mum, and I was serving in the front. We had no staff, that was it.'

From a tiny business – in that first year they turned over barely £100,000 – they have now grown to a £6 million empire. The restaurant represents only a tenth of their business, the outside catering being the remaining percentage. 'In our outside catering we are, and have been

for 25 years, number one in the market. We have been very innovative in the style of service and the equipment we use.' Sanjay invented the original Madhu's carousel, a striking metal contraption to hold numerous serving dishes, which was a trademark of their presentation a few years ago.

A crystal stand has now taken the place of that metal centrepiece. It's instantly recognisable as a Madhu-catered event when the warming candles flicker and the glass carousels twinkle, awaiting the generously-laden serving dishes. When Prince Charles wants to hold an event for the Asian community, Madhu's gets a call from the Palace. When the Prime Minister is entertaining Indian politicians, Madhu's gets a call from Downing Street. On the same day as the World Food Awards in 2010, Madhu's was also catering for Cliff Richard's seventieth birthday party, as well as six other functions.

They couldn't cope with that volume of food in the kitchens of the regular restaurant, so Madhu's have invested in two food production kitchens – one in Southall and one in nearby Hayes. They cater for over 300 events in a year with an average of 500 guests each. They employ 300–350 staff for outside catering, and don't use agencies, preferring to keep staff that have been Madhu-trained. They use their own people, front- and back-of-house, to maintain their quality and reputation. Some of the team have been with the company for 30 years. 'That's the secret of our success,' says Sanjay. 'Although we employ a lot of people, we don't have a great turnover of staff. We pay them slightly more than they would get anywhere else, we look after them and we feed them well – not just a "staff curry" but the same food as the guests, and the chef may even prepare specialities for the staff. These things go a long way, and I know they cost money, but my view is to eat less of the pie yourself and make sure that everyone's got a smile on their face.

'There is no one in the family who is *not* a good cook. Everyone seems to know how to cook, and that probably comes from my Granddad, who passed that passion on to my Dad, who was what I would call a Master Chef. Besides one guy that I met in Mumbai – Satish Arora, who was Executive Head Chef for the Taj Group – I don't think I have come across an Indian chef with the same skills as my Dad. He could cook you potatoes and they would be the best potatoes you have ever tasted; he could be cooking a sauce for fish, and before he put the fish in you could smell the fish, you knew that the sauce was especially for fish.'

Madhu's haven't changed the recipes – they were Sanjay's grandfather's and father's dishes – and their chefs cook to Sanjay's specification. 'Where Madhu's differs is that we do not deviate from that. This is one of the very few restaurants that serve chapatis: that's what nine out of ten Asians eat at home, but how many Indian restaurants do you know, out of the 8,500 in the country, where you can have a chapati? I'll be surprised if it's more than about twenty. Thinking of meat cooking, how many meat dishes do you get that are actually cooked on the bone? The tastes are much more flavoursome, but how many restaurants do that?'

Tandoori Salmon, Jeera Chicken and Nyama Choma (an Indian/Masai dish) are all popular with regulars who enjoy the culinary influences from Kenya. They use tilapia fish from Lake Victoria. They cook Machusi Ku Ku, a Swahili word for chicken curry, but the recipe is traditional Indian/Pakistani. Or you could order Buzi Bafu – lamb chops slow-cooked in a special sauce. 'Our menu has evolved in 30 years, but one thing that hasn't changed is the slow cooking process. Thank God, my restaurant is not just a business – I am still as passionate today as I was 30 years ago. We are here to make money, but that comes at number three or four on the agenda, after maintaining quality, keeping our staff happy, getting bums on seats, keeping our business at the forefront.

'Our clientele is about 50/50 Asian/other. We are a destination restaurant, where people book and come for an evening out and to try something that they won't get elsewhere, and that's why people are prepared to drive here. After the fire (which nearly destroyed the premises a few years ago), I came very close to moving the restaurant into central London. But Southall is where our roots are, and I didn't have the heart to do it. Instead I decided to bring it up to a standard where everyone would feel comfortable dining here,' Sanjay is proud to say.

Madhu's
39 South Road, Southall UB1 1SW
Phone 020 8574 1897 **www.madhusonline.com**

CHILLI CHICKEN

This is my Dad's recipe. It's a hot dish, but full of flavour, not only from the chilli, but from the other spices too, all of which you will probably already have in your larder. It's a good stand-by dish, and if you only have 20 minutes to knock something out quickly, you can do a chilli chicken, although it's so good that you'll make it even when you're not in a hurry.

If you don't like it so hot, then just use a little less chilli – but remember, it is called Chilli Chicken and it would be a shame to dilute it too much!

SERVES 4

125g butter
20g ginger paste
30g garlic paste
2 teaspoons green chilli paste
    (or 1–2 chillies)
1 teaspoon red chilli powder,
    or to taste
2 teaspoons dried fenugreek leaves
    (kasoori methi)
50g Onion Masala (see below)
150ml tomato purée
salt
800g chicken, cut into small pieces
leaves from ½ bunch (approximately
    50g) of coriander, chopped
1 green chilli, chopped, to garnish

For the onion masala
500g onions, sliced
50ml clarified butter or ghee

Make the onion masala first. Melt the butter or ghee in a saucepan, add the onions and cook over a gentle heat until brown in colour (10–15 minutes), then purée with a handheld blender. (The unused masala can be stored in the freezer.)

Heat a pan over medium heat, Melt the butter and add the ginger, garlic and green chilli pastes, and sauté for a couple of minutes until the spices are cooked through. Add the red chilli powder and fenugreek leaves, and mix well. Add 50g of the onion masala and the tomato purée; stir well and cook for 5 minutes. Add salt to taste.

To this gravy add the chicken pieces, mix well and keep stirring at regular intervals. Add a little water if the dish begins to dry out.

After 15–20 minutes check that the chicken is opaque and cooked through; add the chopped coriander, mix well and serve hot. Garnish with a sprinkle of chopped chilli and serve with a green salad.

CHAPATI

Chapati is the most popular bread in the Indian home – nine times out of ten, if an Indian housewife is cooking a bread it will be a chapati. Madhu's is one of the few restaurants that serve this traditional bread, but they are easy to make at home, and can accompany any Indian meal. Especially good for mopping up sauces or for making into a wrap.

SERVES 4

250g chapati flour (atta), plus extra
*   for dusting*
approximately 125ml cold water
1 teaspoon salt, or to taste
1 teaspoon vegetable oil
ghee (optional)

Make the chapati dough by mixing together the atta flour, water, salt and oil. Knead well. This should be a firm but pliable dough. Allow the dough to relax for 10–15 minutes, wrapped in clingfilm or under a tea towel.

Divide the dough into ten equal portions. Cover the dough with a damp cloth so it does not dry out while you are rolling out each chapati.

Roll each ball into a disc about 2mm thick. Dust a little flour on your board to avoid sticking. Remove any excess flour from the surface of the chapati after rolling.

Bring a frying pan to a medium heat. Place a chapati on the heated pan and cook for 30 seconds or so, until the underside has light-brown spots. Flip over and cook the other side. Press the edges down with folded kitchen paper to ensure they are cooked. Put aside in a thermal box or under a tea towel to keep warm while you cook the remaining chapatis.

To serve, add a little melted ghee on top of each chapati if desired.

MAKHANI DAL

This is one of our signature dishes, a Punjabi dal that's a favourite with both the Indian diners and the Europeans – people love it for its creamy richness. It's not a difficult dish to make and any leftovers can be frozen (although there probably won't be any!). Most Indian homes have at least one pressure cooker, because it's such a time-saver when it comes to making dal.

This makes a hearty side dish, or a lovely meal on its own with any Indian bread.

SERVES 4–6

For the dal
250g black lentils
2 litres water
$\frac{1}{2}$–1 teaspoon red chilli powder
salt

For the tadka
100g butter
6 garlic cloves, chopped
50g tomato paste
2 teaspoons garam masala
2 teaspoons ground cumin
$\frac{1}{2}$ teaspoon ground black pepper, or to taste
2 teaspoons powdered fenugreek leaves (kasoori methi)
50ml double cream

Put the lentils and water in a deep pan and bring to the boil. Add the chilli powder, cover and continue to boil gently for about an hour. Check after this time that the lentils are tender; if not, continue cooking until they are all softened. Add salt to taste. (If you have the opportunity, soaking the lentils overnight will reduce cooking time; in this case use a little less water for cooking.)

For the tadka, heat a pan and add 50g of the butter. Let it melt and then add the chopped garlic, and sauté for a few seconds until golden brown; add the tomato paste and mix well. After 5 minutes, or when the oil begins to separate, add the garam masala, cumin and black pepper, and mix well. Allow to cook for a further minute.

Add this tadka to the boiled dal, stir well and bring the pan of dal back to the boil for another 10 minutes, uncovered, crushing the lentils down slightly.

Add the powdered fenugreek leaves, double cream and remaining butter to the pan. Stir in thoroughly and simmer for 5 minutes.

GOBHI SURKH ANGAR

Indians love Chinese food and they have embraced it with the same enthusiasm as the British have shown for Indian food. All the spices here are those you'd use in Indian cooking, but there is the addition of soy sauce to give the dish a recognisable Chinese flavour.

Rakesh Verma, our new head chef, is a talented and innovative young man, who really understands what Madhu's represents, and this is one of his recipes.

SERVES 4

1 head of cauliflower, cut into florets
1 head of broccoli, cut into florets
150ml vegetable oil, for frying (or sufficient for 1–2cm depth)
spring onions, sliced into rounds, to garnish

For the sauce
3 tablespoons vegetable oil
4 garlic cloves, chopped
1 teaspoon red chilli paste
1 tablespoon sugar
2 tablespoons tomato purée
2 tablespoons water
100ml soy sauce
salt

For the batter
100g plain flour
100g cornflour
1 teaspoon salt, or to taste
150–200ml water
1 teaspoon black cumin seeds (shai jeera)

To make the sauce, heat a frying pan over a medium heat and add the oil and the chopped garlic, and sauté for a few seconds until golden brown in colour. Add the chilli paste and cook for 1 minute, then add the sugar, tomato purée and water, and mix well. Add the soy sauce, mix and remove from the heat; add salt to taste. Keep aside to cool.

To make the batter, sieve the plain flour, cornflour and salt into a mixing bowl. Stir in enough water to form a thick batter. Add the black cumin, mix in and keep aside.

Par-boil the cauliflower and broccoli in plenty of salted water for 8–10 minutes. Drain and leave to cool.

Heat the oil in a deep pan or fryer over a medium heat. Coat the cauliflower and broccoli in the batter and fry in batches for a couple of minutes until golden brown in colour on all sides. Remove and drain on kitchen paper.

Just before serving, heat the sauce in a wide, shallow pan, then add the broccoli and cauliflower and stir to coat.

Serve hot, garnished with rounds of spring onions.

GAJAR KA HALWA

I'm sure you will all recognise this dish – it's one of the more common desserts on Indian restaurant menus. It's there because it's something that's popular in Indian homes, it's simple and straightforward to make, and you can buy carrots in every single supermarket. There are no special ingredients except for milk powder, but you can get that everywhere. It's a very traditional Punjabi recipe – comforting and sweet.

SERVES 4

500g grated carrot
1 litre full-fat milk
50g sugar
100g milk powder
100g butter
10g pistachio nuts, shelled and
   chopped

Place the carrot, milk and sugar in a heavy-based non-stick pan, bring to the boil and then simmer for 30 minutes, uncovered.

Add the milk powder and butter, and stir in very well. Cook this mixture over a high heat, stirring continuously, until the mixture is completely dry and the butter starts coming to the surface.

Serve hot, garnished with the chopped pistachio nuts.

DhaYAlan Paul GERaRD McCann and LAra ZanZarin

MINT LEAF LOUNGE

Mint Leaf Lounge is a large and versatile restaurant and bar and a destination for those in the know who want to enjoy striking food alongside delicious and memorable cocktails in the City. It has successfully balanced fine dining with popular high-end bar culture. Mint Leaf Lounge is just as famous for one of the longest and most impressive cocktail bars. The 16-metre bar is backed by an ingenious feature of wall lights and river-washed pebbles. The Lounge can accommodate up to 300 standing or 90 for a seated dinner. The private dining rooms, cocktail bar and lounge areas, and mezzanine champagne bar provide a variety of options for group of all sizes.

Gerard McCann is General Manager at Mint Leaf Lounge and Mint Leaf Restaurant in Haymarket. 'In 2002, the owner had a vision of bringing to the London restaurant scene an Indian restaurant that was authentic yet innovative, contemporary and healthy in its cooking, and all in an environment that was quite obviously not Indian in any way.' The owner brought on board Julian Taylor as designer, and Gerard McCann. They started work in earnest in December 2002 and opened the restaurant in April 2003.

Their mission was to educate an international front-of-house team in the cuisine, the recipes, the content, the passion, the history behind the food, and introduce it to their guests in an interesting and relaxed, smart-casual, setting. 'Bolted on the side of the restaurant is this fantastic cocktail bar. It's very much somewhere people can come and indulge in fantastic modern Indian food in a setting where they could enjoy cocktails first, then the food, then stay on to have more cocktails. Mint Leaf offers a tempting selection of classic, as well as exotic cocktails – everything from a Bourbon Old-fashioned to a Rose-Petal Martini that will waft you to the marble halls of a Moghul palace. Their Margaritas have a subcontinental twist, with infusions of either chilli or cinnamon.

That was the beginning of the journey of Mint Leaf. 'We are seen as something more than just a restaurant. At Mint Leaf the food is a very important element, a key element, but not the only element – the cocktail bar and the wine list also play a major part in what we do.'

Executive Head Chef Dhayalan Paul was born and grew up in Tamil Nadu in the south east of India. 'It was a very competitive environment because you had to decide what you wanted to be at a very early age. Everyone was trying to score high marks at secondary school in order to become a doctor or engineer. To do anything else risked accusations of a poor upbringing.' It sounds like this might be a story of the would-be young chef turning his back on convention and following a culinary path. But this is where Dhayalan Paul breaks the mould: he had his eyes set on a very different horizon.

He did not have a dream of being a doctor, engineer or advocate like his father. He intended to become a cricketer and to play for his country, and he was dedicated to that plan.

General manager Gerard McCann and chef Dhayalan Paul

Yes, it was a career on the pitch rather than in the kitchen that excited Dhayalan during those formative years. 'I left home and went to Madras (now Chennai), the capital of Tamil Nadu to play competitive cricket with the guys who get chosen to represent the country.' He was only 14 years old and continued on that sporty path for seven years, until he realised his predicament. 'I found that I needed not just talent, but a "godfather" to get into the Indian cricket team – someone to promote me. I wasn't too keen on that.'

It was evidently time for a rethink. There was a person in Dhayalan's young life who inspired him and gave him a

broad culinary perspective that was to serve him well in future. 'At home I had always hung around in the kitchen, because that was the way to get to eat before the meal was served! We had a housemaid, Mary, who was very influential. She would always have food on the table, and gave me mis-en-place jobs in the kitchen, like peeling the garlic and onions. She had previously worked for an Anglo-Indian family, so there were lots of different influences in her dishes. That experience was very important to me when I came to make the decision between cricket and cooking.'

'So I studied English Literature at Madras Christian College, and then enrolled on an undergraduate course at Catering School in Chennai. I then trained at the Taj, where I started as a lowly commis chef. I think a lot of people, after doing the course, go straight on to management, and they don't appreciate what it takes to do the menial tasks. I was then hired by the Hyatt, who were opening a brand-new hotel, initially as a South Indian Breakfast Chef. I also worked in the Commissary, which did the prep for the entire hotel, everything from chopped green chillies to speciality restaurant ingredients. From there I went to Butchery for six months, which was really beneficial as knife skills are paramount.'

Chef Paul had the opportunity to move, with his wife, to Dubai. 'I went into the Moroccan restaurant at the Madinat Jumeirah Hotel, as part of the opening team. There I met Alun Sperring, senior sous-chef of the restaurant (now chef/proprietor of the Chilli Pickle in Brighton), and he taught me what it takes to be a good chef. It was the best thing that happened to me, though at the time I thought it was the worst: we were neighbours, so he would wake me at 6.45 in the morning and take me in to work, even though the shift was not supposed to start until 10.30am!'

Dhayalan worked with Alun for a couple of years, but he really wanted to come to the UK. Alun helped him to get a job with Vivek Singh at Cinnamon Club (see page 63). Vivek immediately put him in the most difficult section of his kitchen, the grill. Chef Paul says it was inspiring and motivating: 'I was happy and my agenda was to soak up as much knowledge as possible, to learn by osmosis.'

'I spent a year with Vivek at the Cinnamon Club, and as part of the opening team at Cinnamon Kitchen. In 2009 I was invited to be head chef at Mint Leaf Lounge and worked with Chef Gopal whom I knew from college. He was at the helm of Mint Leaf restaurant in Haymarket and has assisted with the recipes offered here.' When Chef Gopal left, Chef Paul became Executive Head Chef of Mint Leaf and Mint Leaf Lounge. 'My goal is to create innovative Indian food and push boundaries, to encourage the customer to come back for more.' He is passionate about providing his diners with a memorable experience: 'That starts with the reception, and continues with the food.' These are traditional dishes with contemporary flourishes to suit the restaurant and its discerning high-energy guests. He wants to elevate Mint Leaf with a menu that reflects his evident love for fresh produce and authentic flavours. He has gone from cricket whites to chef's whites, but his enthusiasm for this culinary career is just as strong as it had been for his sport.

Lara Zanzarin is the mixologist at Mint Leaf. She oversees one of the best-stocked cocktail bars in London, and is responsible for creating some of the most evocative and original Asian-inspired cocktails. 'I like to think that I have the same opportunity to make an impression on our customers with our drinks, as do our chefs with their flair for food.

'We change the menu periodically – whenever we find something interesting, or suppliers introduce a new liqueur or spirit, we experiment with it and come up with exciting combinations. We have lots of regulars who are always keen to try a new cocktail. We make some of our own infusions: vanilla rum, vanilla vodka, ginger vodka, vodka with lemon, gin with lemongrass, gin with chilli, tequila with almond, tequila with coffee... combinations that suit our style of restaurant and the palates of our guests, who are looking for cocktails that complement our food and continue their Asian experience into the bar.'

Mint Leaf has seamlessly combined a well-respected Indian restaurant offering classic as well as innovative food, with a bar that encourages Mint Leaf guests to linger a little longer, and to indulge in something more elevated than the clichéd six pints of lager.

Mint Leaf Lounge & Restaurant
12 Angel Court, Lothbury, Bank, London EC2R 7HB
Phone 020 7600 0992 **www.mintleaflounge.com**

ADRAKI PASLIYAN
(GRILLED LAMB CUTLETS WITH LEMON RIND AND DRIED GINGER)

This is a delicious lamb starter which needs very little garnishing apart from a few salad leaves. There are only three or four spices here and they all go in together to make a marinade. It's honestly a three-step dish: mix the marinade, put the lamb in the marinade and then grill. These chops would be delicious in summer cooked on the barbecue outside.

SERVES 4

8 lamb cutlets, French trimmed, fat off
   (see note)

For the marinade
zest of 1 lemon
30ml olive oil
2 teaspoons royal cumin seeds (shahi
   jeera, black caraway)
a pinch of ground turmeric
1 teaspoon salt, or to taste
2 teaspoons ground ginger
1–2 teaspoons red chilli powder
   (optional)

Mix all the ingredients for the marinade in a non-metallic bowl, add the lamb cutlets to the bowl and coat with the marinade. Cover with clingfilm and rest them for 30 minutes in the fridge.

Preheat a griddle, then cook the cutlets for 1 minute on each side. Alternatively, preheat a grill to a high setting and grill the cutlets for a couple of minutes on each side, until well coloured.

Serve hot with a mixed salad.

Note: French trimming means to scrape the meat from the end of the bone so as to leave a 'handle' on the chop. You can ask your butcher to do this if you wish.

PAN-SEARED SCALLOPS WITH PICKLED CUCUMBER AND CHILLI MANGO RELISH

This is a light but flavoursome dish, with the sweetness of the seafood contrasting with the sharpness of the pickled cucumber. You can buy scallops in their shell, and these will have the orange roe attached, but we don't need the shells or the roe for this recipe. These days, scallops are easily found in good fishmongers and almost every large supermarket. Look for scallops which are firm, white and smell of the sea - we like to use Scottish ones.

SERVES 4

250g fresh, dry and roe-less scallops
30ml vegetable oil
Maldon sea salt, to taste

For the pickled cucumber
25ml white wine vinegar
20g white granulated sugar
1 teaspoon fennel seeds
1cm seedless dry red chilli, crushed
300g or 1 medium cucumber, peeled
  and shaved lengthways with a
  potato peeler or very sharp
  vegetable knife until you get to the
  seeds

For the chilli mango relish
250g mango pulp
3 green chillies or to taste, deseeded
  and finely chopped

3 tablespoons coriander cress or finely
  chopped coriander leaves

To make the pickled cucumber, add the vinegar and sugar to a saucepan and stir for a few minutes over a medium heat until the sugar dissolves. Add the fennel seeds and crushed chillies. Simmer over a low heat for 4 minutes. Remove the saucepan from the heat and add the shaved cucumber strips to the mixture. Allow to cool.

To prepare the relish, pour the mango pulp into a bowl and add the chopped chillies; stir for a minute to infuse the flavours.

Lay the scallops out on a clean kitchen towel or paper to remove excess moisture.

Add the oil to a non-stick pan and heat for 4 minutes over a low heat. Increase the heat to medium and carefully add the scallops to the hot oil, laying them away from you to avoid splashing. Cook the scallops on all sides until they take on a caramel colour – about 2–3 minutes.

Drain the cooked scallops on a kitchen towel or paper. Sprinkle with sea salt just before serving.

To serve, lay the pickled cucumber on a serving plate and arrange the scallops on top. Drizzle the chilli mango relish over the scallops and sprinkle with the chopped coriander, or decorate with sprigs of coriander cress.

PAPDI CHANNA CHAAT
(SPICED CHICKPEAS AND WHEAT CRISPS, TOPPED WITH SWEETENED YOGHURT AND TAMARIND CHUTNEY)

Chaat is the word we use to describe savoury snacks in India. We love to eat them at roadside stalls, and people will have their favourite vendor, who will specialise in a particular type of chaat. The best stalls can be recognised by the number of people waiting to be served.

These snacks can be a mixture of potatoes, crisp fried breads and chickpeas, with various relishes and garnishes. My version uses whole-wheat crisps called papdi: here we mostly buy these ready-made from the local Asian supermarket and make our chaat at home.

SERVES 4

50g tamarind paste
2 teaspoons fennel seeds
2 teaspoons ground ginger
salt
500ml water
200ml Greek yoghurt
50g icing sugar
400g tinned chickpeas
75g red onion, finely chopped
20g coriander leaves, finely chopped
10g chaat masala
20g channa masala (available in
   Indian supermarkets)
1–2 teaspoons red chilli powder,
   or to taste
30g jaggery or brown sugar
100g papdi (wheat crisps, available in
   Indian supermarkets)

In a saucepan, mix together the tamarind paste, fennel seeds, ground ginger, salt and water, and allow it to simmer on a low heat, while you continue with the next steps, stirring occasionally.

In a bowl, whisk together the Greek yoghurt and icing sugar, cover and chill in the fridge.

Drain the chickpeas, rinse and allow to drain in a colander. Tip the chickpeas into a mixing bowl and roughly mash. Add the chopped onion, coriander leaves, chaat masala, channa masala and chilli powder, cover and refrigerate until needed.

Check the consistency of the tamarind sauce: when it has thickened to a syrup, add 20g of the jaggery and simmer for a few minutes. Check the seasoning and add more jaggery if desired, to get a sweet and sour taste. Continue to simmer for a few minutes until it thickens a little more, remove from the heat, transfer to a bowl, allow to cool, cover and chill.

Place the spiced chickpeas in a serving bowl and top with papdi. Generously garnish with sweetened yoghurt and top this with a drizzle of the chilled tamarind chutney.

DAL PALAK

Palak is the Hindi word for spinach, and this lentil dish has lots of it. Many Indians eat dal of some description every day, just with some rice or bread. The leafy greens add to the colour and nutritional value. It's a comforting dish that can be made more or less spicy by adjusting the quantity of chilli.

SERVES 4

200g split yellow moong lentils
600ml water
1 teaspoon plus a pinch of ground
   turmeric
2 tablespoons vegetable oil
20g cumin seeds
6 garlic cloves, chopped
10g green chillies, split
100g onions, roughly chopped
1–2 teaspoons Kashmiri chilli powder,
   or to taste
20g ground cumin
200g tomatoes, finely chopped
250g baby spinach leaves
1–2 teaspoons salt, or to taste
40g butter (optional)
50g coriander leaves, roughly chopped

Wash the lentils thoroughly, cover with cold water and leave to soak for 30 minutes, then drain.

Bring the water to the boil in a saucepan, add the lentils and a pinch of turmeric, and simmer for 10–15 minutes.

Heat the oil in a large frying pan or wok over a medium heat, add the cumin seeds and fry for a few seconds until they crackle. Add the garlic and fry for a few seconds until golden. Add the split green chillies, followed by the onions, and cook for 7–10 minutes, until well browned.

Add 1 teaspoon of ground turmeric, the chilli powder and ground cumin; stir for a minute or two to cook the dry spices through.

Add the tomatoes and cook for 4–5 minutes until they melt and incorporate into the onions, and all excess moisture evaporates. Add the baby spinach leaves and salt. Cook for 2–3 minutes.

When the lentils are tender, add the spinach mixture into the lentils and allow to simmer for a few minutes. Add the butter if using, and garnish with chopped coriander leaves.

Serve hot with Indian bread or a rice dish.

COCKTAIL RECIPES

In these recipes, one measure is equivalent to 50ml or 1½ fluid ounces. Each recipe serves one.

To make a simple syrup, put equal quantities of sugar and water in a pan, bring to the boil and stir until the sugar is dissolved. Allow to cool. Always use good-quality fresh fruits and syrups.

POM POM

Gin with fresh pomegranate, lemon juice and coriander – a signature cocktail at Mint Leaf.

1 measure of Bombay Sapphire gin
1 measure of coriander syrup
  (see below)
juice of ½ a lemon
1 measure of fresh pomegranate juice
1 tablespoon pomegranate seeds

Pour the gin, coriander syrup and lemon juice into a tall glass. Half-fill with crushed ice. Muddle (pulverise with the back of a spoon or blunt instrument), check the taste for balance, fill to the top with crushed ice. Slowly pour the pomegranate juice over the ice to create a layer of red over the green of the coriander, and decorate with the pomegranate seeds. Add a couple of straws, and enjoy.

Coriander syrup
Blend ½ cup of finely chopped coriander leaves with 1 cup of sugar syrup (available from wine merchants or make your own, as above), strain through a not-too-fine strainer, to allow tiny bits of coriander to pass through, for colour. This will keep in the fridge for up to one week, but it is best made fresh when you need it.

ELDERFLOWER MARTINI

Gin with cardamom and St. Germain elderflower liqueur.

2 cardamom pods, crushed, plus an
  extra one to decorate
1 measure of gin
1 measure of St. Germain elderflower
  liqueur
juice of ½ a lemon

Chill a martini glass in the freezer for a few hours. Mix all the ingredients in a cocktail shaker, top up with ice cubes and shake well. Taste for balance, then strain into the frosted martini glass. Float a cardamom pod on top to decorate.

TIJITO

Rum, fresh mint and lemongrass,
ginger beer and fresh lime.

2-cm lemongrass stalk, shredded and
  crushed
a sprig of mint leaves
1 measure of white rum
juice of ¹/₂ a lime
non-alcoholic ginger beer, chilled

Add the lemongrass, half a glass of
crushed ice, then the mint, rum and
lime juice to a tall glass. Muddle and
taste for balance. Fill the glass with
more crushed ice, then top up with
ginger beer.

AniRudh Arora

MOTI MAHAL

Head chef Anirudh Arora was born and brought up in Delhi. His father served in the army and his battalion, the historic Napiers, had an officers' mess with sterling silver cutlery and all the paraphernalia of formal dinner settings, and that vision of old-fashioned opulence and refined taste fired Ani's interest.

The family lived for a year in Kashmir, in the late 1980s, where they regularly had a *wazwan*, a Kashmiri banquet of about 30 courses. The chef came to the house and Ani's father asked him to cook about a kilo of lamb curry, but the chef said he didn't know how to cook less than 5 or 6 kilos of anything, so they had to phone all the neighbours to invite them over to help eat the prodigious feast.

Ani's mum wanted him to be a doctor; his father, who had aspired to be an engineer in his school days, wanted him to follow that career path. At one time Ani wanted to become a navy pilot. He told his father that he was not interested in taking up engineering, and eventually they agreed that he would follow in his father's footsteps and join the army. Ani started working for the entrance exams, and noted that the studies for the National Defence Academy were similar to those for Hotel Management! In a fit of inspiration he sent in the papers for both, and he admits he flunked everything except Hotel Management – something that pointed conclusively to his culinary destiny.

The moment he arrived at catering college, he knew he wanted to be a chef, and an Indian cuisine chef at that. He attended the Institute of Hotel Management in Lucknow, which is said by many to be the food capital of India. Biryanis come from Lucknow, as do the Nawabs, those provincial viceroys of the Moghul era, who through their love of fine food encouraged an elevated style of cuisine that still exists. The residents of that region still have an appreciation of epicurean excellence, Ani's grandfather amongst them. Ani is convinced that, 'to cook good food you need to eat good food. For some reason people in Lucknow do both – whether Indian or not. Chinese food tastes better there, too – maybe the taste buds are enhanced.'

Like students anywhere, the aspiring young chef wasn't exactly flush with cash during those years. The course was a three-year diploma in catering at that time, attending college for the first year, then out to hotels for work

experience. Trainees were only paid a stipend – 250 rupees in those days, which didn't even cover Ani's bus fares. He refused to accept such a paltry sum, but at the end of his training the college said that he had to, so he invested it in a knife, a bottle-opener and a full tank of fuel for his scooter!

When Chef Arora left college, he was picked by Oberoi's because of his academic standing within his batch year, and was the youngest Indian chef in that huge empire. He worked for them for over five years, opening three restaurants, including the Indian cuisine restaurant at the famous Udaivilas super luxury resort in Udaipur. 'I went as far as I could as an Indian-speciality chef within the company, and after that, the only option was to diversify and become more of an executive chef, but I didn't want to do that. So I quit, came to London looking for fresh

opportunities, and opened Benares in Mayfair (see page 11), and after two years moved on to Moti Mahal.'

When the original Moti Mahal first opened in Delhi in 1959, the restaurant was a huge success. Regular guests included India's first Prime Minister, Jawahalal Nehru, his daughter Indira Ghandi, as well as the Kennedys. The London branch opened in 2005. Ani recalls, 'It was our ambition to have a show kitchen – the original in Delhi had had one in 1978, and when we came to London the owners wanted to incorporate that feature here.' Moti Mahal is an 84-seater restaurant, and on a regular evening might do 120 or 125 dinners, with that show kitchen, offering views of the tandoors and hanging kebab skewers, at the forefront.

The restaurant is light, bright and has a contemporary air. It's a simple, but classical cuisine concept – they have a focus on the foods from along the length of the Grand Trunk Road, which runs from Bangladesh and Kolkata in the east to Delhi, the north-west and into Pakistan and Afghanistan. One finds recipes from rural India, from the Nawabs, from Delhi, from the North-West Frontier. Anirudh recalls, 'I have travelled along the Grand Trunk Road – many parts of it over the past six or seven years, but before that I lived and worked around it.' How much more romantic that sounds than boasting of spending one's career on the A1.

'I didn't appreciate the Jhelum River in Kashmir when I lived there, and only now do I realise that I will never have that experience again, and I miss it. Similarly, I didn't appreciate the Grand Trunk Road when I lived on it, only when I left it. I used to drive my scooter to college on it every day. I used to eat Indian scrambled eggs at a vegetarian truck-stop, so I had to sit in the corner where nobody would see. The owner used to make breads and dal, cooked on charcoal, and the flavour was exceptional. He had a small chilli tree in the corner, and you could ask him to put some of those chillies in your food. I am always trying to recreate that elusive and exotic taste, and that mirage continues to beckon. Nostalgia is not just about the heart, it's also about the flavour.'

There are stylish innovations at Moti Mahal, such as the complementary salad plate with the house chaat masala, a touch that hints at the generous hospitality to follow.

The menu is divided into two categories: On the Grand Trunk Road, and, unsurprisingly, Off the Grand Trunk Road. 'The GT Road is land-locked, so there is no seafood on it, and we have to divert from the Grand Trunk Road for fish. There are some classic dishes which I don't alter, although I might substitute monkfish in a particular recipe. My spices come from India, but all the meat, fish and vegetable ingredients are local.

'I know for sure that Tandoori Lamb Chops will sell, and Murgh Makhni will be popular. I'm proud of our classics, but food is a fashion, and you have to keep evolving – if you don't, others will. Game is seen more often on Indian menus these days, and our guests appreciate our venison when cooked in the tandoor. Trends are changing: before 2006 people used to worry more about the tablecloths, wallpaper, cutlery, crockery. Now they have added good food and a clean environment to the top of their list – the focus is the food.'

When Anirudh first came to the UK he says he could not understand the references to 'fresh' tomatoes or 'fresh' aubergine – surely there *were* only fresh ones? But he realised that he hadn't considered the array of tinned or frozen food here. 'In India everyone used to shell the peas every Saturday, and the flavour was different. From the late 1990s frozen peas arrived in India and you didn't even have to cook them! Because there is a big Indian community in London, you can get everything that's available in India, and perhaps even more.'

What of Anirudh's ambitions? 'I would like to have a restaurant of my own eventually. Indian cuisine has evolved in London in the nine years I've been here, and over the last five years in regional restaurants as well, and I would like to start a restaurant in the countryside, where I can open the back door and get out into the fields, and not see five lorries waiting to be unloaded, a dry-cleaners, the Evening Standard vendor, and a Dyno-Rod van parked there!'

Moti Mahal
45 Great Queen Street, Covent Garden, London WC2B 5AA
Phone 020 7240 9329 **www.motimahal-uk.com**

BHARWAN MIRCHA (STUFFED CHILLIES)

This is a beautiful dish of pan-fried red chillies. We use the large variety of chilli that is ideal for stuffing and cooking. It's said that the smaller the chillies, the hotter they are – these are mild in flavour and the shape allows for even cooking when stuffed. A stunning vegetarian option.

SERVES 4

4 red banana chillies

For the stuffing
3 tablespoons vegetable oil, plus extra for frying
1 teaspoon black mustard seeds
1 tablespoon peeled and finely chopped ginger
2 green chillies, chopped
5 curry leaves, chopped
2 carrots, very finely diced
60g peas, defrosted if frozen or fresh if available
3 potatoes, boiled and finely diced
1 teaspoon ground turmeric
1 teaspoon chilli powder, or to taste
½ teaspoon garam masala
juice of 1 lemon
30g Cheddar cheese, grated
salt, to taste

2 tablespoons mint and coriander chutney (see below)

Cut the red chillies in half lengthwise and scrape out the seeds.

Heat the oil in a large frying pan over a medium heat. Add the mustard seeds and fry them for a few seconds until they crackle. Add the ginger, green chillies and curry leaves and sauté for 1 minute.

Add the carrots and peas and cook for 1–2 minutes or until tender. Add the diced potatoes, turmeric, chilli powder and salt and continue cooking for another 2–3 minutes. Pour over the lemon juice, add the garam masala and gently stir. Check for seasoning. Remove from the heat and allow to cool.

Add the grated cheese to the cooled mixture and stir in the mint and coriander chutney. Stuff the chilli halves with the mixture.

Add a little vegetable oil to a large non-stick pan over a low heat. Fry the red chillies on all sides until heated through and the flesh of the chillies starts to change colour. This should take around 5 minutes.

Serve with a green salad.

MINT AND CORIANDER CHUTNEY

2 bunches of mint
1 bunch of coriander
8 spinach leaves, young and fresh
1 tablespoon peeled and finely chopped ginger
6 garlic cloves
2 green chillies, roughly chopped
2 tablespoons natural yoghurt
1 teaspoon mango powder (amchoor)
1 teaspoon ground cumin
1 teaspoon salt or to taste
juice of 1 lemon

Rinse and drain the herbs and spinach. Pat dry with kitchen paper if necessary.

Put the ginger, garlic and chillies in a blender or food processor with the mint, coriander and spinach leaves. Add the yoghurt and blend until you have a smooth paste. Add a little water if necessary.

Transfer the paste to a bowl. Stir in the mango powder, cumin and salt. Pour in the lemon juice and stir once more to combine, and check for seasoning. Use immediately; any remaining chutney can be put into an airtight container and stored in the fridge for up to 2 days.

HALEEM

Haleem comes from Hyderabad and Pakistan. The versions are all quite similar, but in Hyderabad they use porridge (bulgur wheat or cracked wheat) rather than lentils, whereas in Pakistan it's both porridge and lentils. Haleem was once considered a poor man's dish – lots of porridge and/or lentils and just a little meat. It's a complete meal in one dish. I love haleem because, although it's a lot of effort to cook, when you put a lot of effort in, the resulting dish tastes better. It's slow-cooked and resembles a delicious paste when finished. I like chopped onions and green chillies with a squeeze of lemon on top of mine. Eat it with naan bread spread with lots of butter.

SERVES 4

100g mixed yellow lentils (moong, masoor, channa dal)
125g bulgur wheat (cracked wheat)
3 tablespoons vegetable oil
6 cloves
3 cinnamon sticks
6 bay leaves
3 onions, sliced
500g lean lamb, cut into 2-cm dice
2 tablespoons ginger-garlic paste
1–2 teaspoons red chilli powder
2 teaspoons ground cumin
salt
1 teaspoon garam masala
3 tablespoons ghee
few sprigs of mint leaves, chopped
few sprigs of coriander leaves, chopped

To serve
1 lemon, cut into wedges
naan, buttered

Wash the lentils and soak in cold water for 2 hours, then drain. Tip the lentils into a heavy-based saucepan, add enough water to cover, and boil the lentils over a medium heat for about 30 minutes until thick. Keep aside.

Wash the wheat and also soak in cold water for 2 hours, then drain. Tip the wheat into another pan, add water to cover, boil uncovered for about 20 minutes until soft – add a little more water should the pan seem to be drying out. (Bulgur wheat comes in a variety of grain sizes, so cooking times vary.) Keep aside.

Heat the oil in a large saucepan, add the cloves, cinnamon sticks and bay leaves and fry for a few seconds until they start to crackle. Add the sliced onions and cook for 4–5 minutes until golden brown. Remove a quarter of the onions onto kitchen paper and keep aside.

Add the lamb to the pan and sear over a high heat for 5–8 minutes, turning to brown all sides. Add the ginger-garlic paste and cook for another minute. Add the red chilli powder, ground cumin and salt to taste, and cook for a minute.

Just cover the lamb with water, cover with a lid and cook over a gentle heat for 45–50 minutes until the meat becomes soft and tender. Shred the cubes of meat into small pieces using two forks.

Add the boiled lentils and wheat to the meat and cook over a medium heat for about 20 minutes until the entire mixture turns into a porridge consistency. Keep stirring all the time or the mix will stick to bottom and burn. Add the garam masala, ghee and salt to taste.

Turn off the heat and garnish the dish with chopped mint, coriander, and the reserved browned onions. Serve hot with lemon wedges and well-buttered naan.

TEETAR KA ACHAR (PARTRIDGE PICKLE)

This is the sort of dish that I learned from my father. The spice mixture gives flavour, and the partridge keeps really well for a few days if the meat is covered with oil. Use mustard oil for its pungent taste. You can even add a little more vinegar if you think the dish needs extra 'tang'.

SERVES 4

12 dried red chillies
2 partridges, skin left on, boneless
   (ask your butcher to do this)
200ml mustard oil
2 teaspoons red chilli powder
2 tablespoons ginger-garlic paste
salt
2 teaspoons black mustard seeds
few sprigs of curry leaves
2 tablespoons chopped ginger
10 garlic cloves, chopped
2 green chillies, chopped
1/4 teaspoon asafoetida
2 tablespoons ground coriander
100ml white vinegar

To make the chilli paste, remove any stalks from the dried chillies, soak the chillies in hot water for an hour; drain and blend to a smooth paste, adding a little water if needed.

Cut each partridge into large pieces, wash, drain and pat dry with kitchen paper.

In a bowl mix together 50ml of the oil, 1 teaspoon of the red chilli powder and half the ginger-garlic paste, and season with salt. Put the partridge pieces in the bowl and turn to coat with the spice mix. Cover and leave to marinate for a few minutes.

Preheat the oven to 200°C/Gas Mark 6. Heat a non-stick pan over a high heat; sear the partridge pieces on both sides, then place on a roasting tray and cook in the oven for 8–10 minutes. Keep aside.

Heat the remaining oil in a heavy-based pan to a medium temperature; add the mustard seeds and allow them to crackle. Add the curry leaves, chopped ginger, garlic cloves and green chillies, and cook, stirring, for a minute. Add the remaining ginger-garlic paste, stir, then add the remaining red chilli powder, asafoetida and ground coriander and cook just until the garlic turns golden brown. Remove from the heat and pour through a metal strainer into a heat-proof container; return the oil to the pan and retain the spices for use later.

Add 1–2 tablespoons of the red chilli paste and the vinegar to the oil over a medium heat, and cook for 10–12minutes until the oil separates. Remove from the heat, add the partridge and fried spices, and check the seasoning.

Allow the partridge pickle to cool, and store in an airtight container in the fridge to mature. Serve after two days. The pickle will keep in the fridge for up to a week.

BOULANI

This is an Afghani bread. I often visit Delhi where there is a big Afghani population. These people have a lot of food stalls where they sell their regional specialities in the evenings. Their dishes are not very spicy, relying on the flavours of the raw ingredients. It's not different from Indian food, but it's a particular type of Indian food. This is a bread that has a sweet filling of leeks or spring onions. We roll out the dough into circles, put the filling on one half and fold it over. This isn't the way it's usually done in India, which is more of a stuffed dumpling flattened out, but this version works very well as the filling is more evenly distributed.

SERVES 4

For the dough
10g fresh yeast (or dried yeast
    alternative)
1 teaspoon sugar
a little warm water
500g plain flour
250g whole wheat flour
salt
2 tablespoons vegetable oil

For the filling
2 large bunches of spring onions
    (or 2 leeks)
$1/2$–1 teaspoon salt
1 teaspoon red chilli powder
2 green chillies, chopped
10ml vegetable oil

For the mint yoghurt
150ml yoghurt
2 tablespoons dried mint
$1/2$–1 teaspoon red chilli powder
salt

In a mixing bowl, whisk together the yoghurt, dried mint, chilli powder and salt to taste until smooth. Cover and put in the fridge until serving.

Put the yeast in a mug with a teaspoon of sugar, and add a little warm water. Set aside.

To make the filling, chop the spring onions (green part only) or leeks into fine shreds, tip into a bowl, and sprinkle the salt over. Turn to mix the salt in and leave for 5 minutes.

Gently squeeze the onions or leeks to remove excess moisture, and place them in a mixing bowl. Add the rest of the filling ingredients and mix well. Keep aside.

Sift the plain flour, whole wheat flour and a large pinch of salt into a large mixing bowl and stir in the oil. Make a well in the centre and add the yeast mixture and about 250ml warm water, and knead until it becomes a soft dough. Leave the dough in a warm place to relax for 15–20 minutes.

Separate the dough into 12 equal portions and, using some flour to stop it sticking, roll each one to a thickness of 5mm with a rolling pin, keeping the circular shape.

Divide the filling into 12 portions. Place a portion of the filling on one side of the rolled dough. Spread the filling evenly across one half of the dough. Fold the other half over the top of the filling to form a semi-circle shape. Pinch the open sides together to seal, in the same way as one would for a Cornish pastie. Dust a baking sheet with a little flour and place the crimped breads on the sheet, leaving a little space around each one to prevent sticking.

Heat the oil in a pan on a low heat; dust off excess flour from the boulani and fry in batches for 2–3 minutes on each side until golden. Drain on kitchen paper and keep hot while you fry the remainder.

Serve hot with the mint yoghurt.

PISTACHIO RICE PUDDING WITH COCONUT FOAM AND CARAMELISED PINEAPPLE

This layered dessert is best served in glasses for visual impact. The top is a foam of coconut and dark sugar cream, and for this we use a cream whipper that's available from cookshops – it's like a soda siphon for food. Kheer is a traditional Indian rice pudding, but for this dish I've made a version using pistachios which give not only flavour, but colour, and it makes a delightful dessert on its own. The pineapple with the molasses sugar is the bottom layer of the three and could equally be served with just some whipped cream or vanilla ice cream. There's sweetness from the fruit and a unique richness from the molasses.

SERVES 4

For the pineapple
2 pineapples, skin and eyes removed
150g molasses sugar or muscovado
    sugar

For the pistachio kheer
200g rice
50g pistachios, plus a handful to
    decorate
1 litre full-fat milk
75g sugar
$\frac{1}{2}$ teaspoon ground green cardamom

For the jaggery and coconut foam
1 gelatine leaf
85g jaggery, grated
1 tablespoon muscovado sugar
300ml double cream
100ml coconut milk
zest of $\frac{1}{4}$ lemon

Preheat the oven to 200°C/Gas Mark 6.

Cut the pineapple into quarters, remove the core and weigh 450g of prepared pineapple into a bowl. Add the molasses sugar to the pineapple and, using your hands, rub the sugar into the pineapple. Transfer the pineapple to a lined baking tray and roast in the oven for 25 minutes, glazing it during the cooking time by spooning the melted sugar back over the pineapple two or three times.

Remove from the oven, allow it to cool and shred it finely by pulling apart with two forks. Transfer the shredded pineapple with the melted sugar to a clean container, and refrigerate.

To make the pistachio kheer, rinse the rice, then soak in cold water for 1 hour. Drain. Boil a large pan of water, add the rice and cook, covered, for 10–15 minutes until soft. Drain.

Place the boiled rice in a blender, add the pistachios and 200ml of the milk, and blend to a coarse paste.

Boil the remaining milk in a heavy-based non-stick pan and add the rice and pistachio paste. Cook over a medium heat for 5–6 minutes until the milk thickens. Add the sugar and cook for a minute or two until it dissolves. Stir in the ground cardamom, then transfer the mixture to a clean bowl and allow to cool to room temperature before covering and transferring to the fridge.

To make the jaggery and coconut foam, soak the gelatine in cold water for about 5 minutes until it has become soft and jelly-like.

Melt the jaggery and sugar in a saucepan over gentle heat, add the cream and coconut milk, and bring to the boil. Remove from the heat and add the lemon zest, leave for a minute to allow it to infuse.

Squeeze the gelatine to remove excess water and add it to the warm cream mixture, whisking well to dissolve the gelatine into the cream. Pass the mixture through a fine sieve and pour it into a cream whipper. Charge with two gas pellets, shake vigorously and refrigerate for 2 hours so that the mixture thickens.

To assemble the dessert, place the cooked pineapple in a clear glass bowl, add a layer of cold pistachio kheer and squirt the foam on the top. Decorate with sliced pistachios.

Note
If you don't have a cream whipper, you can put the cream and gelatine mixture in a bowl in the fridge until needed, then blend with a handheld blender before spooning over the dessert. The effect won't be the same but it will taste just as delicious.

SRIRAM AYLUR

QUILON

The Quilon's journey began in 1999, when vice-chairman of Indian Hotels RK Krishna Kumar decided to capitalise on the success of his iconic Bombay Brasserie (see page 25). He gave Chef Sriram Aylur the opportunity to establish a prestigious restaurant in the heart of London. The building where Quilon is located was the former lodging for guests of Buckingham Palace, the big house around the corner. It still has a cosy and evident charm. The low wooden ceiling in the form of a gently undulating wave gives an intimate and casual ambiance, and the light earth-coloured walls are hung with panels of ceramic medallions that mimic the scales of a fish. There are back-lit niches containing decorative beaten metalwork inspired by design elements from homes in Kerala; the geometric pattern on the screens and on the bar is also a traditional motif from that region. The lower floor houses the private dining area, with its long, 16-seater table and dedicated kitchen.

Quilon offers its guests a refuge from busy lives, with a location convenient for those employed in government and politics. Quilon habitués have been known to come for Christmas lunch but to remain for dinner. Bollywood stars, Indian sports personalities, international singers and artists all have Quilon as their preferred restaurant. The staff wouldn't ever divulge names and the paparazzi will not be stalking around the entrance, allowing diners to relax in discreet privacy.

The restaurant was named after the old Indian port town on the Arabian Sea which was a great centre of trade in Kerala. The city has changed its name frequently and was known as Desinganadu, Kollam and Quilon at various times. It has been a hub of the seafaring industry from the days of the Phoenicians and the Romans. There was a sizable Chinese community in Quilon during a period of trade and diplomacy between that city and China. Marco Polo visited the city in 1275 in his capacity as a mandarin. From the beginning of the 16th century the Portuguese, the Dutch, and then the British established trading centres in Quilon.

Quilon the restaurant is said to import more South Indian spices than any other Indian restaurant in Britain, and Sriram grinds and mixes them artfully to create unique recipes just for Quilon. 'Initially the British public could not comprehend an Indian restaurant that didn't serve naan and chicken tikka.' His biggest challenge in those days was

in sourcing authentic ingredients: 'We offer the cuisine of Kerala, Karvar, Mangalore and Goa. The dishes are light and contain no cream, but rely on fresh seafood, vegetables and herbs. They are all authentic dishes, but with a slight contemporary twist. The Mangalore chicken is made in exactly the same way as it would be in India, but we reduce the amount chilli at Quilon. The public is now much more receptive to different types of cuisines because they travel, particularly with tourism to Kerala and Goa now being so popular.' Sriram is adamant that this is 'progressive' Indian cuisine, not fusion.

The chef at Quilon is, on first meeting, a quietly spoken and unassuming man. His gentle manner reflects his evident

confidence in his work. He is about balance and harmony in so many ways. Born in Mumbai, Sriram was bound to have at least a passing interest in the culinary arts – his father had a catering company, so his first steps into his father's kitchen heralded the beginning of a long relationship with food. 'I remember being fascinated by the aromas from the kitchen,' says Sriram. He was always inspired by the way his father used to work in his restaurant and, when he had charge of a restaurant of his own, he adopted his father's considerate working practices.

Every Sunday there was a family feast, an informal affair with lots of people, both invited and uninvited. Food was taken seriously with consideration given to the ingredients and the menu. Sriram says he still misses the conviviality of those occasions. The dishes naturally drew upon the progress of the seasons and the fresh foods that came with those changes, although as a child Sriram loved to eat street food and looked forward to those opportunities. He still manages to return to visit his parents in Mumbai two or three times each year, but admits that he doesn't eat as much street food as he did in his youth.

Sriram had initially wanted to be a lawyer, but his father started a new restaurant in Warangal, Andhra Pradesh, so he decided to stay at home to help launch the enterprise. He had found his passion and eventually left home for the first time to follow what was to become a successful career. In 1984 he joined the Institute of Hotel Management, Catering Technology and Applied Nutrition. 'I had a lot of fun and was hooked within a month,' he recalls. He had evidently not realised what the future had in store for him, often having to wake at 6am, and then not finishing work until 1am. But despite that, he enjoyed his new-found freedom. Eventually his father recognized his son's ability and made him a partner in the business. Sriram says that was the best training he could have wished for. He stopped the long hours when he became head chef, but he says it's still a tough life – 'You must love the profession to be able to stay at the top.'

In 1989 he joined the prestigious Taj Group of hotels. He eventually launched Karavali Restaurant which was awarded a place in the Top Five Restaurants in India in 1995 by *The Statesman*. In 1997 *The Telegraph*, a national daily newspaper in India, ranked him as one of the top five chefs in the country – quite an accolade when you consider the number of worthy chefs throughout the subcontinent. Travel for the Taj Group expanded his horizons: French food, in particular, made an impression, while Japanese care in presentation, robust Italian flavours and spicy Thai food all increased his awareness of the diverse culinary palates beyond his home country. He has loved learning.

It was in 1999 that Quilon opened and in 2001 the restaurant was recognised as 'the best Indian restaurant' in the Good Curry Guide awards. In 2008, Sriram Aylur was awarded a Michelin Star by the eponymous guide to gastronomy. In July 2011 he was named 'Beer Drinker of the Year' by the All-Party Parliamentary Beer Group – he doesn't drink volumes of beer himself, but has created a special five-course all-British beer menu. Previous winners have included HRH The Prince of Wales, so he's in good company.

At Quilon light food is the style – healthy, but indulgent. Chicken curry, biryani, black cod, dosas and crab cakes are all popular. The menu is influenced not only by the seasonal availability of fresh produce but also by the inspiration of the chef. The restaurant wants to offer its guests the best of Indian cuisine with the advantages of Western culinary philosophy: for example the lamb is trimmed of fat; prime cuts are selected even for the sauced dishes. Sriram wants to present Indian fine dining via the medium of authentic dishes. 'Art forms need to progress to assure their continued existence and it's that way with food,' says Sriram.

Indeed, this chef does love art and galleries, theatre, movies, fashion and jewellery design. Presentation is always important and is reflected in his unfussy attention to detail. Fascination with proportion perhaps comes from his interest in architecture. Quilon offers traditional yet progressive cooking, West Coast food rather than fusion. The chef has worked with Indian housewives to learn authentic cooking techniques and unique family recipes, which he then draws upon to create polished cuisine worthy of being described as classically Indian.

Chef Aylur likes to cook at home, but he sets high standards for a domestic kitchen, and has designed his own. His elder son loves Italian, but all the family enjoy food of every kind. The children sometimes dictate what Dad needs to cook. He dedicates all his free time to his family: wife and children are the cornerstones of this man's life. He says he seldom accepts invitations which don't include his boys. Sriram's elder son is already a good cook, but the chef thinks that it might just stay a hobby – or will he follow in his father's footsteps?

The Quilon
41 Buckingham Gate, St James's, London SW1E 6AF
Phone 020 7821 1899 **www.quilon.co.uk**

CAULIFLOWER CHILLI FRY
(GOBI KEMPU)

This is street food from Bangalore – simple, easy to make and very popular. It's not a fancy dish, but our guests love it and it's been on the restaurant menu for many years. It's easy to make at home too. Many people don't like cauliflower because they consider it bland, but here the chillies and curry leaves add both heat and flavour.

SERVES 4

500g cauliflower florets, thinly sliced
vegetable oil, for deep frying

For the batter
150g cornflour
50g rice flour
1–2 tablespoons red chilli paste,
*   or to taste*
1 egg
salt
100ml water

Spices for tempering
1 tablespoon vegetable oil
2–3 green chillies, or to taste, split
1 sprig of curry leaves
2 tablespoons yoghurt
salt

In a large bowl, mix the cornflour, rice flour, chilli paste, egg and a large pinch of salt into a thick batter, adding approximately 100 ml water, or as needed.

Heat the oil in a deep pan, wok or fryer over medium heat, until shimmering.

Stir the cauliflower in the batter a little at a time, and drop the individual pieces into the hot oil. Do this in batches, so as not to overcrowd the pan. Fry for a couple of minutes, turning, until golden and crispy. Remove from the oil, drain on kitchen paper, and keep warm until all of the cauliflower is cooked in this way.

Heat 1 tablespoon of oil in a large frying pan or wok, add the green chillies, curry leaves, yoghurt and a pinch of salt. When the yoghurt boils and almost all the moisture has evaporated, add the fried cauliflower and toss to coat. Serve immediately.

TOMATO RASAM

This is a popular recipe because it's easy to make and to drink. It is lovely on a cold day, and is a quick-fix for a fever, cold or cough. It does not require any exotic ingredients, and most of them you will already have at home. Traditionally poured over rice, this thin spicy mixture can also be served in a small glass as a hot appetiser.

SERVES 4

50g toor dal
700g tomatoes, chopped
1 teaspoon black peppercorns
2 teaspoon cumin seeds
2 whole dried red chillies, or to taste
1 small garlic clove, roughly chopped
1 tablespoon vegetable oil
1 teaspoon black mustard seeds
8 curry leaves
1/2 teaspoon ground turmeric
850ml water
1 tablespoon tamarind paste
salt
sugar
chopped coriander leaves, for garnish

Wash and drain the lentils several times until the water runs clear. Place in a saucepan, cover with water, bring to the boil, cover and simmer for 20 minutes. Drain and set aside.

Purée the tomatoes in a blender. Set aside.

In a frying pan over a medium heat, dry roast the peppercorns, cumin seeds and dried red chillies for 1 minute, remove to a bowl and allow to cool, then very coarsely crush in a pestle and mortar or grinder with the garlic to make a spice mix.

Heat the vegetable oil in a large frying pan over a medium heat, add the mustard seeds and curry leaves and allow the seeds to crackle for a few seconds. Stir in the puréed tomatoes and turmeric and bring to the boil. Pour in the water, stir in the lentils, spice mix and tamarind paste. Simmer for 15–20 minutes. Add salt to taste, and a little sugar if your tomatoes are not very sweet.

Strain through a fine sieve into glasses or a serving jug, and sprinkle with chopped fresh coriander before serving.

LEMON RICE

This traditional dish is made in most parts of southern India. It is the beautiful colour and flavour of turmeric that makes it interesting, and the tanginess of the lemon makes it flavourful. You can even eat this by itself – it's a one-pot dish with everything in it to make it a complete meal.

SERVES 4

400g basmati rice
1 litre water
3 tablespoons vegetable oil
2 tablespoons black mustard seeds
2 teaspoons urad dal
4 teaspoons channa dal
10g whole cashew nuts
1–2 whole red chillies, or to taste
1½ teaspoons ground turmeric
10 curry leaves
juice of 2–3 lemons
salt

To garnish
oil, for deep-frying
1 sprig of curry leaves

Bring the rice to the boil in 1 litre of salted water, turn the heat as low as possible and cook, covered, for 10 minutes; set aside and keep warm.

Heat the oil in a small saucepan over a medium heat, add the mustard seeds and fry until they crackle; add the urad dal, channa dal, cashew nuts, chillies, ground turmeric and curry leaves, and sauté for 2 minutes. Add the lemon juice, salt to taste and simmer for 5 minutes.

Pour this mixture over the cooked rice, mix and adjust the seasoning.

For the garnish, heat the oil in a wok or deep pan over a high heat, and fry the curry leaves for a few seconds until they are crisp. Transfer to kitchen paper to drain.

Serve the rice hot, garnished with fried curry leaves.

FISH IN BANANA LEAF

A very traditional recipe, because banana leaf is available all around the coasts of India. The idea of cooking a piece of fish wrapped in a leaf is appealing because it cooks not only from the heat below the pan but also in the steam trapped inside the leaf. The leaf does impart some flavour to the fish, but you can use foil or baking parchment if you can't get banana leaf.

SERVES 4

20g chilli paste, or to taste
10g ginger-garlic paste
1 tablespoon lemon juice
1/4 teaspoon ground turmeric
salt
4 banana leaves
8 halibut chunks (or tilapia fillet),
    about 700–800g
vegetable oil, for frying

For the tomato-onion masala
1 tablespoon vegetable oil
1 onion, finely chopped
2 tomatoes, finely chopped
1/4 teaspoon chilli powder
1/4 teaspoon ground turmeric
100ml water
salt
1/2 teaspoon garam masala

To make the tomato-onion masala, heat the oil in a saucepan over medium heat, add the onion and fry for 3–4 minutes until golden brown. Add the tomatoes and continue cooking for a further 3–4 minutes until they are soft. Add the chilli and turmeric and sauté for a few minutes. Add the water, salt to taste and the garam masala, cover with a lid and cook on a low heat for 15 minutes.

In a bowl combine the chilli paste, ginger-garlic paste, lemon juice and turmeric, and add salt to taste.

Wash and dry the banana leaves and cut into 8 pieces, each sufficient to make an envelope for a piece of fish. Soften the leaves by heating them in the microwave for 10 seconds.

Pat the fish dry with kitchen paper. Place a piece to one side on each banana leaf and fold the sides to create a parcel. Secure with a wooden toothpick, if necessary.

Heat a frying pan over a medium heat, sprinkle in a little oil and add the fish parcels (in batches if necessary). Cook for a few minutes, turn over and cook the other side for a couple of minutes. Open a parcel and check that the fish is cooked through. (Alternatively, the parcels can be put on a baking sheet and baked in an oven preheated to 200°C/Gas Mark 6 for 12–15 minutes.

Serve with the hot tomato onion masala, either served separately in a jug or poured directly over the fish.

ASPARAGUS AND MANGETOUT

In Kerala they call this dish Thoran, which just means 'stir-fry'. We have used that principle, but have incorporated vegetables that are not available in India, preferring to take advantage of fresh local produce here. This dish takes only five minutes to cook, and goes with any meat or fish. I think that makes it very interesting and very different. When we Indians see vegetables such as these, they look familiar, but the resulting dish is unique, and that's more exciting. You can use French beans, spinach or almost any vegetable that can be stir-fried, and it will taste fresh and vibrant.

SERVES 4

150g mangetout
1 tablespoon olive oil
1 sprig of curry leaves
$1/2$ teaspoon black mustard seeds
1 bunch of asparagus, peeled and
    diced
pinch of crushed black pepper
salt
1 teaspoon lemon juice
1 tablespoon fresh grated coconut or
    dessicated coconut

Blanch the mangetout in boiling water for 1 minute, refresh with cold water, drain and set aside.

Heat the olive oil in a frying pan over a medium heat, add the curry leaves and mustard seeds and let them crackle. Add the asparagus and blanched mangetout, and stir. Add the pepper, salt to taste and lemon juice and stir again. Add the coconut, and toss. Add just a few tablespoons of water, cover with a lid and cook for a few more minutes until the asparagus is lightly done, but still crunchy.

Transfer to a bowl and serve immediately.

mANISH SHARMA

There is a corner of Soho that will be forever Bollywood. Sitaaray is the unique and iconic restaurant that seems to double as an Indian film portrait gallery. There is a twinkling array of etched glass mirrors, several glittering chandeliers and walls crammed with photographs of some of the best-loved stars of the Bollywood silver screen – black and white shots of dashing actors and smouldering actresses from every decade and posters of musicals, epics and comedies.

The design of Sitaaray is striking, memorable and glitzy. Its intimate ambiance attracts a regular clientele, as well as those who are in the area to take advantage of the local theatres – that show-biz element again. The first floor is sought by small groups who can occupy semi-private booths for the evening, each one with its themed selection of pictures to jog the memories of some and to inspire others. An area dedicated to heroes, another to musicals – homage is paid to every genre. The music and the film flickering from monitors add to the atmosphere. This is a restaurant for the movie aficionado, as well as those looking for a stylish meal out. Even those who know nothing of the Indian film industry might be encouraged to flick through *Time Out London* magazine to catch the latest subcontinental cinematographic offering after the last Sitaaray kebabs and curries have been consumed.

Sitaaray and its sister restaurants Tamarai and Chor Bizarre (see page 49) are owned by Rohit Khattar, who sits on the Managing Director's couch. Having Sitaaray (meaning 'star' in Hindi) isn't a mere whim of an enthusiastic entrepreneur – film has always been his passion. He grew up watching four films a day in the projection booth of his grandfather's cinema, the Broadway in Kashmir. Aside from his three London restaurants, he runs numerous entertainment facilities and restaurants in India. More pertinent to Sitaaray is the fact that Rohit owns probably the largest private collection of Indian cinema posters and photographs in the world, and has chronicled the history of Indian cinema from the first to the most recent films.

The restaurant has a unique dining concept. Diners are presented with an endless supply of those aforementioned kebabs and curries, and can call for extra portions of this particular dal or that grilled delicacy. Chef Manish Sharma explains, 'Our cuisine is a mix-and-match of the kebabs, mostly North Indian kebabs, and curries. We always like to take on board the suggestions from our customers, and this improves our knowledge of what our guests enjoy or would like in the future. People should not be bored with the food that a restaurant serves, and we have introduced innovations like our Lamb Pepper Kebab, and Idli, a South Indian dish, which we serve with a vegetable starter snack.' Manish doesn't mention the naan bread at Sitaaray, but it, too, is exceptional. That, along with the other dishes on offer, arrives hot and steaming, on demand and in a continuous succession.

Manish Sharma is a shy young chef who doesn't naturally court publicity, although he is confident and animated when discussing his passion – food. He was born and brought up in Delhi which has long been considered a hub for good food. His home was near an area known as Purani

Dilli which is famed for its speciality shops, and the locals are serious about their food. It's a market for prepared and fresh ingredients – visitors seek out popular dishes like papdi chaat, phulka, tikkis, and other savouries and desserts. They are all produced in this neighbourhood, so it was easy for Manish to see exactly how these things were made: 'A lucky chance for me, living there.'

His first steps on the journey to becoming a chef began when he was just a child. 'When I was small my father used to cook very good food. He installed a tandoor at home and got me to bring charcoal, and he taught me lots about the dishes. He was a teacher, not a chef. When I came to leave school I wanted to join a hotel management and catering course. It was then that I found that this was my forte, and my teachers encouraged me to follow the kitchen side. The realisation that this was the thing I could do best in life came slowly, step by step.'

Manish joined Old World Hospitality as a management trainee – a small company, but with a reputation for culinary excellence in India and now in London. 'I have been given lots of opportunities by the company, who have supported me throughout my career. I came to England in 2005, after working at the Old World Hospitality's celebrated India Habitat Centre in Lodhi Road, Delhi. I also trained with a Thai chef at the Oriental Octopus restaurant, where I was in the opening team. I helped to open Chor Bizarre in Noida (which was modelled on the original Chor Bizarre in nearby New Delhi), and then the company brought me to London to work in Chor Bizarre – India's Restaurant in Mayfair. When Sitaaray – India's Grill was being planned, I transferred to this restaurant, and we opened in December 2007.'

The restaurant has its regular followers. Some Sitaaray customers want a pre-theatre menu, and there is also a demand for a post-show meal. Lunchtime is often a problem for Indian restaurants: 'curry' has never been viewed as a noon tradition in the UK but that is changing, now that many restaurants are offering lighter fare or smaller plates. 'We are introducing a two-course menu for lunchtimes. People don't want to eat too much and fall asleep in the office in the afternoon! If we only offer unlimited kebabs, those who do enjoy that menu will overindulge, and will ask me, "Where's the bed?" and they won't want to leave the restaurant!'

At home Manish takes charge in the kitchen. 'The food you make is dependent on your mood: if I am happy, the food I cook is better. I saw this in my mother, too, and one's frame of mind makes a difference. It is something that comes from inside. People who work in the industry just for the money have their own agenda and style of cooking, whereas if you love coming into work you can enjoy yourself. If the shift starts here at 11am, I'm here at nine. And the learning never stops.' Manish doesn't keep that knowledge to himself, though. He uses some of his time to teach the young chefs about the food they are preparing. 'I talk to the college guys here about masalas, we go to the market and I introduce them to the different meats, fish, cheeses, spices. Did you know there are 18 different types of cardamom?' asks Manish. No, I didn't, chef. 'When you experiment with the science of food you can really enjoy the learning process. I have a big collection of notes recording what I have done each day, and what's new.'

Sitaaray's range of kebabs followed by main course has a northern Indian theme: 'I don't like too much spice and oil,' says Manish, who enjoys milder dishes with lots of flavour. 'Some South Indian food is too strong for me and difficult to modify for the restaurant. If a guest doesn't want lamb, we will alter the selection of kebabs so we can offer him something different; if he needs gluten-free bread, we will serve idlis or dosa. We prepare our kebabs fresh every day, marinating them in the morning, according to the bookings that we have. We serve three or four curries each day, like Dal Makhani, Butter Chicken, Tikka Masala, Kormas, Baigans, and we change them every few months.'

The two chefs who have impressed Manish most are Chef Manish Mehrotra, Head Chef at Tamarai pan-Asian restaurant (another in the group and conveniently connected by a flight of stairs to Sitaaray), and Rajiv Malhotra, the executive chef of Old World Hospitality. 'Their working methods, their techniques, their attention to the needs of their guests and their command of the culinary arts make them the best I have seen. They have taught me a lot, they have critiqued my work and sorted out my mistakes, and I respect them very much professionally.'

Sitaaray offers fantasy and conviviality, along with its classy and colourful memorabilia, but it's the predictable quality and generous portions of delicious comfort food that will ensure your return.

Sitaaray – India's Grill
167 Drury Lane, New London Theatre Building, London WC2B 5PG **Phone** 020 7269 6422 **www.sitaaray.com**

PEPPER SHAMI KEBAB

This is a famous dish, both in India and in restaurants here. I have added peppers to make it more visually appealing, and they help to keep the kebabs delicate and moist. The kebabs have a mild peppery taste, and fresh mint and garlic give it a different dimension. This new version is very popular in Sitaaray – half the customers specifically ask for Shami Kebab.

You can cook the mince mixture in advance and freeze it in batches.

SERVES 4

150g channa dal
450g lamb mince
1½ tablespoons chopped mint
15g red pepper, finely chopped
15g yellow pepper, finely chopped
15g green pepper, finely chopped
1 tablespoon finely chopped coriander
   leaves
1–2 cloves garlic, finely chopped and
   fried until golden
1 egg
2 tablespoons ghee or vegetable oil

For the masala
10 green cardamom pods
2 teaspoons fennel seeds
¼ teaspoon ground cloves
a pinch of mace powder
1 teaspoon ground black pepper
¼ teaspoon red chilli powder,
   or to taste
1 teaspoon ground cumin
¾ teaspoon ground cinnamon
2 teaspoons ground turmeric
1 teaspoon salt, or to taste
2 green chillies, or to taste
4–6 cloves garlic, finely chopped
15g fresh ginger, finely chopped

Soak the channa dal in cold water for 1 hour, then drain. Boil in plenty of water for 15–20 minutes, and drain again.

Crush and remove the husks from the cardamom pods, retain the black seeds.

Heat a small frying pan to medium heat, add the seeds and dry spices and stir for a few seconds until they start to give off their aromas. Remove from the heat and tip into a bowl to prevent further roasting.

Put the lamb mince in a saucepan, add the salt, chillies, garlic, ginger and the roasted spices, and 2 tablespoons of water, and cook over a medium heat for 10 minutes, stirring frequently.

Add the par-boiled channa dal, cover with a lid and cook over a low heat for 20 minutes. Stir occasionally to ensure that it is not sticking to the bottom.

When cooked, let it cool, then pass it through a mincing machine, or use a processor or blender to produce a smooth paste. Add the mint, peppers, coriander, fried garlic and egg to the meat and mix well.

Take small quantities of the mixture and roll between moistened hands to make patties of a suitable size: small to go with cocktails, or large as a main-course item.

Add the ghee or oil to a medium-hot frying pan and fry the patties for a few minutes on each side, until a light golden-brown colour. Drain on kitchen paper.

Serve hot with garnishes such as mint chutney.

DILL CHICKEN TIKKA

This is an easy and flavourful dish and combines readily-available ingredients. These days people are using a lot more dill in India – it has a very distinct flavour. In the restaurant we cook it in a tandoor, but at home you can use a regular oven. Care with the marinade is important. This dish doesn't require any additional chutneys, it can just fill a wrap for a light meal on its own.

SERVES 4

20g ginger-garlic paste
1 1/2 teaspoons lime juice
1/2 teaspoon or to taste, salt
2 green chillies, chopped
1/2 teaspoon ground white pepper
400g chicken breast, skinned and cut into chunks
80ml Greek yoghurt
12g (about 1/2 pack) dill, chopped
40ml double cream
10g cashew nut paste
15g butter, melted

For the garnish
6g (about 1/4 pack) dill, chopped
250ml Greek yoghurt
chaat masala

In a non-metallic bowl, mix together the ginger-garlic paste, lime juice, half the salt, chillies and white pepper as a marinade. Add the chicken and stir to coat, and set aside in the fridge or a cool place for 1 hour.

Put the yoghurt and dill for the garnish in a small bowl and mix well. Leave in a cool place.

Put the yoghurt for the second marinade in a small bowl, add the dill, double cream, cashew nut paste and the remaining salt, and mix it thoroughly.

Pour the yoghurt mixture over the chicken, mix gently to coat, and set aside in the fridge or a cool place for 30 minutes.

Preheat the grill to a high heat (or prepare a barbecue and allow the coals to burn until they become white). Thread the chicken pieces onto skewers if desired, place the chicken on the rack and cook for several minutes to a light golden colour. Turn and repeat on the other side, ensuring that the meat is cooked through to the centre.

Remove the chicken from the heat and baste with melted butter. Put onto a serving dish and garnish with a sprinkle of chaat masala. Place a little of the dill-yoghurt sauce over the chicken as decoration and serve the remainder in a bowl at the table.

COCONUT AND TOFU SHAMI

This dish was a bit of an experiment, and it has proved to be very popular. This recipe is unusual in that it uses tofu as an alternative to the more common paneer, which makes it something of a fusion dish. It has the delicate flavour of the coconut, while the tofu soaks up all the flavours of the other ingredients. Snub-nosed chillies don't add much heat, but they do bring an aromatic flavour, and lemon zest gives freshness. This is a practical dish because it keeps well for a few days in the fridge, and would be good to serve to vegetarians at a barbecue.

SERVES 4

200g fresh tofu
60g coconut milk powder
60g dessicated coconut
10g fresh ginger, finely chopped
2 cloves garlic, finely chopped
1 red chilli, snub-nose, finely chopped
1 green chilli, finely chopped
2–3 tablespoons finely chopped
    coriander leaves
¹/₂ teaspoon salt, or to taste
zest of 1 lemon
vegetable oil or ghee, for frying

For the green coriander chutney
¹/₂ bunch (approximately 50g)
    coriander, finely chopped
¹/₂–1 green chilli, or to taste, de-seeded
    and roughly chopped
juice of ¹/₂ lemon
a pinch of salt

For the garnish
chopped dates

To make the chutney, blend all the ingredients to a fine paste and spoon into a serving bowl. Set aside.

Mash the fresh tofu in a bowl, add all other ingredients apart from the oil, and mix well. Form into eight round patties.

Heat a non-stick pan to medium and add the vegetable oil or ghee. Fry the patties on both sides for a couple of minutes until light golden brown. Drain on kitchen paper.

Serve hot with dates and green coriander chutney.

MURG MEETHI MALAI

This dish has lots of fresh fenugreek. It can be served as a main course, but it also works as a snack or with drinks. A light recipe with a little cream, it goes well with Indian breads or rice. Fresh methi (fenugreek) is used a lot in our restaurant. Cloves and cardamom are also important, as well as the tempering of the asafoetida (asafoetida is a digestive and considered to be a healthy ingredient) – I'm particularly interested in the healthful properties of food.

SERVES 4

2 tablespoons vegetable oil or ghee
1 teaspoon green cardamom pods, cracked
1/2 teaspoon whole cloves
5-cm cinnamon stick
1 teaspoon black peppercorns
2 pinches asafoetida
300g onion, chopped
25g fresh ginger, finely chopped
4–5 cloves garlic, finely chopped
1/2 teaspoon ground turmeric
1/2 teaspoon red chilli powder
2 teaspoons ground cumin
2 teaspoons ground coriander
250g tomatoes, chopped
20g tomato paste
150g onions, thinly sliced and fried until brown
400g chicken breast, cubed
15g dried kasoori methi (fenugreek leaves)
200g fresh green methi (fenugreek leaves)
200ml double cream
1 tablespoon chopped coriander leaves
salt

Heat a large frying pan over a medium heat, add the oil or ghee, then the green cardamom pods, cloves, cinnamon stick and peppercorns, and heat until they crackle. Add the asafoetida and chopped onions and sauté until the onions are translucent.

Add the ginger, garlic, turmeric and red chilli powder, and sauté for a couple of minutes, then add the ground cumin and coriander, chopped tomato and tomato paste, and cook for a further 10 minutes.

Add the fried onions, salt to taste, and the chicken, and cook for 15 minutes. Add the kasoori methi powder and fresh methi, and continue cooking for a further 5–6 minutes, or until the chicken is cooked through. Finally, stir in the double cream and fresh chopped coriander, and simmer gently for 2 minutes.

Serve hot with rice or bread.

HARYALI MACCHI TIKKA

There are lots of fresh ingredients in this recipe, especially mint, and it makes a light and healthy starter. There's a little tang from the lemon juice, and it isn't a very spicy dish. I have added curry leaves for a little innovation, to give colour and a smoky flavour. Many South Indian dishes use either mustard seed or curry leaves – curry leaves are even said to help with ailments like heat stroke. This is a simple, adaptable dish: you can remove the chillies if you want a milder finish.

SERVES 4

1 tablespoon lemon juice
1½ tablespoons ginger-garlic paste
400g pieces of firm white fish (any fish you like), cut into 5–7 cm cubes
1–2 green chillies, or to taste
½ small packet (20g) mint leaves
¼ bunch (25g) coriander leaves
10g (a large handful) curry leaves
35ml thick yoghurt
1½ tablespoons mustard oil
large pinch of ground white pepper
salt, to taste

Place half the lemon juice, the ginger-garlic paste and salt in a non-metallic bowl, and stir to combine. Add the pieces of fish, turn to coat, and set aside to marinate while you continue with the preparation.

Put the green chillies, remaining lemon juice, mint leaves, coriander leaves and salt to taste into a blender or mini-processor and blend to a smooth paste. Pour into a bowl with the yoghurt and mix thoroughly; add the mustard oil and white pepper, and mix.

Add the pieces of marinated fish to the bowl, coat with the spice paste and allow to stand for 30 minutes in a cool place.

Pre-heat the oven to 200°C/Gas Mark 6, or bring the grill up to full heat.

Place the fish pieces on a grid and bake or grill for 6–8 minutes, or until the fish is just cooked through.

Serve hot with a mint chutney or your favourite relish.

REZA MAHAMMAD
AND BRINDER NARULA

STAR OF INDIA

The Star of India is iconic, and so is its effervescent owner, Reza Mahammad. He amused us with his food and travel television series *Delhi Belly*, where he visited restaurants in India before flying home to London to replicate recipes in his own kitchen. Reza basically taught himself how to cook. 'I filmed at the flat and I used to cook and entertain every weekend – it was something I loved to do. I realised that there was no other way to learn but to do a lot of entertaining, and to cook for friends. One can talk a lot about it, but the only way to learn is to do it oneself. On your own, it can take up to two days to prepare a meal for a group.' Reza has a well-respected chef, Brinder Narula, who looks after the kitchen at the restaurant.

'The Star of India has been in the family for 58 years now. My father passed away in 1978 when I was at school in India, and still only 16. So I did a quick course in hotel management in Mumbai, just to get an inkling of what I was going to face when I got back! We had a manager to look after the restaurant in the meantime, and I returned to England in 1980. Working at the Star and in other restaurants was my rite of passage.

'My father had come to England in 1937, one of the earlier Indian immigrants, and worked as a chef at Veeraswamy's, then helped to set up the kitchen at the Cumberland Hotel. He opened the Shah restaurant in 1952, then Star of India in 1954.'

Food was, in a sense, a legacy, but Reza admits he had no understanding of food and cooking as a youngster. He learned a lot whilst he was in India, staying with his grandparents. He remembers the big vats in which they would make mango jam or Indian sweets – everything was cooked over live coals, and they would get him to stir the jams and chutneys, and he was fascinated. 'In all Indian households there is a background of good food and eating. In any Indian home you will always hear: "My mother is the best cook in the world!" Food plays an integral part in Indian society, and it brings the family together.'

Reza had dreams for his restaurant, which has had several reincarnations over the decades. 'When I took over the restaurant, I was only 17 or so, and having to learn the ropes was a nightmare. But instinctively I knew that the decor – the flock wallpaper of Indian restaurant

tradition – was so "not me", and it had to change,' he asserts with a flourish, then a giggle. It's now unfussy and contemporary, although the ceiling is striking. The first decorative theme was 'From flock to baroque', and in the 1980s had the ceiling tented, added chandeliers, and the colours were black, white and grey. In the 1990s Reza changed to a 'Sistine Chapel' Italianesque design. The Renaissance-style ceiling has remained, but the walls have been changed to neutral colours with textures, and the murals are covered over.

'When I moved away from home and was living independently in a flat for the first time – I'll never forget the day – I phoned my mum and said, "Mum, how do I cook a biryani?" She fell about laughing, and asked why I needed to cook a biryani. And I explained that this was

something I wanted to do for myself, and much was done by guesswork. So often I find I jump in at the deep end. I would have a party for 10 people, and that was manageable, but a friend wanted me to cook for 50, and that was beyond my realm, but I did take on the challenge – 50 could just as well have been 100 as far as I was concerned! My portioning was hopeless. I simply multiplied everything by five and there was so much waste! And you're cooking for days to prepare everything. You only learn through experience. Similarly, when you spice a dish, you don't double the amount of chilli when you double a dish – it doesn't work like that.

'I do like to cook and I get a lot of ideas from cookbooks, but I always try out my own variations, to put my own twist on it, and then it becomes my own recipe. I say, "Do the same as me: take ownership of the dish, and that way the sky's the limit – you can mix and match in your own creative way."' Reza vows that Star of India will keep up with the times. 'We have to stay current – there are so many restaurants out there now, competition is much fiercer than it used to be and we have to stay on our toes.' These days Reza is busy with media projects, and planning a cookery school in France, but he still has his family restaurant as a base and an inspiration for his continuing culinary journey.

Chef Brinder Narula comes from a family where food was very important; his grandmother was an excellent cook, and that's where his inspiration came from. She loved cooking, and loved feeding people. She preferred slow cooking, and would cook over coal. A dal would cook overnight and Brinder says the flavour was much more

pronounced than one would find when cooking on a gas or electric stove. 'Mother and grandmother used to argue over the coal fire: my mother wanted to get that messy coal out of the kitchen! But eventually we realised why the coal fire was so important. One of the items on our menu is a favourite of mine from home, Ma ki Dal (Mother's Dal), which is black lentils cooked for a long time over the tandoor, and it's her recipe that inspired me.'

When Brinder left school he wanted to be an engineer, but didn't make it to one of the top colleges, as the competition was so fierce and he lost interest in pursuing that career. His brother-in-law suggested he go into hotel management, and he was accepted at the Institute of Hotel Management at Pusa, Delhi – one of the most celebrated in India. At that time he didn't particularly want to be a chef, and imagined he would be a hotel manager. But he started enjoying the cooking course. He discovered that baking was very methodical and scientific, very step-by-step with beating the eggs, folding in the flour, learning why you don't mix the butter in first. At the end of that course Brinder joined the chef training programme and was selected to go to the Oberoi School of Hotel Management, which is famous for its kitchen training.

'This is where all those famous guys had been: Atul, Vineet, Navin, Vivek. I trained there for two years, and then became a baker and confectioner. I did that for four or five years and loved it, but bakers in India are not that well known. So then I came out into the mainstream kitchen and cooked European, Italian, Thai cuisine, and finally my own Indian cuisine. I always think that starting in baking gave me a more scientific approach to cooking. For that reason I can appreciate how one can change the character of a dish simply by altering the stage at which one might introduce an ingredient. I was at the Oberoi New Delhi for seven or eight years, and then they asked me to become a chef trainer, and I did just that for three years. I feel honoured and proud to be able to say that some of the chefs who are now famous were my pupils – Atul, Vivek...'

Brinder was chosen to be the executive head chef at Oberoi Mumbai, one of the leading hotels in the world. The restaurant was called Kandahar, where the food is said to be comparable to that at the world-renowned Bukhara restaurant in Delhi. He was then invited by restaurateur Andy Varma to come to London, where he opened the restaurant Vama on Kings Road. In 1999 he found his place at Star of India.

'The style here is traditional yet innovative, so we have regional classics like Lal Maas from Rajasthan, Kozhi Chettinad from the south of India, then unique dishes that I created for different palates, using local ingredients like venison. In London you get a different perspective: people here want to explore new dishes, and this allows chefs to showcase their talents and creativity, and of course Reza is very supportive of that philosophy. It is said that the best Indian food outside India is here in the capital.'

Star of India
154 Old Brompton Road, London SW5 0BE
Phone 020 7373 2901 **www.starofindia.eu**

HIRAN KE PASANDE
(VENISON ESCALOPES)

We get our venison from the Highlands of Scotland, and this is one of the most popular dishes at Star of India. These are thinly-sliced fillets cooked in a spiced onion sauce, and it's a dish that always works well – very tender and rich. We serve it with matchstick potatoes here. Game always looks very sophisticated on menus, and people in the UK love to try different meats cooked in interesting ways.

SERVES 4

800g venison striploin
2 tablespoons vegetable oil
4 bay leaves
2 cloves
2, 3-cm cinnamon sticks
2 star anise
4 green cardamom pods
1 teaspoon fennel seeds
$\frac{1}{2}$ teaspoon fenugreek seeds
4 onions, thinly sliced
1 tablespoon finely chopped or grated
    ginger
4 garlic cloves, finely grated or crushed
1 teaspoon ground turmeric
1 teaspoon chilli powder
1 teaspoon ground cumin
$\frac{1}{2}$ teaspoon ground coriander
$\frac{1}{2}$ teaspoon garam masala
6 gratings of nutmeg
1 tablespoon tomato purée
salt
2 tablespoons chopped coriander
    leaves

For the garnish
potatoes, cut into fine juliennes,
    soaked in a bowl of water
oil, for deep-frying
salt

Remove the silverskin (the white connective tissue or membrane) from the striploin with a sharp knife. Place the thick side of the meat away from you and thin side towards you, and cut the venison diagonally to make escalopes (slices).

Heat the oil in a heavy-based pan, add the bay leaves, cloves, cinnamon, star anise, cardamom and fennel and fenugreek seeds, and let them crackle. Add the sliced onions and fry until they are golden brown.

Add the grated ginger and garlic, fry for a minute and then add the venison. Keep stirring and searing the meat for about 2–3 minutes. Stir in the remaining powdered spices and keep stirring to prevent them burning, adding a tablespoon of water if needed. Pour in a cup of boiling water, reduce the heat to a simmer and cover the pan for 10 minutes.

Add the tomato purée and cook for 2 minutes. Check for seasoning. Sprinkle fresh coriander over, and remove the pan from the heat.

To cook the potatoes, heat the oil to 180°C in a deep pan or fryer. Strain all the water from the potatoes, pat dry on a kitchen cloth and fry until golden. Drain on kitchen paper and sprinkle a little salt over.

Serve the venison topped with a heap of straw potatoes.

MURG KHUMB BAHAR (STUFFED CHICKEN SUPREMES WITH WILD MUSHROOM SAUCE)

Here are chicken breasts stuffed with mushroom duxelles and onion with a hint of nutmeg – we cook it in the tandoor, but you can use your regular oven. The chicken is finished in a mild creamy sauce, and it really works well. The most difficult process is making a pocket in the breast – once you've mastered that, it's a very simple dish to make.

I love mushrooms with anything, and I think this recipe is a delight. Mushrooms are not the usual run-of-the-mill item on Indian menus, but they are becoming more popular. I trained in Simla in the north of India – it's a hill station and that area is famed for its lovely mushrooms. You can serve this dish with rice or naan.

SERVES 4

4 chicken breasts, 200g each, skinless, with wing bone if possible

For the stuffing
200g cup mushrooms
30g butter
1 onion, chopped
salt
freshly ground black pepper
4 gratings of nutmeg
4 tablespoons chopped coriander leaves

For the marinade
1 tablespoon grated fresh ginger
4 garlic cloves
juice of 1 lemon
100ml single cream
50g cream cheese
50ml yoghurt
1/4 teaspoon ground cardamom
   (or 5 green cardamom pods, ground)
salt
freshly ground black pepper

For the sauce
30g cashew nuts
1 tablespoon vegetable oil
2 onions, sliced
100ml Greek yoghurt
50g wild mushrooms, sliced
10g butter
a little chicken stock or water, as
   needed
20ml single cream
1 tablespoon chopped coriander leaves
salt
pepper

To make the stuffing, wash and then boil the mushrooms in water for 4–5 minutes until cooked through. Allow to cool, then finely chop or mince them. Melt the butter in a non-stick pan, add the chopped onions and cook them until they just begin to colour, then add the chopped mushrooms and cook until these are free of any liquid. Season and add the nutmeg and chopped coriander. Leave to cool.

Remove any fat or membrane from the chicken breasts. Make a horizontal incision with a sharp knife just next to the bone side, creating a pocket deep enough to hold the stuffing. Fill a piping bag with the stuffing and gently push the stuffing into the chicken breasts from the point of incision.

Gently press the chicken breast to even out the stuffing.

In a mixing bowl, whisk all the marinade ingredients together to a smooth consistency. Coat the stuffed chicken breasts with the marinade, then leave the chicken in the fridge for a minimum of 4 hours.

Preheat the oven to 200°C/Gas Mark 6. Place the chicken breasts on a greased baking tray and roast for about 15 minutes. The stuffed chicken breasts can also be chargrilled on a barbecue for even better flavour, but ensure that the chicken is cooked all the way through if you choose this method.

To make the sauce, soak the cashew nuts in warm water for 15–20 minutes. In a saucepan, heat the oil, add the sliced onions and fry until golden brown; add the yoghurt and strained cashews. Take the pan off the heat and purée the sauce with a handheld blender until smooth. Sauté the sliced wild mushrooms in butter, pour the sauce in and mix. Add a little water or chicken stock if necessary to get a sauce consistency.

Cut each grilled chicken breast into two or three slices, gently place them into the sauce and simmer for 3–4 minutes, then add the cream and fresh coriander. Serve hot with pulao rice or naan.

SUNEHRI KHASTE

(CRISP SAFFRON AND CORIANDER ROLLS FILLED WITH PANEER AND RED ONIONS)

I wanted to make a light version of a kati roll. This particular variation has a lovely crunchy texture, and is served with a tangy tomato chutney. It has great visual appeal when served with some simple salad leaves. Cut the rolls at a slant for an attractive presentation.

We often make these for cocktail parties – just cut the rolls into smaller slices.

SERVES 4

For the filling
200g paneer
1½ teaspoons vegetable oil
1 teaspoon cumin seeds
1 tablespoon finely chopped or grated ginger
1 green chilli, slit, deseeded and chopped
1 red onion, sliced
½ teaspoon chilli powder
1 teaspoon chaat masala
juice of 1 lemon
2 tablespoons chopped coriander leaves

For the crêpes
a few threads of saffron
2 eggs
100g plain flour, sifted
150ml milk
a pinch of salt
¼ bunch of coriander leaves (approximately 25g), very finely chopped
1 teaspoon vegetable oil
1 tablespoon flour, dissolved in a little water to make a glue

For the crust
200g sevian (vermicelli)
1 egg
1 teaspoon plain flour
salt
freshly ground pepper
oil, for deep-frying (optional)

Put the saffron threads in a small bowl, pour on a tablespoon of warm water and set aside to soak.

To prepare the filling, cut the paneer into matchstick-sized strips. Heat the oil in a wok or a non-stick pan and sprinkle the cumin seeds in. Let them crackle, then add the ginger and green chilli and stir for a minute. Add the red onion, fry for about 2 minutes, then add the paneer, chilli powder, chaat masala, lemon juice and chopped coriander. Gently stir for another minute, then remove from the heat and leave to cool. Check the seasoning.

To make the crêpe batter, whisk the eggs and flour in a mixing bowl until smooth, then add the milk and whisk until a light batter is achieved. Add a pinch of salt, the soaked saffron (with the soaking water) and coriander.

Smear an 18–20-cm crêpe pan or flat non-stick pan with a little oil, and heat to medium. Pour in enough of the batter to just cover the bottom of the pan, cook until the underside shows light-brown spots, then flip to cook the other side for just a few seconds to dry out the batter. Transfer to a plate and continue until all the batter is used.

Divide the filling evenly between the crepes, placing a sausage-shaped portion of filling about a third of the way down each crêpe. Fold the sides of the crepe in, and roll it, from the top, as for spring rolls, and seal the edges with a tablespoon of flour dissolved in a little water to act as a glue.

Crush the vermicelli with both hands in a flat tray. Beat the egg and flour in a bowl and add the seasoning. Dip each roll in egg batter and coat them with vermicelli evenly all over.

Deep fry the rolls in hot oil at 180°C until golden brown, or bake in a preheated oven at 190°C/Gas Mark 5 for 10–12 minutes.

Cut into two on a diagonal, and serve with a fresh leafy salad and tomato chutney.

SHAKARKANDI, GUCHCHI AUR PALAK QUORMA
(SWEET POTATO, MOREL AND SPINACH QUORMA)

This is a good combination of a couple of slightly unusual vegetables, all in a korma sauce. Sweet potatoes are beginning to appear more on Indian menus – we've tried using them in various forms, and this recipe is one of the best. Sweet potato is quite popular in India, mostly as a snack cooked on a char-grill or cooked in the dying embers overnight, seasoned with salt and mango powder. It's also sold as a street food, cut into cubes with spices sprinkled over.

SERVES 4

500g sweet potato, cut into 2-cm dice
salt
ground white pepper
2 tablespoons vegetable oil
12 morels (about 100g)*

For the stuffing
30g paneer
1/4 teaspoon chaat masala
1/4 teaspoon sesame seeds, roasted
a few coriander leaves, chopped
salt
freshly ground black pepper

For the batter
1 egg, white only
1 tablespoon cornflour
1/2 tablespoon plain flour
20ml milk, or as required
oil, for frying

For the sauce
30g charmagaz**
60g cashew nuts
2 tablespoons vegetable oil
3 onions, sliced
1 tablespoon ginger-garlic paste
2 tablespoons Greek yoghurt
large pinch of saffron, soaked in
   1 tablespoon of milk

1/4 teaspoon ground green cardamom
1/4 teaspoon garam masala

To finish
100g spinach, stalks removed, washed
   and shredded
50ml single cream or coconut milk
a few coriander leaves, chopped

* Dried morels can be bought from most supermarkets if fresh ones are hard to find; just soak them in a cup of warm water for an hour, wash in running water to remove grit and then use.
** Charmagaz: A mixture of four seeds – pumpkin, cantaloupe, watermelon and cucumber; sometimes almonds in place of cucumber seeds. If you can't find these, use an extra 30g cashew nuts.

Preheat the oven to 200°C/Gas Mark 6.

Place the sweet potato cubes on a baking tray, sprinkle with salt and freshly ground pepper; drizzle a little oil over and bake in the oven for 30–40 minutes, or until cooked through and golden at the edges.

To prepare the morels, trim off the stalks if they are attached, wash the morels carefully (as they sometimes contain grit), leave them upside-down in a sieve to dry.

For the stuffing, grate the paneer into a bowl, add the chaat masala, sesame seeds and chopped coriander. Mix well and season. Fill the morels with the filling.

For the batter, whisk the egg white in a mixing bowl with a pinch of salt, add the cornflour and plain flour and continue whisking until smooth. Pour in the milk a little at a time and whisk to make a thin but clinging batter of a double-cream consistency.

Heat enough oil in a deep pan or fryer to deep-fry the mushrooms. Dip each morel into the batter and fry them until light golden.

For the sauce, soak the charmagaz and/or cashew nuts in just enough hot water to cover them; leave for 10 minutes and then blend to a paste. Heat the oil in a heavy-based pan, add the sliced onions and fry until golden brown; add the ginger-garlic paste, fry for a minute, then add the yoghurt and cook for a further minute. Remove from the heat and use a handheld blender to purée the sauce until smooth.

Return the sauce to the heat, add the nut paste, soaked saffron and its soaking milk, and the powdered spices; if the sauce is too thick, add water to create the desired consistency. Add the spinach, morels and sweet potatoes to the sauce, check the seasoning, heat for 2–3 minutes over a low heat and pour in the single cream or coconut milk. Sprinkle over some chopped fresh coriander.

Serve with steamed rice or naan.

BEET SAMOSA WITH CARDAMOM ICE-CREAM

This is a common vegetable but presented in a different way – as a dessert. The beetroot is cooked along with khoya and clarified butter, just as if you were making a fudge. It uses khoya as a prime ingredient, and the filling becomes very creamy, as the khoya is like a solid form of condensed milk. This recipe can be used for carrots and for pumpkin in the same way, so you can have three varieties of sweet samosas. Serve with cardamom ice cream.

SERVES 4

For the cardamom ice cream
4 green cardamom pods
250ml milk
250ml single cream
1 teaspoon ground cardamom
4 eggs, yolks only
150g sugar

For the filling
1 tablespoon clarified butter or ghee
200g beetroot, peeled and grated
75g sugar
100g khoya (mawa), grated
1 teaspoon ground green cardamom
1 tablespoon slivered almonds
1 tablespoon slivered pistachios

For the tuile shells
4 eggs, whites only
130g caster sugar
50g plain flour, sifted
zest of 1 lemon
50g butter, melted

For the pastry
1 packet samosa or filo pastry, approximately 200g
1 tablespoon plain flour, dissolved in a little water to make a glue
oil, for frying, or melted butter if baking

To garnish
sprigs of mint
crystallised beetroot (thin slices of beet simmered in sugar syrup and dried in a low oven)

To make the ice cream, split open the green cardamom pods with a rolling pin. Bring the milk and cream to the boil in a pan with the cardamom pods and ground cardamom, then strain.

Whisk the egg yolks and sugar in a mixing bowl. Pour in the strained milk and cream, stirring continuously. Pour into a pan and place over a low heat; cook until the custard thickens and coats the back of a wooden spoon. Do not boil as it will curdle the mixture. (You may use a double boiler if you are not confident cooking over direct heat.) Strain the custard through a fine sieve and allow it to cool. Churn in the ice-cream maker according to the manufacturer's instructions, then transfer to a lidded plastic box and freeze for few hours.

To make the filling, heat the ghee or clarified butter in a heavy-based pan, add the grated beetroot and cook for 4–5 minutes, stirring continually. Add the sugar and cook for a further 4 minutes (on adding the sugar the beet will become soft). Add the grated khoya, ground cardamom and slivered nuts. Remove from the heat and allow to cool.

Preheat the oven to 170°C/Gas Mark 3.

To prepare the tuile shells, whisk the egg whites and sugar until they form soft peaks; add the flour and lemon zest. Whisk in the melted butter. Make a stencil by cutting out a 10-cm diameter hole in the top of an ice-cream box (or a piece of card). Place the stencil on a greased baking tray and place a spoonful of the mixture in the centre. Spread to the edges to form a circle when the stencil is lifted away. Repeat to make four in total. Bake for about 6 minutes or until the tuiles are just light golden in colour. Remove one tuile from the baking tray and place it on the bottom of an upside-down individual brioche or fluted tartlet mould and hold for a few seconds until the tuile starts to set. Continue in this way with the remaining tuiles. Leave on the moulds to cool.

Separate the samosa pastry sheets, fold them into triangles, fill with a spoonful of beetroot mixture and seal with a thick batter of plain flour and warm water as glue. Fry the samosas in hot oil at 180°C for a couple of minutes on each side. (If using filo pastry, cut into strips about 10 x 25cm, place a spoonful of the filling in one corner, fold over diagonally, and continue folding to create a triangle of a couple of layers of the pastry around the filling; brush with melted butter before and after baking in the oven at 180°C/Gas Mark 4 for 15–20 minutes.)

Serve the hot samosas with a scoop of cardamom ice cream in tuile shells, garnished with mint and crystallised beetroot.

ALFRED PRASAD

TAMARIND

Tamarind opened in 1993 and this award-winning Indian restaurant in the heart of stylish Mayfair continues to be at the forefront of the Indian dining revolution. It was one of the first London restaurants to present an uncompromisingly subcontinental fine-dining experience to the general public, sans the red-flock wallpaper and the painting of the Taj Mahal.

The slightly anonymous stained wood and glass façade offers not a clue to the style of this restaurant. A flight of marble stairs with contemporary wrought metalwork leads the guest to a sumptuously chic, old-gold-accented dining room with pillars and antiqued mirrors. The décor has changed little over the years, although those mirrors replaced panels of red fabric. Tamarind offers a hint of exotica with gold-plate chargers and dark-wood chairs. The dining room is a low-lit and tastefully understated complement to confident restaurant design. The ambiance is of calm intimacy without overt Indian accents. The open kitchen is separated from the dining room by gilded glass, so the guests can watch the artistry of the tandoor chefs at work.

Mayfair attracts the great and the good, and its location means that Tamarind regularly plays host to its loyal following of 'men from the ministry' and celebrities, not only from the UK and India but from all over the world. If it had a guest list, it would boast a throng of Bollywood and Hollywood stars who have this restaurant as their dining destination of choice.

Alfred Prasad is the Executive Chef at Tamarind and an acknowledged master of contemporary Indian cuisine in London. Celebrity chef Gordon Ramsay says of him: 'Alfred deserves the widest recognition. A lot of people take Indian food for granted, but this man is always pushing the boundaries.' This said, Chef Prasad would not want to be considered 'cutting edge'. He excels at presenting exceptional Indian food, and traditional dishes new to the European restaurant scene.

Alfred was born in Wardha in Maharashtra, which was a centre for the Indian Independence Movement, and the location of Mahatma Gandhi's Ashram. He was only a year or so old, however, when his father, a doctor, took the family to live in Kathmandu where they stayed for two years. Moving around India, they were eventually to settle in Chennai (formerly Madras) in southern India.

It is not only Alfred's travels that have given him an understanding of that country's complex culinary heritage. He has a background which has allowed him to learn and appreciate his own family's broad cooking culture. His father is a Tamil Brahmin and his mother is Anglo-Indian. A combination of hearty meat dishes from his mother's Hyderabad home, and pure southern vegetarian dishes cooked by his father's mother created a colourful tapestry of flavours to explore. Alfred says he admires the skill of vegetarian cooks in particular – he believes that meat dishes are more easily made rich and sustaining, whereas vegetables often need more thoughtful and imaginative treatment to showcase their best qualities. With two distinct food traditions to draw upon, he was bound to develop broad tastes. He considers that early exposure to a multitude of cuisines encourages children to enjoy a raft of exciting foods, and they will be less likely to become fussy eaters.

Being the second of four children, he had a ready audience for his first culinary efforts. At weekends he would help chop vegetables and peel prawns, and as his family kept chickens he would have the job of plucking feathers and cutting up raw poultry. It was this introduction to ingredients which stood him in good stead when starting his training at the Hotel School in Chennai. He remembers that he was among the more fortunate and confident students, as many of his classmates had never before touched uncooked meat. A six-month period of work experience in the kitchens of the ITC Park Sheraton finally confirmed his career choice.

He graduated from Chennai's Institute of Hotel Management and was handpicked, along with six others in India, to undergo advanced chef training with the ITC Welcome Group at Maurya Sheraton, New Delhi, which is famous for its two flagship restaurants, Dum Pukht and Bukhara. The celebrated Bukhara restaurant, voted Best Restaurant in the World in 2008, specialises in the cuisine of the North-West Frontier. He learnt about Indian fine dining from the late Master Chef Mandanlal Jaiswal. (The menu developed by Chef Jaiswal is still followed at Bukhara.) Alfred says that this man was one of his major culinary influences. Chef Jaiswal ruled the kitchen with an iron fist, but he was a remarkable chef whom Alfred admired for his skill and professionalism.

He moved to London in 1999, having been invited by Namita Punjabi to join the team at Veeraswamy, the oldest

Indian restaurant in London. He stayed for a couple of years, learning about the perceptions and expectations of Indian food that Europeans had at that time.

He joined Tamarind in 2001 as sous-chef, an opportunity that he describes as too good to miss. A year later he took over the reins from Atul Kochhar (see page 11). It was a testament to the skill of this new Executive Chef that he maintained the coveted Michelin star once Atul left to start Benares, a neighbouring restaurant. The chefs still have great respect for one another. Alfred was, at 29, the youngest Indian chef to receive a Michelin star, and staked his unarguable claim as a leader of the new generation of skilled and charismatic Indian chefs. He has retained the Michelin star, and has been the recipient of several other prestigious accolades. Chef Prasad was named in Restaurant magazine's top twenty 'Movers and Shakers' for 2004, and as one of the 'Rising Stars' predicted to make it big in *Delicious* magazine. Alfred was also added to the 2004 Debrett's *People of Today*, the annual publication which lists high achievers in British society. He puts his success down to passion, hard work and solid training.

Alfred is highly respected for his personal and original slant on traditional Indian cuisine. His seasonal dishes take advantage of fresh ingredients to further enhance his recipes, whilst at the same time ensuring that they retain their charm and authenticity. He is not a fan of fusion food, preferring to remain faithful to a wide yet classic palate of Indian spices.

He returns to India as often as he can in order to search for culinary secrets still held in family cookbooks or passed from mother to daughter. The discovery of those hidden gems is what thrills Alfred – food archaeology as well as alchemy – an Indiana Jones of the subcontinental gastronomic arena. He fears that many lesser-known dishes will be lost as fewer people cook at home, preferring to eat out or order take-aways. If Alfred was ever to write a cookbook he says it would be filled with those fast-disappearing dishes. Both he and his wife enjoy seeking out the less-trodden paths around India to restaurants known only by the locals, in the hope of finding an authentic dish that is unknown outside its neighbourhood.

It is important to him to present each meal as a complete sensory experience, and he enjoys being able to celebrate the immense diversity of India through his cooking. He has an evident appreciation of the subtleties of regional cuisine, but is not afraid to use his inventiveness; for example, scallops were unheard of on menus back in India, but Alfred uses what is fresh here in Britain and adapts recipes to incorporate that freshness, flavour and texture.

Alfred Prasad has been a worthy ambassador for the fine-dining Indian revolution in London, and continues to inspire his appreciative audience.

Tamarind
20 Queen Street, Mayfair, London W1J 5PR
Phone 020 7629 3561 **www.tamarindrestaurant.com**

FISH CURRY

This is my take on the best bits of a few southern Indian regions combined in this fish curry, with its delicately spiced, distinct flavours of mustard, curry leaves and fresh ginger. Being tomato-based (traditional Indian tomatoes act as souring agents, unlike the salad tomatoes in Britain), the tartness is balanced with coconut milk which smoothes out the sauce on the palate. This is the kind of fish curry that I grew up eating. Best with steamed rice; some like it spicier, some milder – the ratio of the green chilli and chilli powder to the coconut milk will result in a more fiery or a sweeter sauce.

This is best made using an oily fish. Kingfish is rarely available outside Billingsgate market, so trout would be a fantastic alternative; mackerel and herring would also work well.

SERVES 4

4 tablespoons vegetable oil
½ teaspoon fenugreek seeds
½ teaspoon black mustard seeds
2 sprigs of curry leaves
1 tablespoon finely chopped ginger
2–3 onions, finely chopped
½ teaspoon ground turmeric
3–4 tomatoes, puréed
500ml hot water
½–1 teaspoon red chilli powder
2 tablespoons ground cumin
2 tablespoons ground coriander
800g fish cubes (preferably kingfish, but see introduction)
120ml coconut milk
leaves from ½ bunch of coriander (approximately 50g)

Heat the oil in a heavy-based frying pan over medium heat, throw in the fenugreek seeds (they tend to burn very quickly, so make sure the oil is not too hot). Add the mustard seeds next and allow them to crackle before adding the curry leaves, ginger and chopped onions. Stir occasionally and cook until the onions are golden-brown.

Add the turmeric, sauté, then add the puréed tomato and water, followed by the remaining ground spices. Boil over a high heat for 20–25 minutes, by which time the volume of liquid will have reduced and oil will begin to float on top of the mixture.

Turn down the heat, add the cubes of fish and simmer for about 8–10 minutes or until the fish is done.

Add the coconut milk and stir gently. Bring to the boil, then remove the pan from the heat, add the chopped coriander and serve hot.

POTATO AND PEAS CURRY

This is a recipe from my wife, who got it from her mother, and it's a recipe from Sind province, the area around Karachi, which is now in Pakistan. Their food was originally very distinct, although over the years it has absorbed local flavours, spices and techniques, so Sindi food is unrecognisable from the original, but it has greatly enriched the Indian food repertoire.

This is such a comfort food – a curried version of 'potatoes and peas'. It's just a question of controlling the heat, timing and volume of water; the end result is always rich. Cooking the potatoes from raw also helps to flavour the gravy, and it doesn't matter if the pieces of potato are a little overcooked because the starch will thicken the gravy which is excellent mopped up with bread or roti. Leftovers can be dried a little more and used as a sandwich filling or in a wrap.

SERVES 4

2 tablespoons vegetable oil
pinch of asafoetida
$^1/_2$ teaspoon cumin seeds
$^1/_2$ teaspoon chopped fresh ginger
1–2 green chillies, finely chopped
1 sprig of curry leaves
600g potatoes, cut into cubes
  (see Note)
$^1/_2$ teaspoon ground turmeric
salt
4 tomatoes, puréed
$^1/_4$ teaspoon chilli powder
$^1/_2$ teaspoon ground coriander
150ml water
4 tablespoons green peas
1 tablespoon chopped coriander leaves

Heat the oil in a saucepan over a low heat, add the asafoetida and cumin seeds and sauté until lightly browned. Add the ginger, green chillies and curry leaves and sauté for 2 minutes. Add the potatoes and sauté for a further 2 minutes, then add the turmeric and salt and sauté for another minute.

Add the puréed tomatoes, chilli powder and ground coriander, mix well and cook over a low heat for a further 2 minutes. Pour in the water and stir well, cover with a lid, put on medium heat and simmer for 10 minutes, or until the potatoes are cooked. Now throw in the green peas and chopped coriander, stir well, cover and simmer for a further 5 minutes.

Check the seasoning and serve hot.

Note: The cooking time depends upon the size of your potato dice: the recipe assumes 1-cm dice. If you prefer larger dice, you might need to add more water to allow for the extra cooking time.

MASALA SCRAMBLED EGGS

A variation of a Parsi classic breakfast dish known as 'akuri'. The Parsis are migrants from Persia, and they have tremendously enriched the food and culture of India. It's like your regular scrambled egg but with *lots* more flavour, and the tomatoes give it a runnier texture. Excellent on toast or with chapatis, or as a sandwich filler. With the spices toned down it's kid-friendly food. It's so versatile.

SERVES 4

4 eggs
120ml milk
2 tablespoons vegetable oil
1 onion, chopped
1–2 green chillies, chopped
$^1/_2$ teaspoon chopped fresh ginger
$^1/_2$ teaspoon ground turmeric
$^3/_4$ teaspoon chilli powder, or to taste
2 tomatoes, chopped
salt
leaves from $^1/_2$ bunch of coriander
   (approximately 50g), chopped

Beat the eggs in a bowl with the milk.

Heat the oil in a non-stick pan over a medium heat, add the onion and green chillies and sauté for 3–4 minutes until the onions are translucent. Add the chopped ginger, turmeric and chilli powder and sauté for a further 5 minutes.

Add the tomatoes and cook until they are soft, adding a little water if necessary. Add the beaten egg and milk mixture and salt, and cook stirring constantly over a medium heat until the eggs are done.

Garnish with chopped coriander leaves. Best served with toast or chapatis for a delicious Indian breakfast.

GREEN PEPPER PULAO

Passed down from my Mum's side of the family, she used to refer to this as 'Spanish rice' because the sweet pepper is also called the Spanish pepper in India. Essentially it is a very flavoursome pulao, made with or without a stock cube for extra flavour, sweetened with browned onions, tomatoes and peppers. The peppers are added at the last stage of cooking to retain colour and crunch. This isn't like a biryani which is a meal on its own, but an alternative pulao for special occasions. If you wish, finish with coconut milk. The aromas when you open the pot are exquisite.

SERVES 4

500g basmati rice
20ml vegetable oil
1 teaspoon cumin seeds
2 cinnamon sticks
3 green cardamom pods
4 cloves
1–2 bay leaves
900ml water
salt
1 tablespoon ghee
1 green pepper, diced
1 tomato, quartered
25g fried onions (optional)
leaves from ½ bunch of coriander
   (approximately 50g), chopped

Wash and soak the rice in water for about 10 minutes.

Heat the oil in a heavy-based pan that has a tight-fitting lid over a medium heat. Add the cumin seeds, cinnamon, cardamom, cloves and bay leaves and sauté for 2 minutes.

Strain the soaked rice and add to the pan. Sauté for a couple of minutes, add the water, then salt to taste. Add the ghee and stir gently with a spatula or wooden spoon. Leave to simmer over a low heat for 8–10 minutes, or until most of the water has been absorbed by the rice.

Add the diced green pepper, quarters of tomato and fried onions (optional). Gently stir once again. Cover with a tight-fitting lid, reduce the heat to its lowest level and leave to simmer for 10 minutes. Turn off the heat and leave to stand for a further 10 minutes with the lid removed.

Transfer to a serving bowl and garnish with chopped coriander leaves.

CHICKEN CURRY

A perfect match with the Green Pepper Pulao (see page 249). If entertaining friends, these would form a very good core to the meal, with a couple of salads and another vegetable, and lentils perhaps. This is a simple recipe, best cooked with chicken on the bone (if using boneless chicken, add a stock cube to add a little more flavour). Traditionally it's more of a stew, so when cooked on the bone and gently simmered, the sauce is naturally more flavoursome.

There are several variations, for example, finishing it with coconut milk gives it a creaminess; ground fresh coconut gives it more body, like a khorma; you can use nut pastes like cashew paste or almond paste to make it richer for a special occasion; or add baby spinach leaves at the last minute to add variety.

SERVES 4

4 tablespoons vegetable oil
2–3 3-cm cinnamon sticks
3–4 green cardamom pods
4–5 cloves
2–3 onions, finely chopped
2 green chillies, chopped (optional)
1 tablespoon ginger paste
1 tablespoon garlic paste
$\frac{1}{2}$ teaspoon ground turmeric
1 teaspoon red chilli powder
4 teaspoons ground cumin
2 tablespoons ground coriander
3–4 tomatoes, puréed
8 chicken drumsticks (about 800g),
  skin removed
500ml hot water
$\frac{1}{2}$ teaspoon garam masala (optional)
chopped leaves from $\frac{1}{2}$ bunch of
  coriander (approximately 50g

Heat the oil in a heavy-based saucepan over a medium heat, then add the cinnamon, cardamom and cloves. Sauté for 30 seconds, then add the chopped onions (and chopped green chillies, if using) and sauté over medium heat, stirring occasionally, until golden brown.

Add the ginger and garlic pastes, stir well for a couple of minutes, then add the turmeric, chilli, cumin and ground coriander and sauté for a further 5 minutes. Add the puréed tomatoes, stir and allow to simmer for 10–15 minutes or until the oil separates from the masala and begins to float on top of the mixture.

Add the chicken drumsticks and cook over high heat for 5 minutes, stirring constantly. Add the hot water, bring to a boil, cover with a lid and then simmer until the chicken is done (approximately 20 minutes).

Sprinkle with the garam masala powder (optional) and chopped coriander leaves, check the seasoning and serve hot.

KaRam SeThi

The name Trishna may be familiar to anyone who has travelled to Mumbai. Trishna London is the sister restaurant of Trishna in Mumbai, which is widely acknowledged to be one of the best seafood restaurants in the world – quite a reputation to uphold.

The London premises were originally an Italian restaurant, and the Trishna team had to take it back to basics and start again. The London premises were originally an Italian restaurant, and although Trishna's interior designers completely revamped it, it does still retain the cool colours reminiscent of the southern Mediterranean: contemporary lines with little evidence that this is an Indian restaurant, apart from some evocative 1930s travel posters inviting one to visit a country populated, it seems, by beautiful dusky water-carriers.

Trishna's interior was created by B3 Designers. Its clean and minimalist feel is offset by tumbled marble, smoked oak, brickwork and glass. Owner and Head Chef Karam Sethi explained, 'I *wanted* it not to scream "Indian restaurant" at the customer, but to reflect the seafood theme by being light and fresh. Chairs are from Denmark and the lights are by a Finnish designer.' Trishna has an enviable location in a quiet side street in the stylish and vibrant neighbourhood of Marylebone, which has become a hub for those seeking high-end boutique shopping and inspired eateries. Trishna's outside seating gives a nod to sunny southern Europe.

Karam Sethi was born and brought up in London. His parents are from Delhi, but have lived in Britain for over 35 years. His stays in India have given him a love for his gastronomic heritage, and he obviously has an appreciation of fine European cuisine. He is a lad with a culinary grasp of two continents. 'My interest in Indian cooking stemmed from always having cooks in the house – at my grandparents' home in India – and having three meals a day prepared by the chefs, with fresh vegetables coming into the kitchen every day.'

He was first inspired by European food during family holidays to France: 'We used to go to Normandy every summer, and Normandy is full of sweetcorn and vegetable fields. My mother used to stop the car, jump out, dive into the corn fields, and come out ten minutes later having collected a basketful. Sometimes it was onions, and I remember putting them on the barbecue, and the sweetness of those onions is the best thing!

'So I always watched her cook, and remember, by about age 11 or 12, getting into the kitchen where she would teach me the basics of Indian food. She was my main inspiration.' Trishna is very much a family-run restaurant. 'I have a brother who deals with the financial side of the restaurant, and my sister is helping out with the administration. We have all enjoyed eating out at good restaurants, but there has been no formal family background in catering. We used to go to Gaylord on Mortimer Street, and at that time – the late 80s and early 90s – it was considered to be the best North Indian restaurant around.' Karam was introduced to an even wider spectrum of cuisines – Thai and Malaysian – when he had the opportunity to travel to the Far East, while more time spent in France had him sampling French restaurant fare, although he didn't have the opportunity to enjoy those same dining experiences in London until he was in his late teens.

When Karam was 15, his school sent him on a work-experience' trip. He went to Stuttgart for a month and worked in a hotel as commis-chef, gutting and scaling fish, de-boning meat and poultry and dealing with offal, day in, day out. It was a real eye-opener. He realised the need to be passionate about what you are doing. 'From then on, I wanted to get up in the morning and come to the kitchen, it was something I loved doing.'

While Karam was still a teenager, he took a gap year and went to Delhi to work in the celebrated Bukhara restaurant at the Maurya Sheraton. 'I had a place at university, but at the last minute I decided I wanted to go into food. That year really taught me the basics of how to run a kitchen.'

There were a couple of tandoori chefs at Bukhara who took the 'English' Karam under their experienced wings and taught him everything: 'These two simple guys were from the village of Dehradun and had been there for years. They were world-record naan-makers, turning out 600 naans per hour or something like that! It was tough being a Brit going into the kitchens, but these guys made the effort to get to know me and help me out.'

When he returned to Europe, Karam took a Business Management degree at university and worked at various restaurants in London and in Marbella, later working at Zuma Japanese restaurant in Knightsbridge for a year.

'Then I teamed up with a fellow head chef and set up a catering company serving Japanese and Indian food. I was looking for a venue for my own restaurant during that time, and after 18 months opened here in November 2008.' He had travelled to Delhi, where he was looking to open a restaurant, but soon realised he was too young to achieve that. Fortunately he had been introduced to the owner of Trishna in Mumbai, who was considering opening something similar outside India. That entrepreneur did not have the contacts to set up a restaurant in London, so Karam made a brand agreement with him whereby ownership would be independent and he would be able to use the Trishna name. It was both a help and a hindrance, as some people came into Trishna London expecting something similar to the food served in Mumbai, but of course so many of the ingredients are completely different.

The main menu inspiration is from the coastal regions of India, so there's a lot of seafood, as well as game and poultry. The spicing is the kind you'd find in the home, and there are never more than two or three elements on the plate – it's not over-complicated, just simple and tasty food where the flavour of the main ingredient comes through and the spices act as an enhancer. Trishna has built and maintained its culinary status on that very ethos.

Karam says his biggest influence has been working in Zuma. 'The success of that place is unbelievable, probably the greatest turnover of any restaurant in London, the organisation, the kitchen set-up, the systems, the sheer volume of food served every night. It also taught me about the simplicity of food: flavourful, seasoned well, presented in a "clean" manner.'

Trishna has a good client base. Mondays to Wednesdays they entertain residents from Marylebone, and some of those enthusiasts may come two or three times a week. There is a good mix of corporate workers from the City, Baker Street, Bond Street and Mayfair. At weekends they see a lot of Indians and a lot of clients from North London. Hariyali Bream has been on the menu since they opened, as have Lamb Chops, and Seafood Biryani. The signature dish here, as well as at the Mumbai Trishna, is the Crab in Butter, Garlic and Black Pepper – the recipe which made the Mumbai restaurant famous.

At home on Sundays, Karam likes eating and cooking simple things: challa bread, a fry-up, club sandwiches, and snacky things, nothing elaborate. Karam and his two siblings might be at home with Mum at the weekend, or the three 'kids' might go out to a restaurant. It's a change for him to be front of house and enjoying food cooked by others.

Trishna is a success, but what next? 'For the future, I am looking for a second place in Soho, along Goan lines – Goan tapas, maybe. There are lots of similarities between a Spanish tapas menu and a typical Goan menu.'

Trishna might have taken the name of an iconic restaurant in India, but Karam has successfully carved out a reputation for his own restaurant that is becoming every bit as enviable. The name 'Trishna' is said to mean hunger, thirst or desire, all of which will be sated by a visit here.

Trishna
15–17 Blandford Street, London W1U 3DG
Phone 020 7935 5624 **www.trishnalondon.com**

All these dishes have been on the restaurant menu, and all the main ingredients are British: wild bream, wild sea bass, Devonshire pollack, wild Yorkshire guinea fowl, Dorset crab, Maldon oysters, which reflects the philosophy of the restaurant.

HYDERABADI FISH TIKKA WITH DILL RAITA

This has quite a peppery flavour. You get a sweetness and nuttiness from the butter, and the heat of the pepper is tempered by the raita. This could also be cooked whole in a fish-cage on the barbecue. Alternative fish are trout, mackerel and salmon.

SERVES 4

500g gurnard fillet, cut into 8 equal pieces, pin-boned and scaled

For the marinade
15g black peppercorns, roasted in a dry pan for 30 seconds to 1 minute until they give off their peppery aroma, then coarsely ground
3 tablespoons butter, melted
½ teaspoon ground turmeric
1 tablespoon lemon juice

For the dill raita
4 tablespoons finely chopped dill
2 teaspoons salt
150ml Greek yoghurt

Mix all the marinade ingredients together in a non-metallic bowl. Coat the fish with the mixture, cover and marinate in the fridge for 30 minutes.

Preheat the oven to 230°C/Gas Mark 8.

Transfer the fish and any adhering marinade to a baking tray and bake for 7–8 minutes.

To make the dill raita, simply combine the ingredients and serve alongside the gurnard tikka.

COASTAL FRIED FISH, CHIPS AND CRUSHED PEAS

The dish is my take on British fish, chips and peas. The subtle spicing from the coriander and hint of green chilli in the crumb, coupled with the freshness of the peas and crunch of the chips, is a perfect partnership. Cod or haddock would also work well if pollack is unavailable.

SERVES 4

For the coastal fried fish
2 tablespoons ginger-garlic paste
1 tablespoon lemon juice
4 pollack fillets (about 400g total), pin-boned and skin removed
2 tablespoons cornflour
4 tablespoons water
1 tablespoon finely diced ginger
3 cloves garlic, finely diced
½–1 tablespoon diced green chilli, or to taste
2 tablespoons chopped coriander leaves
1 shallot, finely diced
1 teaspoon salt, or to taste
2 teaspoons coriander seeds, roasted and crushed
60g Panko breadcrumbs (crunchy dried Japanese breadcrumbs)
vegetable oil, for deep frying

For the chips (salli)
2 large King Edward potatoes
2 teaspoons chaat masala
2 teaspoons chopped coriander leaves

For the crushed peas
250g petits pois, thawed
1 teaspoon chopped mint
½ teaspoon chopped green chilli
1 teaspoon diced ginger
salt
2 teaspoons finely diced banana shallot

Cut the potatoes into matchsticks. Soak in cold water for an hour, then drain and pat dry on kitchen paper. Deep fry in oil heated to 190°C for 3–4 minutes, then drain on kitchen paper and set aside.

Put all the ingredients for the crushed peas, apart from the banana shallot, in a blender and grind to a coarse paste. Stir in the banana shallot dice and set aside.

Mix the ginger-garlic paste with the lemon juice in a non-metallic bowl; add the pollack fillets and turn to coat.

While the fish is marinating, combine the cornflour, water, ginger, garlic, green chilli, chopped coriander and shallot to make a paste. Add salt to taste. Coat the pollack with this second marinade, and set aside for 30 minutes.

Combine the coriander seeds and panko on a plate, and coat the pollack on both sides with the mixture.

Deep fry the fish in oil heated to 190°C, in a wok or other suitable fryer, for 3 minutes, turning once, until both sides are golden brown.

When ready to serve, re-fry the chips for 30 seconds and drain them on kitchen paper. Garnish with chaat masala and coriander.

Serve the crushed pea mixture and chips alongside the fried pollack.

COASTAL SPICED GUINEA FOWL
WITH A MASOOR LENTIL SALSA

The main flavour is heat, not from chilli, but from cloves, and a subtlety from the star anise. The brown Masoor lentil salsa is quite cooling and refreshing after the smoky guinea fowl.

SERVES 4

4 guinea fowl supremes
4 teaspoons lemon juice
salt
4 teaspoons ginger-garlic paste
4 star anise
2 dried Kashmiri chillies
6 cloves
1 tablespoon fennel seeds
2 tablespoons mustard oil
1 tablespoon Greek yoghurt
melted butter, for basting

For the mantoor lentil salsa
200g masoor lentils
2 tablespoons diced red onion
2 tablespoon diced tomato (seedless)
2 teaspoons chopped green chilli
4 teaspoons finely chopped fresh
   ginger
1/2 teaspoon salt, or to taste
2 tablespoons mustard oil
2 tablespoons chopped coriander
   leaves
fennel cress, to garnish

To make the salsa, soak the lentils in cold water for 1 hour, then drain. Place the lentils in a pan of boiling water and cook for 10 minutes on a high heat. The lentils should be *al dente*. Drain and cool. Combine all the other ingredients with the lentils and set aside.

Coat the guinea fowl with the lemon juice, salt and ginger-garlic paste, and set aside for 1 hour.

To make the spice marinade, dry roast the star anise, chillies, cloves and fennel seeds in a pan. Remove the spices from the pan and allow to cool. Grind these in a spice grinder (a coffee grinder is fine) to a fine powder.

Combine the mustard oil, yoghurt, spice powder and salt to taste in a bowl to form a smooth paste, and coat the guinea fowl supremes. Set aside for 1 hour.

Preheat the oven to 200°C/Gas Mark 6.

Roast the guinea fowl for 12 minutes. Remove from the oven and leave to rest under foil for a further 12 minutes. Baste the cooked meat with a little melted butter.

Serve the guinea fowl with the lentil salsa alongside, garnished with fennel cress.

HARIYALI BREAM WITH TOMATO KACHUMBER

The tang of the kachumber against the bream is quite subtle, so it cleans the palate. Wild bass, halibut or gurnard are good alternatives if bream isn't available. In the restaurant we cook our tomatoes in a tava over the tandoor, but I have adapted the recipe so you can use the oven.

SERVES 4

4 bream fillets, pin-boned and scaled, skin on

For the marinade
4 tablespoons baby spinach paste (spinach leaves puréed in a blender)
2 green chillies, chopped
8 tablespoons coriander paste (leaves and stalks puréed in a blender)
4 teaspoons ginger-garlic paste
2½ tablespoons mustard oil
1 teaspoon dry fenugreek leaf (kasoori methi powder)
4 tablespoons Greek yoghurt
½ teaspoon ground turmeric
salt

For the tomato kachumber
16 baby plum tomatoes, cut in half
1 tablespoon diced ginger
2 spring onions, diced
1 tablespoon mustard oil
1 tablespoon lime juice
3 tablespoons tomato pulp
   (roast 4 tomatoes on a baking tray
   for 20–30 minutes at 170°C/
   Gas Mark 3 or until softened
   through. Remove the skin and seeds
   and chop the flesh into a pulp)
salt

Combine all the marinade ingredients in a blender to form a smooth glossy paste. Put the bream in a non-metallic dish and coat with the marinade, cover and place in the fridge for 2–3 hours.

Preheat the oven to 230°C/Gas Mark 8. Transfer the fish and any adhering marinade to a baking tray and bake for 10 minutes.

To make the kachumber, mix all the ingredients together, season to taste and serve alongside the bream.

JASBINDER SINGH, CLAUDIO PULZE AND LUIGI GAUDINO

ZAIKA

The name Zaika means 'fine flavour' in one of the local South Indian dialects and this restaurant has been known for that since its opening in 1999. With 85 seats, plus another 30 at the bar, it's not the largest of restaurants, but it has great architecture and ambiance. It's a Grade-II-listed former bank building which would be described as having 'many original features, with a striking dining room' if you saw it in an estate agent's window. It was built when Kensington was being developed in the 1850s.

Claudio Pulze has never described himself as an entrepreneur. 'One particular reviewer branded me as that – Michael Winner, about 15 years ago – but I only do restaurants, it's all I have ever done.' Claudio studied at catering school in Italy: 'I ended up in this business as a punishment from my father. I wasn't particularly good at school, and so one summer my father decided to send me to work. A 5-star hotel had just opened in Turin; a neighbour of ours was a curtain-maker for the hotel, and suggested that I work there for the three months over the summer.'

Once he got there he fell in love – not just with the food, but with the beautiful cars, the beautiful people, the chandeliers and the glamour. Claudio has worked all over the world, and in 1974 he came to London. A friend of a friend was opening a restaurant in Knightsbridge; Claudio had a little money, so they pooled their resources. Now he says he is just a restaurateur who can't stop opening restaurants!

'When I started, a couple of waiters and I had a few thousand pounds saved up between us, and we were able to start a business. Now, you go to a bank to open up a 50- or 60-seater restaurant, which will cost you six or seven hundred thousand pounds, and they won't lend you the money – they probably wouldn't even lend to me, never mind to two unknown waiters with a good idea. The process of natural evolution has been taken away.'

Claudio loves food and he has broad tastes, but the common denominator is that the food must be good. 'To me, food is like the clothes I wear: today I might wear jeans, tomorrow shorts, the day after, linen trousers; we may put labels on food, but to me there is good food, bad food and insignificant food, food just to fill the stomach. Good food does not have to be fancy food, or complicated, it has to be the best possible ingredients treated with the utmost respect.'

Claudio was introduced to Vineet Bhatia, the chef at Star of India (see page 229) at that time. He thought his food was fantastic, and they agreed that they would open a restaurant together. Claudio was offered a site in Fulham Road, and Zaika was born.

'Those were the days when talent could flourish. It has become much more difficult now. I know young people who have an equal amount of talent to those celebrated chefs back then. But times have changed. London has the most sophisticated restaurant scene anywhere in the world. New York is pretty close, but they don't have the variety that London has. London is unique: every cuisine is represented here at top level.'

The present address was once Claudio's British restaurant, but he moved Zaika from its original location in Fulham to take advantage of the smart neighbourhood and stunning architecture. 'This is a listed building, and we can't fix anything to the walls. But I think people attach too much importance to the decor. It's a matter of personal taste: you can spend five million pounds fitting out a restaurant, and a customer will walk in and say "Ugh, tacky!" I've done it myself. To me, a restaurant has to feel comfortable, and has to serve a purpose.'

Zaika is impressive and manages seamlessly to marry Gothic Victorian stonework with statues of Ganesh. There are many of these carvings of the 'remover of obstacles', and this elephant god is obviously taking care of the restaurant. He gazes over a cosy and stylish space that is popular with Asians as well as Europeans. 'Affluent Indian people have to be comfortable with the ingredients, and find something that they recognise. So a slab of steak with a slice of foie gras on top – how many Indians would eat that? It's not a question of authenticity: to serve that kind of dish is going against the traditions, the culture of a country. If you do that everything gets so diluted that you can't recognise the core.' Claudio appreciates the cultural constraints, but is nevertheless eager to introduce his audience to new concepts, and Western ingredients given an Indian twist

Luigi Gaudino is general manager at Zaika. 'When I came to London, I didn't speak much English so I joined a small restaurant. For three years I spent all my spare time in bookshops reading everything I could find about wine, learning English at the same time.' Luigi joined Zaika in 2002; he was already working at Claudio's restaurant in Jermyn Street, Al Duca. Zaika had just been awarded a Michelin star – in 2001 Zaika and Tamarind (see page 241) were the very first Indian restaurants to gain one. Luigi is a talented sommelier and is responsible for the restaurant's creditable wine list.

'At that time there were few Indian restaurants with an extensive wine list. We designed tasting menus with wine pairings and since day one, the restaurant has tried to present Indian food in a different way: Indian "nouvelle cuisine" perhaps – Indian ingredients, but plated, rather than sharing dishes. We use only three, perhaps a

Zaika owner, Claudio Pulze

General manager, Luigi Gaudino

maximum of four, spices; they are a catalyst, rather than the main ingredients,' explains Luigi. 'Everyone knows that, traditionally, beer and lassi go well with Indian food, but even beer doesn't work with very spicy dishes – you just burn your palate! So we followed common sense, and the European philosophy of matching wines to food, and that has been a great success. We use some ingredients that are not Indian, but with Indian spices. We must not forget that we are in London, and London is a very cosmopolitan city, which allows us to add those sorts of twists. Desserts

are not a big part of Indian restaurant culture, so we play with ingredients to take a familiar dish and present it in a more modern way. We are not inventing anything – there's not much left to invent these days – but you have to be creative all the time.'

But obviously food is the key to the success of any restaurant – or at least it should be. Chef Jasbinder Singh is very much a man who is content leaving the front-of-house to Luigi, but he is passionate about his food and dedicated to presenting the best. 'There are some restaurants that are not doing as well as they could – serving chicken tikka masala, using frozen food, especially frozen fish (which is just like cotton wool!), and ordering their food just once a week. The most important thing is job satisfaction – if you are not dedicated to your work you can't give your best.

'I got a chance to work with the Oberoi Group at the Hotel Cecil in Shimla. Later I was given the opportunity to cook at the house of His Holiness the Dalai Lama, and I worked there as head chef for five years, learning about Tibetan, Indian and Thai cuisine.' Cooking for large numbers doesn't strike terror into this shy man: Jasbinder prepared food for all the visitors to the Dalai Lama, sometimes as many as 15,000 people in a day!

Chef Jasbinder has embraced some non-Indian ingredients. 'We use olive oil in place of ghee, for its healthy properties, lighter food but still rich, and cleaner and more delicate on the palate; yoghurt instead of double cream as it is easier to digest.' Jasbinder's food is refined and the presentation memorable. He introduces innovation and imagination to his dishes and also some humour. A smoked-chicken cigar with a garnish of matches is surely unique to Zaika.

High ceilings, dark wood panels and silk upholstery make this a chic and calming retreat. This former bank building must have given confidence to its investors, as it now does to its diners.

Zaika
1 Kensington High Street, London W8 5NP
Phone 020 7795 6533 **www.zaika-restaurant.co.uk**

CHICKEN MOMOES

Instead of making your own dough, you can substitute ready-made Chinese wonton wrappers. The chicken stuffing can also be formed into balls without the wrapping and steamed. These are no longer traditional Tibetan Momoes, but make a delicious cocktail nibble.

SERVES 4

For the dough
250g plain flour, sifted
4–5 tablespoons water, or as necessary, for kneading

For the filling
250g chicken mince
salt
25g red onion, finely chopped
2 green chillies, or to taste, finely chopped

For the sauce
20ml vegetable oil
2 garlic cloves, finely chopped
2 baby shallots, finely chopped
20g celery, finely chopped
20ml tomato ketchup or tomato sauce

For the garnish
2 spring onions, finely sliced
5 tablespoons light soy sauce (optional)
1 teaspoon sugar (optional)

Sieve the flour into a mixing bowl. Make a well in the middle, add a little water and knead to a stiff dough – this should be dry and pliable, but not sticky.

To make the stuffing, put the minced chicken in a bowl, add salt to taste, the red onion and chillies, and mix well.

Divide the dough into approximately 30 balls. Roll each between moistened hands to make a small disc, about 5-7cm in diameter. Put about a teaspoon of the stuffing mixture in the centre, raise the sides to make a round dumpling shape and crimp to seal; or place the stuffing to one side of the disc and fold over to make a half-moon pasty shape.

Using a steamer, or a wok and large bamboo steaming basket, or a colander with a lid over a large pan, bring water as required for your method to a boil and steam the dumplings for 8–10 minutes.

To make the sauce, heat the oil in a saucepan over a medium heat, add the chopped garlic and sauté for 10 seconds. Add the shallots and celery and cook for 2 minutes. Add the tomato ketchup or sauce and mix well, then add the steamed dumplings to the sauce, and turn to coat.

Serve garnished with chopped spring onion.

As an alternative, add soy sauce and sugar to the cooked sauce and serve as a dip for the dumplings.

NILGIRI KORMA

Nilgiri is a range of mountains in the Western Ghats, Tamil Nadu. The mountains are green and so is this korma. Cook this dish carefully – if you add the green coriander paste too early, it will turn black due to the effect of the heat on the coriander. To achieve a rich sauce we use melon seeds, which aren't a common ingredient, but they do combine well with the fresh coconut. If you can't find melon seeds, just add more coconut; the finished dish will be slightly different, but still delicious. In India the meat is mutton or goat, but here it's lamb.

SERVES 4

75g melon seeds (buy them with husks removed), or pine nuts
100g fresh coconut, grated
500g diced leg of lamb, fat trimmed
75ml yoghurt
leaves from a bunch of coriander (approximately 100g)
2–3 green chillies, or to taste, roughly chopped
60ml vegetable oil
20 small green cardamom pods, cracked
4 cloves
100g onions, finely chopped
15g ginger-garlic paste
5 teaspoons ground coriander
salt
5-cm piece fresh ginger, peeled and cut into juliennes (small matchsticks), to garnish

Soak the melon seeds or pine nuts in a small bowl of water for 15–20 minutes. Drain and put the seeds into a blender or mini-processor with the coconut and blend to a smooth paste, adding water as necessary (about 3 tablespoons).

Place the lamb in a non-metallic bowl. Coat with the yoghurt, cover with clingfilm and put in the fridge or somewhere cool for 3–4 hours.

Put the coriander leaves and green chillies into a blender or mini-processor and blend to a smooth paste, adding a little water if necessary.

Heat the oil in a heavy-based pan over a medium heat. Add the cardamom pods and cloves and, after a few seconds, when they start to crackle, add the onion and fry for 5–6 minutes until golden brown. Add the ginger-garlic paste and ground coriander and fry for 15 seconds. Add the marinated lamb and cook over a low heat for about 15 minutes, then add salt to taste.

Stir in the coconut paste and continue to cook for 30 minutes. When the lamb is fully cooked and tender, add the coriander paste and stir to combine. Check the seasoning.

Serve garnished with ginger juliennes and with basmati rice or Indian bread.

CHICKEN THUKPA

This Tibetan dish is a combination of vegetables and noodles – I'd advise using Chinese noodles, as these are the easiest to cook. This recipe uses leeks, green onions and carrots, but green peppers would also work. You can add chicken or lamb, as you wish. The quality of the dish depends on the quality of the chicken stock. It's said to be very good for anyone not feeling very well – it's a bit like a Tibetan 'Jewish chicken soup'.

SERVES 4

450g Chinese noodles
60ml vegetable oil
10g fresh ginger, finely chopped
3 large cloves garlic, finely chopped
1–2 green chillies or to taste, finely chopped
200g chicken breasts, boneless, skinless, cut across into thin strips
200g cabbage, finely shredded
50g carrots, shredded
2 leeks, finely chopped
600ml chicken stock
2 teaspoons cornflour
salt
4 spring onions, finely sliced, to garnish

Boil the noodles according to the instructions on the packet, then refresh them in cold water, drain and keep aside.

Heat the oil in a large frying pan over a medium heat; add the chopped ginger, garlic and chillies. Sauté for a minute until the garlic is just starting to turn golden brown. Add the chicken, cook for 1 minute, then add the shredded vegetables and sauté for a further minute.

Add the chicken stock and bring to the boil. Add salt to taste and the boiled noodles. Mix well. As soon as it returns to the boil, remove from the heat. Mix the cornflour with 2 teaspoons of water and add to the soup. Bring back to the boil.

Serve hot, garnished with the spring onions.

MONKFISH ACHARI MASALA

This dish calls for a firm fish as it needs to hold together after frying – halibut would also work well.
The main aim of the lemon juice is to bring a freshness to the dish. My Mum advised me not to deep-fry the fish, but to shallow-fry it in mustard oil pre-heated almost to smoking point. The oil adds to the pickling spice flavours.

SERVES 4

15g ginger-garlic paste
2 teaspoons caraway seeds
10ml lemon juice
salt
4 monkfish fillets (about 500g in total)
25g gram flour
100ml mustard oil
coriander leaves, to garnish

For the sauce
20ml mustard oil
1 teaspoon asafoetida
2 red chillies, or to taste
2 teaspoons black mustard seeds
2 teaspoons fennel seeds
2 teaspoons onion seeds
100g onion, finely chopped
2 teaspoons ground coriander
1 teaspoon ground turmeric
75g tomatoes, chopped
10ml lemon juice
10ml white vinegar
1 tablespoon sugar
salt

Mix the ginger-garlic paste, caraway seeds and lemon juice together in a bowl and add salt to taste. Then add the monkfish into this mixture, stir to coat and set aside to marinate in the fridge for 30 minutes.

Sprinkle the gram flour over the fish, mix well to coat and leave for a further 30 minutes.

Heat the cooking oil in a shallow non-stick pan over a medium heat and fry the fish for a few minutes until the fish has changed colour to the centre and cooked through; remove to a plate covered with kitchen paper, and keep warm.

To make the sauce, heat the mustard oil in a frying pan over a medium heat until shimmering, and add the asafoetida. Stir for a few seconds – be careful not to let it burn. Add the whole chillies and the mustard, fennel and onion seeds. When they start to crackle, add the onion and sauté until golden brown.

Reduce the heat to low. Add the ground coriander and turmeric and cook for 15 seconds, then add the tomatoes and cook for a few minutes until they become soft. Add the lemon juice, vinegar, sugar and salt to taste, and check for seasoning. It should be sweet and sour with a taste of pickle. Remove the sauce from the heat and allow to cool a little; pour into a blender or mini-processor and blend to a smooth gravy. Return the sauce to the pan and reheat over a low heat.

To serve, arrange the pieces of fried fish on a dish, pour the hot sauce over and garnish with coriander leaves.

MOONG DAL HALWA

This dessert comes from North India and is a good winter dish. It uses the yellow inside of green gram lentils. If yours aren't already split, you can do this yourself – just soak overnight, wash and rinse to remove the green skins. We use olive oil wherever possible in the kitchen, but this particular recipe needs ghee for its buttery flavour.

Serve with a sprinkle of grated khoya (solid condensed milk), almonds (or cashews) and silver verk, to make this simple dish look spectacular. I don't think the khoya here is quite the same as that found in India, but you can still make a lovely dessert.

SERVES 4–6

125g moong dal (skinless split green gram lentils)
125g ghee, melted
125g sugar
100ml milk
50g khoya, grated
10 almond slivers (or cashew nuts)
2 sheets silver verk – edible silver leaf (optional)

Soak the lentils in water overnight in cold water. Next day, drain the water and grind the lentils in a grinder or mini-processor, using as little fresh water as you need to make a thick paste.

Put the lentil paste in a heavy-based pan over a low heat. Slowly add the melted ghee, mixing well to combine. Turn the heat up to medium-high and sauté the lentil paste, stirring it continuously, for 5–6 minutes. Lower the heat to medium-low and continue cooking and stirring for another 5–10 minutes until the lentil paste turns golden brown and the ghee comes to the surface.

Add the sugar and milk, and continue stirring for a few more minutes until everything becomes a fluffy consistency. Add half of the khoya and continue cooking for a few more minutes until it dissolves.

Serve the halwa hot, garnished with the remaining grated khoya, almonds and silver verk, if using, dotted over the top.

GLOSSARY

ENGLISH	HINDI	DESCRIPTION
	Chaat masala	A sweet and sour spice mix, typically including cumin, coriander, ginger, chilli, amchoor and asafoetida, with black salt as the key ingredient. Used to garnish salads, fruit dishes, street foods and drinks.
	Garam Masala	A mix of several spices: cumin, coriander, cardamom, cinnamon, cloves and black pepper are all common ingredients. This is often added at the end of cooking.
Asafoetida	*Hing*	Dried sap of a large fennel-like herb, with a pungent onion-like smell. The smell disappears on cooking. Can be substituted with powdered onion or garlic.
Barberry	*Kashmal; Zereshk (Parsi)*	Fruit of some species of the berberis shrub, rich in vitamin C. Could substitute dried cranberries.
Black Cardamom	*Badi Elaichi or Moti Elaichi*	Black, brown or 'fat' cardamom; a larger pod than the more common green cardamom, with a smoky flavour. Often used as a component in Garam Masala.
Black Peppercorn	*Kali Mirch*	Probably the most common spice in the world.
Black Salt	*Kala Namak*	A type of Indian mineral salt. It is pinkish-grey in colour with a very distinct mineral taste. It is used in Indian cooking as a condiment and is added to chaats, chutneys, raitas and savoury Indian snacks. An ingredient in commercial chaat masala.
Cardamom	*Chhoti Ilaichi or Choti Elaichi*	Green, 'common' or 'true' cardamom; used in many recipes, savoury and sweet, and in Masala Chai.
Carom	*Ajwain (also Ajowan)*	Seed similar in taste and smell to thyme or caraway. Normally dry-roasted or fried to remove the bitterness and develop the flavour.
Cassia bark	*Jangli Dalchini*	Close relative of Ceylon or true cinnamon, but thicker and tougher, with a less delicate flavour.
Chickpea flour	*Gram flour*	An amber-coloured flour with a nutty flavour used in sweets and in batters for fried foods.

Chilli	*Mirch*	Red (Lal), yellow (Pili), green (Hari): Dependent on the variety of chilli and on the degree of ripeness, the colour is no guide to the heat of the chilli, nor is its size. Few Indian dishes are meant to be searingly hot, so adjust the quantity in your cooking to suit the chillies available to you. If you wish, discard seeds and inner membrane to reduce intensity.
Cinnamon	*Dalchini*	The dried inner bark of the Cinnamomum verum tree, used to flavour savoury and sweet dishes. Found in stick or ground forms.
Clarified butter	*Ghee*	Melted butter with the milk solids removed. Keeps longer without refrigeration than traditional European butter.
Clove	*Lavang, Laong*	Dried flower buds of a tree native to Indonesia. Used whole or powdered in garam masala, biryanis and many other sweet and savoury dishes, as well as in masala chai.
Coconut	*Narial*	Fresh or desiccated flesh, as well as cream and milk in liquid or powder forms.
Coriander	*Dhania, Dhaniya*	The leaves are a common ingredient and look similar to flat-leaf parsley. Seeds are found whole or ground.
Cumin	*Jeera*	Cumin is said to be the second most popular spice in the world after black pepper. Cumin is used both whole and ground.
Curry leaves	*Kadipatha*	Shiny, dark green, aromatic leaves. Distinct flavour, indispensible to many South Indian dishes.
Fennel seeds	*Saunf, sounf*	Fennel seeds are used as a spice and a mouth-freshener, and have an aniseed flavour. Used in many savoury dishes, and, coated in sugar, as an after-dinner digestif.
Fenugreek	*Kasoori Methi*	Leaves are used fresh and dried.
	Methi	The cuboid yellow seeds are used as an aromatic spice.
Flour, whole wheat	*Atta*	General term for whole wheat flour, used for Indian breads like chapati, roti, naan and puri.
Garlic	*Lahsun*	Used fresh – chopped, sliced or in a paste. Also available in ground or powder form.

Ginger	*Soonth, Adrak*	A rhizome found fresh in most supermarkets. Available crushed in jars and in powder. Used in sweet and savoury dishes.
Indian bread rolls	*Pau, or Pav*	A European-style yeast bread; often found filled with a spiced vegetable mixture as street food.
Jaggery	*Gur*	Raw palm sugar; you can substitute Demerara sugar, though the taste is somewhat different.
Lentils	*Dal*	*Channa:* sweet nutty flavour, these are the most popular lentils in India. Yellow in colour.
		Masoor: salmon-coloured when dry, they cook quickly, and turn to a yellow purée.
		Moong: mung beans: you can find them whole with green skins, or skinned and split. Yellow in colour and cook quickly.
		Toor: yellow in colour and sometimes sold with an oily coating. Rinse this off.
		Urad: comes in both black and white. The black has a strong, earthy flavour from the skins; used in robust dishes like Dal Makhani. The white skinless dal is mild and often used in conjunction with spices.
Lotus	*Bhein, or Kamal Kakri*	The flowers, seeds, young leaves, and 'roots' or stems (rhizomes) are all edible. Can be found fresh and in tins.
Mace	*Javanti*	The outer layer covering nutmeg, it is sold either in blades (whole) or ground. Has a mild nutmeg flavour.
Mango powder	*Amchur (also Amchoor, Umchoor)*	Dried green (raw) mango powder. Has a tart, citrus taste. Used on chicken and fish, and in marinades as a tenderising agent. Can be substituted with tamarind or lime juice.
Mustard oil	*Sarson Ka Tel*	Mustard oil is often heated almost to smoking point before being used. A pungent oil which can be made with black, brown or white seeds.
Mustard seeds	*Rai*	Black mustard seeds are the variety most often used in Indian cooking.

Papaya	*Papeeta*	The green unripe fruit is used in salads and cooked dishes.
Paprika	*Paprika*	Powdered dried sweet red (bell) pepper. Not a substitute for chilli powder but can be used to reduce heat while maintaining colour in a dish.
Pau bhaji spice mix	*Pau bhaji masala*	A ready-made mix of spices used in the preparation of Pau bhaji.
Pomegranate	*Anar*	Red fruit filled with seeds. Used in both sweet and savoury dishes.
	Anardhana	Fresh seeds, dried seeds and syrup are available. The dried seeds are usually roasted and ground before being used in curries.
Poppy seed	*Khuskhus*	Small black seeds used in both Indian and Eastern European cooking.
Royal cumin	*Shajeer, or Shah Jeera*	Similar to European caraway.
Saffron	*Kesar*	The most expensive spice in the world. Gives a yellow colour and delicate flavour to both sweet and savoury dishes.
Sesame	*Til*	Both black and white sesame seeds are used in sweet and savoury dishes. The oil is mostly used as a flavouring.
Star anise	*Chakri phool*	A beautiful spice with distinct flavour used in Asian cooking.
Tamarind	*Imli*	A pod much prized for its rich tart flavour. Can be purchased as a compressed block, concentrate or sauce from Asian grocers.
Turmeric	*Haldi*	Considered to have antiseptic properties, this yellow root is mostly used as a powder. Gives a yellow colour to rice and other dishes, but should not be used as a substitute for saffron.
Waterchestnut	*Shingara*	A small aquatic vegetable. It looks very much like a regular chestnut but has a unique texture and mild flavour. Mostly found in tins in Europe.
Yoghurt dip	*Raita*	A cooling yoghurt-based preparation served with spicy dishes.

SPICE WEIGHTS AND MEASUREMENTS

	Volume	Weight
Almonds	10	15g
Asafoetida	1 teaspoon	4g
Black cardamoms	2	1g
Black pepper, ground	1 teaspoon	3g
Black peppercorns	10–12	1g
Caraway seeds	1 teaspoon	3g
Carom seeds	1 teaspoon	2g
Cashew nuts	10-12	20g
Cashew nut paste	1 cup	225g
Chaat Masala	1 teaspoon	1g
Cinnamon	5-cm stick	1g
Cloves	10	1g
Coconut, fresh scraped	1 cup	120g
Coconut, grated dried	1 cup	80g
Coriander leaves, chopped	1 tablespoon	5g
Coriander, ground	1 teaspoon	2g
Coriander seeds	1 tablespoon	4g
Cumin, ground	1 teaspoon	3g
Cumin seeds	1 teaspoon	3g
Dry fenugreek leaves	1 tablespoon	1g
Dry mango powder	1 teaspoon	1g
Fennel seeds	1 teaspoon	3g
Fennel seed powder	1 teaspoon	2g
Fenugreek seeds	1 teaspoon	5g
Fenugreek seed powder	1 teaspoon	3g
Garam masala powder	1 teaspoon	2g
Garlic	10 cloves	15g
Garlic paste	1 tablespoon	15g
Ginger	3-cm piece	6–8g
Ginger paste	1 tablespoon	15g
Gram flour	1 tablespoon	5g
Green cardamom powder	1 teaspoon	2g
Green chillies	10	20g
Jaggery, grated	1 teaspoon	10g
Lemon juice	1 tablespoon	15ml
Mace	2 blades	3g
Mint leaves, chopped	1 tablespoon	2g
Mustard seeds	1 teaspoon	4g
Mustard seed powder	1 teaspoon	2g
Onion seeds	1 teaspoon	3g
Poppy seeds	1 teaspoon	4g
Pistachios	10	5 g
Red chilli powder	1 teaspoon	3g
Red chilli flakes	1 teaspoon	1g
Rice	1 cup	190g
Rice flour	1 cup	140g
Salt	1 teaspoon	7g
Sesame seeds	1 teaspoon	4g
Sugar	1 teaspoon	5g
Tamarind pulp	1 teaspoon	5g
Tomato purée	1 tablespoon	15g
Turmeric powder	1 teaspoon	3g

US CONVERSIONS CHART

British and American cookbooks use different measuring systems. In the UK, dry ingredients are measured by weight, with the metric system increasingly replacing the Imperial one, while in the US they are measured by volume.

WEIGHT

7g	1/4 ounce	200g	7 ounces
20g	3/4 ounce	220–225g	8 ounces
25–30g	1 ounce	250–260g	9 ounces
40g	1 1/2 ounces	300g	10 1/2 ounces
50g	1 3/4 ounces	325g	11 1/2 ounces
60–65g	2 1/4 ounces	350g	12 ounces
70–75g	2 1/2 ounces	400g	14 ounces
80g	2 3/4 ounces	450g	1 pound
90g	3 1/4 ounces	500g	1 pound 2 ounces
100g	3 1/2 ounces	600g	1 pound 5 ounces
110–115g	4 ounces	700g	1 pound 9 ounces
120–130g	4 1/2 ounces	750g	1 pound 10 ounces
140g	5 ounces	800g	1 3/4 pounds
150g	5 1/2 ounces	900g	2 pounds
175–180g	6 ounces	1kg	2 1/4 pounds

VOLUME

50ml	1 3/4 fl oz	300ml	10 fl oz
60ml	2 fl oz (4 tablespoons/1/4 cup)	350ml	12 fl oz
75ml	2 1/2 fl oz (5 tablespoons)	400ml	14 fl oz
90ml	3 fl oz (3/8 cup)	450ml	15 fl oz
100ml	3 1/2 fl oz	475ml	16 fl oz (2 cups)
125ml	4 fl oz (1/2 cup)	500ml	18 fl oz
150ml	5 fl oz (2/3 cup)	600ml	20 fl oz
175ml	6 fl oz	800ml	28 fl oz
200ml	7 fl oz	850ml	30 fl oz
250ml	8 fl oz (1 cup)	1 litre	35 fl oz (4 cups)

LENGTH

5mm	1/4 inch	8cm	3 1/4 inches
1cm	1/2 inch	9cm	3 1/2 inches
2cm	3/4 inch	10cm	4 inches
2.5cm	1 inch	12cm	4 1/2 inches
3cm	1 1/4 inches	14cm	5 1/2 inches
4cm	1 1/2 inches	20cm	8 inches
5cm	2 inches	24cm	9 1/2 inches
6cm	2 1/2 inches	30cm	12 inches

INDEX

A

adraki pasliyan 180
Ahuja, Manpreet Singh 50–1
 mango and mint smoked salmon
  with kachumber salad 57
 marrow and lotus root patties 56
 okra with baby corn and spring
  onion 59
 stewed apples, soft cheese,
  strawberry custard 60
 stuffed chicken breasts with a
  saffron sauce and grapes 53
Anand, Sanjay 165–7
 chapati 170
 chilli chicken 168
 gajar ka halwa 174
 gobhi surkh angar 173
 makhani dal 171
apples: stewed apples, soft cheese,
 strawberry custard 60
apricots
 khurmani ki tikki 34
 sauce 105
 stewed white apricots 111
Arora, Anirudh 191–2
 bharwan mircha 194
 boulani 200
 haleem 197
 partridge pickle 198
 pistachio rice pudding with coconut
  foam and caramelised pineapple
  201
asparagus and mangetout 214
aubergine
 grilled aubergine with peanut,
  tamarind and chilli 84
 roasted aubergine soup 110
avocado chutney 133
Aylur, Sriram 203–5
 asparagus and mangetout 214
 cauliflower chilli fry 206
 fish in banana leaf 213
 lemon rice 209
 tomato rasam 208

B

baked tamarind halibut 105
banana leaves: fish in banana leaf 213
banana orange yoghurt raita 109
beef: coconut chilli beef 106
beetroot: beet samosa with cardamom
 ice-cream 239
Benares 11–12, 192
bhaji: Pau 94
bharwan mircha 194
bharwan seena, kesari angur ras 53
Bhatia, Navin 101–3
 baked tamarind halibut 105
 banana orange yoghurt raita 109
 coconut chilli beef 106
 roasted aubergine soup 110
 stewed white apricots 111
Bhatia, Vineet 265
bhein aur lauki tikkis 56
biryani: chicken berry biryani 97
black lentils: makhani dal 171
black-eyed beans: lobia black-eyed
 beans 162
Bombay Brasserie 25–7
boulani 200
bread
 boulani 200
 chapati 170
bream
 Hariyali bream with tomato
  kachumber 263
 herb-crusted black bream with
  Jerusalem artichoke podimas and
  tomato lemon sauce 66
Brilliant (restaurant) 165
broccoli
 gobhi surkh angar 173
 tandoori broccoli 150
bulgur wheat: haleem 197
bund gobi 160

C

cabbage: stir-fried shredded cabbage
 160
Café Spice Namaste 37–9
cardamom ice-cream 239
carrots
 gajar ka halwa 174
 green papaya and carrot thoran 148
cauliflower
 cauliflower chilli fry 206
 gobhi surkh angar 173
chaat 184
chapati 170
chard and waterchestnut pakoras 144
charmagaz 238
cheese
 chena seb sandwiches aur
  strawberry rabri 60
 murgh malai 98
 tandoori broccoli 150
cheese (paneer)
 crisp saffron and coriander rolls
  filled with paneer and red onions
  236
 grilled stuffed paneer 134
chena seb sandwiches aur strawberry
 rabri 60
chicken
 chicken berry biryani 97
 chicken curry 250
 chicken momoes 268
 chicken thukpa 271
 chicken tikka pie with spiced berry
  compote 21
 chilli chicken 168
 dill chicken tikka 223
 masala grilled chicken 133
 murg meethi malai 225
 murgh khatta pyaz 32
 murgh malai 98
 stuffed chicken breasts with saffron
  sauce and grapes 53
 stuffed chicken supremes with wild
  mushroom sauce 235
 tandoori-style chicken terrine 71

Y

Z

ACKNOWLEDGEMENTS

This book would never have seen the light of day had it not been for the vision of the publisher at Absolute Press, Jon Croft, and his commissioning editor, Meg Avent, and art director, Matt Inwood, for turning my dream into reality. Gillian Haslam has done a sterling job of editing and Lara Holmes has worked her usual photographic magic. I owe a great debt of thanks to my dear friend Sanjeev Kapoor for his kindness and advice – a charming mentor.

My very special thanks go to some others who have played a part in my journey over the last couple of years of juggling life and writing. You might not know their names, but their support has been indispensible in keeping me focused:

Mukta Kapoor for her energy and for planning fun in Delhi; Shiyam Sundar who always has kind words and sparkles with chef passion; Monica Bhide, a talented writer and food-loving chum; lovely Raquel Guzman who has done a marvellous job of organising people and dates; Janice Waterhouse who has been a good listener to tales of woe, and who revels in my every small success; Claire Fantides for her support and friendship over a couple of continents; Mridula Baljekar for cheering and feeding me, and teaching me how to peel ginger with a spoon; Lotte Duncan and Anissa Helou for trusting me when I was taking my first steps as a writer. Many thanks to both Glynn Christian for his faith and friendship, and Anne Dolamore, who together made me think that perhaps I could be a real writer one day. Last, but never least, my husband Graham who is the quiet and thoughtful half of the partnership and who encourages me in all I do – I dedicate this book to him with my love.